About the Author

Graham has conducted successful workshops on welding and wrought iron over many years, teaching his students to make both useful and decorative items from steel, as well as showing them how to tackle the many small repairs that need to be done around the home, garden and on the farm.

Graham's articles have appeared in a range of popular magazines intended for the home welder and the farm welder.

Graham's first book about welding, *A Guide To Wrought Iron and Welding*, was published by Nelson Publishers.

Other Books By the Author

A Guide To Wrought Iron and Welding

You're On Air

In Your New Image

Easy Guide To Creative Writing

Easy Guide To Writing Winning Essays

Easy Guide To Science and Technical Writing

Island Of the Barking Dog

Dad Kept Bees

Reach For the Sky

Practical Arc Welding

Welding techniques and projects for the home and farm

Graham J Andrews

Flairnet

Copyright © Graham J Andrews 2016

ISBN : 978-0-9924642-9-5

Published by Flairnet
www.flairnet.com.au
PO Box 645
Narooma NSW 2546

National Library of Australia Cataloguing-in-Publication entry

Creator: Andrews, Graham J., author.

Title: Practical arc welding : welding techniques and projects for
 the home and farm / Graham J Andrews.

ISBN: 9780992464295 (paperback)

Notes: Includes index.

Subjects: Electric welding--Handbooks, manuals, etc.
 Wrought-iron.
 Welding.

Dewey Number: 671.5212

Contact the Author:
Email: graham@grahamandrews.com
Website: www.grahamandrews.com

Contents

Acknowledgements

A book such as this is never the work of just the author. Many people contributed to its writing, editing, proofreading and publication. Along the way there are others who have contributed to its success in the way of encouragement, such as editors who have published the numerous articles on which much of this book is based, the readers who told the editors they enjoyed the articles and benefited from their content, and many more who will be able to identify themselves.

In particular, I would like to extend heaps of thanks to my wife Glenden who spent many hours editing and proofreading the manuscript, and for giving advice on its final production.

And a thank you to Paul Stebbing of Paul Stebbing Constructions who shared many of his own welding projects and many of his techniques to help make this book successful.

Many of the line drawings in the original articles were the work of Torben Johansen.

To all these people, I give my sincere appreciation and thanks.

Preface

It's been nearly thirty years since my first book *A Guide to Wrought Iron and Welding* was published by Nelson Publishers.

A lot has happened in the fields of welding and in publishing since then.

Over those thirty years or so, new equipment has become readily available to help the welder achieve good results. Back thirty years ago, for most home welders a grinding wheel attached to an electric drill was the most common means of grinding off excess metal from the welded joints. Today, primitive equipment like that wouldn't be allowed. Angle grinders, disk cutters and grinding wheels have become so affordable that almost anyone can buy them.

Safety equipment too has advanced over those three decades. Ear muffs for ear protection are almost standard equipment in any workshop to reduce the noise produced from grinding and cutting steels. Or at least ear muffs should be mandatory. New saws used for cutting steel and other metals create a lot of noise.

Eye protection too has given welders a high level of protection for one of their most precious senses. The development of polycarbonate plastics makes penetration by flying pieces of metal and red-hot sparks almost impossible, giving eyes proper protection and saving the sight of the welding operator.

Developments in the fields of metallurgy have advanced the alloys used today so metals have new applications. Along with those advances in metallurgy must go advances in the fields of technology and in equipment available to weld them, and in welding methods to suit that new equipment and the alloys. And testing of welding has advanced so much that an engineer can expect extremely high performance in any metal fabrication they are engaged in.

Advances too have been made in the field of publishing. Much of the material in this book was first published in a range of popular magazines over a couple of decades. Those articles were sought by their readers, and the editors often asked for more and more of them. I was happy to oblige them, and through the editors, I was happy to oblige the readers of their magazines to provide the types of material they wanted.

The information those articles contained has been substantially revised and brought up to date to match the equipment and the metals and the methods that have become available over those three decades.

Graham Andrews
Narooma
New South Wales
Australia

Introduction

Welding can mean many things to many people. It's a way of their becoming creative, making artistic items around their homes. For others, it might be the start of a new career, or even a change in direction in their lives.

Learning the basics of welding — the main object of this book — should be seen as the beginning of change or even, hopefully, to bigger things.

These days, a career is no longer a life-long activity. The average person changes direction perhaps as many as five times during their working life. Often that's through necessity because their job just ... Well, it disappeared one day and they are left with nothing.

For others, staying where they are means endless boredom. Boredom from the routine of their work, boredom from their lack of things to do, their lack of stimulation.

Even if many readers cannot make that change just yet to a new career or change direction in their path of life, this doesn't mean that they can't engage in a new direction in their free time — and, believe it or not, we all have a lot of it if we organise ourselves and if we make time for the more important things in life, like hobbies, creativity, challenge.

There's a complete new field awaiting you when you get started on welding. There's so much you can make from mild steel using your welder — gates, trellises, archways, clothes lines and mailbox stands, wrought-iron gates and ladders, or pergolas. You can build a box trailer, repair machinery, or carry out car repairs.

Many take up welding in a small way to save money. And who doesn't want to do that? Others want to make money from what they do. And who doesn't want to do that too?

It is best to start off with the right equipment. Having the right tools removes much of the frustration and guesswork and sets you on the path to a new and rewarding pastime.

The most important piece of equipment, of course, is the welder itself. Over recent years, the price of tools, including welding equipment, has dropped significantly in price, making the right tools for the job within most — even modest — budgets. Many of the small welding units now available are suitable for beginners or experienced operators, and will give many years of service. This type of unit can be used for projects such as building a box trailer or wrought-iron gates. It is only the serious welder who will migrate to the larger units with higher outputs of power. But that would come much later on.

Try sparking a new interest with welding. There's nothing mysterious about welding and, with the right equipment, the right instruction, there's nothing difficult in it either. After a few practice sessions in your workshop, you will be making simple and long-overdue items for the home. And for the farm, it's hard to imaging how a farmer could survive without welding equipment. It sure is a good substitute for that twisted-wire technology and similar innovations that many farmers around the world are renowned for.

There's a lot that could be written about the psychology of motivation, and of stimulation, and of being progressive, and self-development. This book is not about psychology, but about moving forward in a new field, into a new pastime, career, interest.

The aim of this book is not to be a complete guide to using an arc welder. One would need many volumes to cover everything that could be said about welding with an arc welder. But this book is about showing you, the reader, how to get started, how to learn the art of welding, how to make simple projects, and then progress to more complicated projects such as a box trailer, wrought-iron gates, and other projects you could reasonably be able to spend days of your time creating.

If you are learning to weld for a hobby, there's so much you can make. You are not limited only by the necessities, but you might be limited by your imagination. How big is your imagination? Hopefully it's huge, because the range of items you can reasonably expect to construct from steel is huge.

While the price of steel has risen many times since I started welding more than thirty years ago, the good news is that the price of tools and equipment needed has dropped significantly. Thirty years ago, one could reasonably expect to pay the equivalent of more than a week's wages to buy a basic welder. Now, you can buy a good one for perhaps a day's pay or less. Consumables too have dropped in proportion to wages. That is good news.

Once you have bought the right tools, and this book directs you in the right direction, there will be some consumables such as welding rods, cutting disks, grinding wheels you will need to buy on an ongoing basis. But these are not expensive.

And if you shop around, you might be able to find a steel supplier who will look after you and not charge too much for small pieces of steel or for cutting it.

Many a profitable business has started from a mere hobby. The person learns new skills, develops them to a high level, and progresses to the stage where they are so good at what they are doing that their skills have real value. They are able to charge a reasonable amount for their time. People will pay for anything they cannot do themselves, but they probably won't pay someone else to do what they themselves can do. Not many people can weld!

Once you have gained sufficient experience and expertise in welding, who knows what might be in store for you? If you enjoy your hobby, you will want to work at it more often. And we all know that the more we engage in something, the better we will become at that skill. Of course, the opposite too is true. If we have no interest in what we are doing, we can't reasonably expect to become good at it, can we?

But, whatever your expectations, I urge you to be patient if you have not welded before.

Remember, a trade course in welding usually spans a four-year apprenticeship. This means formal technical qualifications at a recognised educational institution such as a technical college, with on-the-job training where you apply what you have learned during those formal studies.

And if you finish your apprenticeship, you should be good at it.

But that doesn't mean than someone who is self-taught can't make a success out of welding too.

If you dream big, where will your ambitions take you? To distant lands and to those magical islands in the Pacific, perhaps. Some take up welding to build their dream boat. Steel boats are reasonably easy to build, especially compared with the construction of a fibreglass or a timber boat. So if you can weld, there's no reason why, with good skills, planning and the determination, you won't be able to build your own yacht. Or your cabin cruiser. With the money you will be saving by building your own boat, you might be able to extend the imagination even further and go for a boat that is even bigger than the one you had hoped to own all along.

If you work your way through this book—the methods in welding, in cutting, in fitting up, in grinding, and so on, and try working with different steels such as galvanised steel, and the different projects, you will be well on your way to achieving your goals, no matter how high they might be. Remember, there's a whole new world out there for you.

1 History of welding

As a welder, you will be continuing a tradition that started over five thousand years ago. There are welded artefacts that date from the Bronze Age and the Iron Age.

Welding can be defined as the fusion of material by the use of heat. While the methods used in the typical welding workshop today don't really resemble the methods used by the early Egyptians, the people of Eastern Mediterranean or those of the civilisations of the Middle Ages, the process is still all about fusing two or pieces of metal together. Iron and bronze artefacts that show intricate forging and welding processes have been found in the Egyptian pyramids.

For example, small boxes that can today be found in the National Museum of Dublin, were made by fusing sections together. During the Iron Age, Egyptians and artisans from Eastern Mediterranean countries learned to fuse pieces of iron together. Their main need for metal objects would generally have been, but not limited to, tools and weapons. These two classes of items were, apparently, the most essential possessions for their development, survival, or for decimating those whom they opposed. Such items date back around three thousand years, and many such items can now be found in the British Museum in London.

As we move on to the Middle Ages, we see that the art of blacksmithing, that is, the processes of using heat to forge metals, were developed to a high level. Many items of iron were welded by heating the objects and hammering them together. The Iron Pillar of Delhi, India, shows welds from this time in history, and it dates back around 1700 years.

Throughout the development of almost everything in our culture, one development depends to a large extent on something that has been invented, developed or discovered previously.

Many of the splendid palaces of Europe were protected by elaborate wrought-iron gates. These were generally constructed without the use of any welding. The sections, once formed, were often held together by large rivets passing through the sections, and then they were beaten to close the ends to ensure the sections stayed together. Another way to secure sections of gates and other ornate wrought-iron objects together was to use pieces of steel that were bent over the two sections and then bent closed. This, however, did not constitute welding, but simply a means of securing two or more pieces of steel together.

Gas welding was pioneered by Sir Humphrey Davy in England. Sir Humphrey was also credited with the invention of the miners safety lamp that prevented explosions from occurring in underground coal mines, saving many lives.

Davy discovered acetylene gas in 1836, the gas that is used in gas welding and gas cutting today. Gas welding is used for brazing (that is, using brass filler and welding rods), and for cutting. Mixed with oxygen, the combustion can generate very high temperatures, in the vicinity of 3000° Celsius.

Humphrey Davy could be considered an inventive genius by any standards. Another of his important inventions, or discoveries, that is applicable to welding, include the production of an electric arc between two carbon electrodes. The power source for this simple contraption was a battery.

It wasn't until the mid-1800s that the electric generator was invented, and arc lighting and arc welding was able to be developed.

The transformer, which is what an electric welder really is, converts, say, 240 volts and 15 amps, giving a power demand of 3600 watts. The current (the amps) is then increased up to 180 amps or more and the voltage dropped to about 26 volts, or any variation of volts multiplied by the amps to give a result of 3600 watts. Smaller welders draw only 10 amps, giving 2400 watts. The amperage (that provides the heat) is converted to 135 amps, while the voltage is reduced to less than 20 volts.

The last quarter of the nineteenth Century saw the largest number of inventions and discoveries related to welding. Gas welding was developed. Gas cutting, that is, using a mixture of oxygen gas and acetylene gas, burned in a flame, generated enough heat to melt large pieces of steel. Railway lines can be cut quickly and easily using oxy acetylene cutting equipment.

Also developed during this short period of the late 19th Century was arc welding, using the carbon arc and the metal arc methods that have been carried on up to today, and resistance welding. They became important contributors to engineering and development of heavy machinery.

The first patent for the metal electrode was awarded to Mr CL Coffin of Detroit, Michigan. This was the first documented use of metal melted by an electrode being carried across the arc to deposit the molten metal in a joint and thus form the first welded joint.

The metal electrode was developed further by Strohmeyer around the year 1900 in Great Britain. His development of the electrode resulted in a flux coating consisting of clay or lime around the metal core. While not as successful as the coated electrodes of today, the resulting electrode did at least provide a more stable arc.

At about the same time as Strohmeyer's invention, resistance welding methods were discovered, including spot welding, seam welding, projection welding and flash butt welding. Gas welding was more or less perfected at around the same time as Strohermeyer's development of the coated electrode. The gas welding and gas cutting were further developed and perfected by the invention of the welding torch, the means of combining two gasses that could be combusted at the end of a single nozzle.

While these methods of welding were used extensively up to the early part of the 20th Century, the First World War saw rapid development in welding methods and welding equipment, pushed along through necessity brought on by the war efforts. Many companies were formed in America and in Europe to develop welding machines and consumables.

The 1920s saw further development in welding techniques and welding equipment. Automatic welding was introduced to industry, whereby bare wire operating on a direct current was able to build up worn machinery and produce heavy automotive components.

And at around that time, it was realised that it was possible to weld aluminium and metals such as magnesium. Aluminium had always been a problem for welders because a coating of aluminium oxide formed on the surface almost immediately it was cut or filed. This prevented any fusion taking place. But with gas shielding, aluminium welding opened up a whole new field of welding. Most of the shielding is by the use of an inert gas such as argon. Even under the extremes of heat produced by welding, argon will remain inert—that is, is won't combine with oxygen.

Since this time, other types of welding electrodes were developed. There were electrodes that could weld most types of steels. High carbon and alloy steel electrodes were developed. Special rods comprising copper alloys were developed for carbon arc welding and brazing.

And then later in the 1920, there was interest in the development of welding equipment for steel welding where the arc was shielded by inert gases, such as argon and carbon dioxide. Oxygen and nitrogen in the atmosphere, in contact with the hot weld metal, causes brittle and often porous welds that are weak. The gas shielding welding overcame many of the difficulties in this area. Tungsten electrodes were later used for this type of welding, and became knows as TIG (tungsten inert gas) welding.

Today, the coated electrode is still the most popular electrode, but improvements have been made over a number of decades. Improvements have also been made to automatic welding using the continuous wire method.

Pipes and square hollow tubing are formed and then the edges are brought together and welded by the smothered arc welding process. Longitudinal seams in pipes were then possible. While further developed for military applications around the Second World War, the method is still widely used today.

Developments in welding equipment and consumables have led to the pulsed current metal arc welding and the plasma arc welding processes. Electron beam welding processes have almost been superseded already by laser welding methods. With the use of laser beams in welding, very fine beams of energy are produced to create heat that has applications in small spaces. Laser cutting is often used in some workshops where precision cutting is required. Friction welding, where two parts are rotated together at high speed to produce enough heat to melt the surfaces together are gaining support in some industries. For the amateur welder, the home hobby worker, or those starting their vocation in welding, the use of this advanced technology might be further along into the future, as they are specialised applications, using expensive equipment that might be beyond the average humble budget, and is often limited to large companies that specialise in this type of welding, or companies that have a lot of money to spend on technology. For most people for whom this book is aimed, the typical arc welder will suffice for many years.

As welding has developed, so have the standards. Quality inspection of welding, and of those performing the function of welder, need to meet high standards. Those repairing crane jibs, aircraft components, and crankshafts in submarine engines and nuclear reactors, all areas of which an amateur welder at present has no place in the process, the standards of welding, and those operating the equipment must always be the highest. Those starting out in welding today should not give up hope of reaching the highest levels of their profession. Skills take many years to develop to the high standards demanded by industry. If those people don't give up, they too could be up there achieving the highest standards of their chosen occupations.

Guides to welders, guides to weld inspectors, engineers and the correct methods must be applied, otherwise failure will occur, often with disastrous results. Methods used to maintain high quality welds include not only visual inspection, by X-raying the welds to ensure full metal penetration with no gaps, impurities, porosity or other defects; ultra-sonic testing is used, magnetic particle inspection, and computer tomography (similar to the CAT scans of human bodies) reveal even the smallest defect that can lead to failure of the weld.

As new methods of welding are developed, the application of those methods must be enhanced, such as the need to reduce the heat-affected zone as much as possible in critical areas of fabrication or repair.

While these standards don't necessarily apply to all welding applications, such as making wrought-iron gates or making a garden trellis, many areas of industry now demand more. In fact, they demand the best.

As welding methods are developed, the science of metallurgy has kept pace with demands of industry. Instead of one standard of steel, with a certain carbon component, several metals are mixed together in precise quantities to deliver the metal that is ideal for a specific task. The method to weld those new compounds must be developed together. One, without the other, is useless. If a new metal compound were to become available, on its own, it would have limited applications unless the methods, and the operators who could use the processes, were available for those new metallic compounds.

It is reasonable to expect metallurgy and welding processes, and welding operators, to continue to evolve over coming years. And why not? Why limit ourselves to what is only available now? In ten or twenty years from now, new discoveries and methods will make the present techniques look boring and rather inadequate.

As the purity of metals is improved, the strength of materials is improved. Thus the standard to manufacture is improved, so that it might be possible to use less steel that is stronger, resulting in a manufactured item that is lighter, stronger and easier to handle.

As more technological advances are made, these can be used as a basis for further developing welding methods and welding equipment. Each invention provides the platform from which the next step can be taken.

Despite whatever changes may be introduced into welding in the coming decades, welding itself will always be here for as long as humans want to fuse two pieces of metal together. And that seems to be for a long time yet.

The 21st Century still has many years to run. So has the development of metals, and of welders, and of welding methods, and the training and skills of welding operators, and automatic processes. These days, life never stands still for long. Even for welders, exciting times are ahead for us all.

2 About iron and steel

Iron is iron, but steel can be many things.

Probably 90 per cent or more of all arc welding is done with some alloy of iron.

Commercially pure iron is a silvery-grey, very ductile metal of low tensile strength. It is generally too weak for most structural applications. To be useful and strong, it is necessary to give it the hardness and strength it needs. To achieve the strength required in most applications, other elements, mainly carbon, must be added in varying amounts. When the carbon content ranges from 0.01 to 1.5 per cent, the material is known as steel. And from 2.5 to 4.0 per cent, it is cast iron. Cast iron is easy to pour and to mould and to shape in prepared moulds. But it is brittle.

In addition to carbon, other elements are also used to induce strength, ductility and resistance to corrosion, abrasion and impact. Such elements include nickel, chromium, molybdenum and copper. In general the addition of these elements increase hardness and enhance the physical properties of the metal. These steels are used extensively in the popular construction steels such as those used in girders and trusses. Other elements, including tungsten and cobalt, are important in the production of high-speed tool steels, not only to increase hardness, but to retain good cutting edges at relatively high temperatures.

Phosphorus and sulphur are generally considered to be impurities as they are detrimental to the strength and usefulness of steel, except in those steels where free cutting is a prime requisite. These elements are usually kept below 0.05 per cent. Sulphur, for example, in excess of this amount causes porosity and brittleness in steel that is welded.

It is therefore necessary to exercise care when welding free cutting steels, which have a sulphur content higher than this amount. Steels of this type are the cause of much unsatisfactory welding. Unfortunately, no simple test will disclose the amount of sulphur in the steel. The only safe course is to use steels that are known to be low in sulphur.

In making alloy steels, the physical properties depend not only on the elements added, but also upon the heat treatment. The degree and duration of heat and the rate of cooling have a definite effect on the end hardness and grain structure. Steels that possess marked hardening ability, such as those with more than 0.30 per cent carbon, and varying amounts of other elements, harden in proportion to their rate of cooling. Therefore, in welding, the rapid cooling induced by the cold surrounding area causes such steels to become so hard that they are difficult or impossible to machine. Rapid cooling also induces stresses that, unless relieved by later heat treatment, may produce cracks and subsequent failure. To prevent such conditions from occurring, the work or parent metal should be preheated and welded while hot, the exact temperature depending on the type of material and its response required to hardening.

This permits the weld and adjoining metal to cool more slowly and more evenly, reducing hardness and producing a more uniform grain structure throughout.

It should be remembered that the above conditions apply only to steels having more than 0.30 per cent carbon or when other elements are present. By far the majority of welded fabrications today are of structural steel, including angles or angle iron beams, channels and plates. All these steels have low carbon and low hardening ability. When other elements are present in such stock, the amount is so small as to be negligible as a hardening factor, therefore the precaution of preheating is unnecessary except on heavy sections where the cooling effect would be severe, or where precise welding techniques are required.

High tensile alloy steels

These are produced to increase strength without increasing weight. This result is attained by adding elements to give alloys. Such elements include manganese, nickel, chromium and molybdenum. Increasing the carbon content beyond that of mild steel will often achieve steels with the desired properties. The result of this, though, is usually to make the steel more difficult to weld.

Effects of welding

The two most prominent effects of welding these steels are the formation of a hardened zone in the weld area, and, if suitable precautions are not taken, the occurrence in this zone of cracks.

3 The right tools

If you've never welded before, start off with the right equipment.

The arc welder

The most important component of a welding workshop is ... the welder. Obvious, I know, but welders come in all sizes with different capabilities.

The older welders used stick electrodes, and they could take electrodes up to 3.25 mm and possibly larger. Welders that use the electrodes are still in wide use today, and are just as popular as they have ever been. Electrodes of this size are adequate for most general steel fabrication and repairs.

Properly equipped workshops will possibly be wired for high voltages—415

volts, possibly three-phase power that can deliver the required current for all sorts of fabrication. Welders that run on 415 volts are expensive.

For the home welder, and those just starting out, a welder running on 240 volts or thereabouts will be more than adequate. But be careful. Many of these smaller units draw 15 amps, so you will have to ensure that you have a power supply that can deliver 15 amps. Don't be tempted to buy a 15 amp welder if the only outlet you have to run it is rated at 10 amps. You will be asking for trouble. The wiring in your house won't be sufficient to take the extra power drawn from the circuit, and the fuse in the circuit will not take the extra demand.

If you want a 15 amp welder, make sure you have an adequate power outlet rated at 15 amps, or see if you can get an electrician to install one for you. It shouldn't cost too much, and you will need it. If you try running a 15-amp welder on a 10-amp power outlet, you will also be over-loading the wires from the meter box to the power point. Most wires run through the ceilings of houses, where there are very dry roofing timbers, dried out over many years of heat from the sun. If there is a fire, it will spread rapidly.

There's more about running the 15 amp welders from 10 amp power outlets under the chapter Safe Welding.

Electric welding uses mains electricity. The unit (in the smaller home welders) converts 240 volts and 10 or 15 amps, down to a few volts and up to about 150 amps. It is the high amperage that generates enough heat to melt metals together.

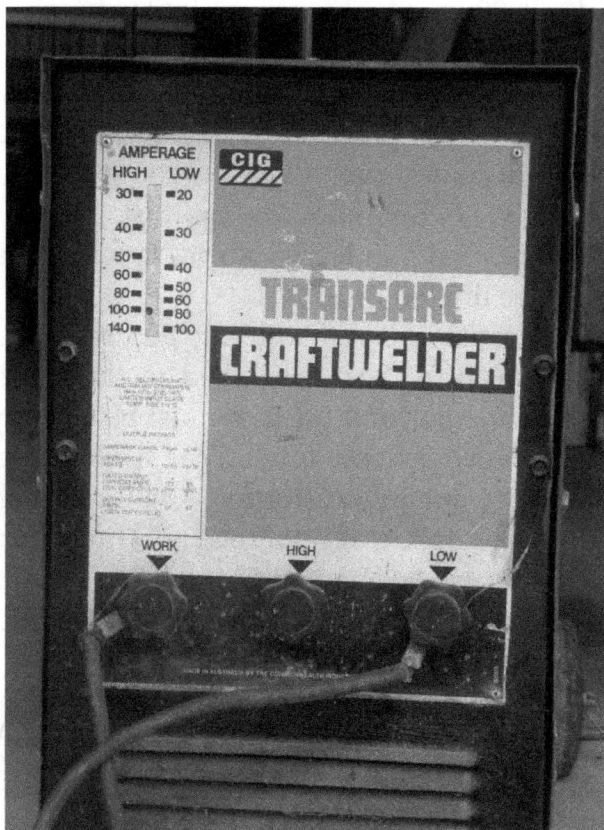

Within this range there are some excellent units that will do admirable work.

These small units have the advantage of being portable — if you expect to do jobs in awkward spots around the house, such as in high places. You can carry them up ladders or stairs if you need to.

But just what can you do with the smaller units? Most of the projects in this book, and general repair work, can be welded with even the smallest, portable machine.

The larger 15 amp units are more expensive, but they are more versatile. They will do many more jobs than the less expensive 10 amp ones. But the extra cost, and the cost of installing the power point must be worthwhile. It's money wasted if you buy the bigger machine and don't use it to its full capacity. But there are jobs that can be done only with a larger machine.

There are some welding jobs that require a higher voltage and lower amperage. These will be mainly repairs using special electrodes, but this feature can be used also when welding very thin metals. The higher voltage will help carry the lower amperage more easily.

Power boards

You will probably want to use a power board so you can run more than one appliance at a time — the welder, the electric drill, grinder or disk cutter, and possibly a radio. Make sure the amperage of the power board is sufficient to take the current drawn on it.

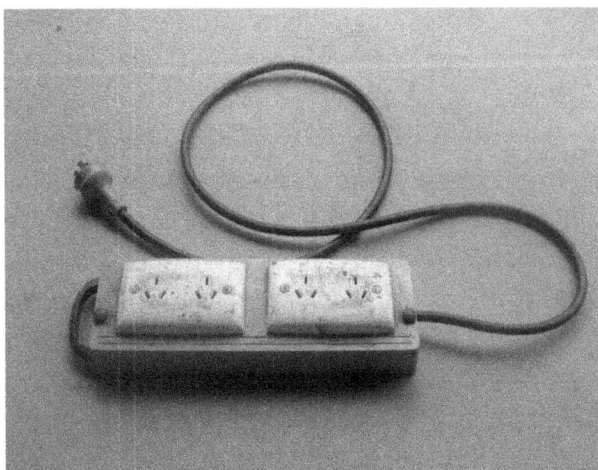

Gas welding

There are advantages with electric welding over gas welding.

One is the cost. It is less expensive, generally, than gas welding, and there are no hidden costs involved. You buy the unit and the electrodes, and that's the total expense. If you don't use the unit for two years, it won't cost you anything for the time it's idle. If you use more electrodes, you buy more of them.

This book is about arc welding, or electric welding, but a few words about gas welding will certainly fit in here.

Gas welding equipment can be quite different. There is a wide range available, so the choice may confuse you.

Most gas welding units will do two things — they weld (and that includes brass welding, or brazing) and they cut steel. Most manufacturers claim that their units will cut steel 12 millimetres or more thick. Certainly, if you are making numerous projects, and you have a lot of cutting to do, particularly of the thicker steels, then oxy equipment will make the job much easier. The rate of cutting steel plate 10 millimetres thick can be up to about 20 centimetres per minute. Imagine that job using a hacksaw!

But gas welding has some disadvantages. It is slow. The process can take quite a while to perfect, and only then can you expect to achieve good results. By contrast, brazing isn't too hard to learn, but its applications may be limited.

Because the gas welding process is so slow, a lot of heat is applied to the steels being welded, and the heat must be kept on the job for a long time. That's when the welder's enemy — distortion — will make its presence felt. And there's not much an amateur can do about it. The intense heat will twist the steel, and it's very difficult to straighten.

The process involves heating the steel to red heat, and then applying a filler rod and melting that on to the two pieces of steel being welded together. In contrast, with electric welding, the electrode touches the steel, and the process is almost instantaneous. Distortion is minimal.

Certainly with very large projects, such as building a steel boat, the job is too big to consider using oxy equipment. Electric welding will get you half way around the world on your yacht before you have used an oxy welder on the first few frames!

Oxy welding does have one advantage that electric welding cannot overcome. It can be used where there is no electricity. If you are on a property where there is no electricity, or no generator to drive an electric welder, and you need to weld equipment or repair a shed frame, then electric welding won't help you very much. You will need a portable generator that can deliver sufficient amperage. Gas welding is mobile in this way, and can be taken anywhere—even on your boat if you wish to carry out repairs in the middle of the Pacific Ocean.

Whereas electric welding equipment is bought outright, this isn't so with gas welding equipment. You buy the basic equipment, such as torch, hoses and regulators, but the gas bottles are not yours, and they never will be. They must be hired from a gas supply firm for an annual rental. If you don't use your welder for two years, then you still pay the rental on the bottles. That's money tied up for as long as you have the welding equipment. This amount must be paid annually, and in advance. The gas refills are expensive, too. That, of course, is in addition to the rental on the bottles. The rate of usage of the gases depends on what you are welding or cutting. The larger the flame and nozzle, the faster the rate of consumption of gases. Extensive cutting will empty an oxygen bottle in about twenty minutes. So after twenty minutes, you have to go out to your industrial area and replace the oxygen bottle with a new one.

These are some of the reasons why many people purchase electric welders rather than a gas unit.

So back to the electric welding—the main purpose of this book.

All the projects in this book can be made by using an electric welder.

Welding electrodes

Naturally, a welding unit will be the most important component of your tool kit, but there are other tools and accessories you will need. With the electric welder, you will require a range of welding electrodes. Depending on the task and the gauge of steel you are welding, and what the item is for, you will have to select the electrodes appropriate to the job. For most jobs, the electrode gauges that you will use most will be 2.5 millimetres and 3.25 millimetres. This is the diameter of the rod. There are other sizes available, but you could do without these to begin with.

Don't look at each job and decide to buy the smallest pack of electrodes on the market. You will use a lot of electrodes with many of the projects, even the smaller projects listed in this book. You will need electrodes of different diameters, and for welding different steels. There are electrodes for just about any application you can think of, and probably even more after that. You can weld cast iron, stainless steel, special steels with unique compositions for which you will need special electrodes.

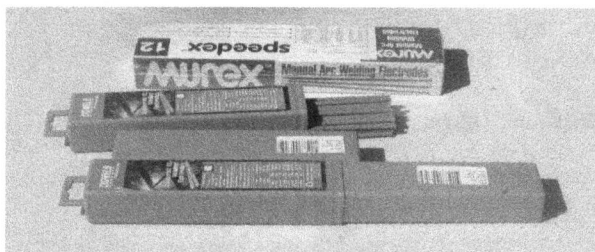

But to get started, and to have an adequate supply on hand to get you on your way, buy a 5-kilogram carton each of general purpose electrodes rated as E6012 or E6013. Buy electrodes of 2.5 mm diameter and 3.25 mm diameter. If you need small electrodes for welding thin steel, buy thin electrodes (but make sure your competency is adequate to weld very thin steel). If you have a need to weld stainless steel or cast iron, you can buy special electrodes when you need them. For the home welder, and the general amateur enthusiast, it is unlikely they will be welding materials such as these in the early days of welding.

Cutting the steel

Before you can work with steel, you will need to cut it. A hacksaw is quite suitable for small pieces of steel, although a bit slow for large pieces. It is nevertheless quiet. Replacement blades are available, with teeth sizes of 18 teeth per inch for general work, and 24 or more teeth per inch for cutting fine pieces of steel.

If you always use a sharp saw, your work will be much easier. A blunt saw will take a lot longer to cut through steel, and it won't cut straight. This means that you will have a lot of grinding and filing to do to get your work straight. You'll break blades too, so don't buy them one at a time, buy half a dozen when you go to the hardware store. They are inexpensive and they won't stretch even the tightest budget.

Cutting disks and angle grinders or disk cutters are available too. These are efficient but extremely noisy. For most jobs they will sure speed up the cutting of even the thickest steel pieces. Grinders will be useful for removing excess weld metal on completion of your project.

Disk cutter

A disk cutter is essential if you are doing any serious welding and steel fabrication. With this tool, you will be able to buy a range of disks. Some will be useful for grinding the welds to remove excess weld metal and make the weld much neater. You can, by using a grinding disk, bevel the edges prior to welding them so that you can better ensure weld metal penetration into the joint. It's hard to believe anyone could do any welding without grinding the surfaces.

With cutting disks, you will be able to cut through steel. I don't mean railway lines, but you will be able to cut through angle iron, pipes, square tubing, rods both round and square, and flat bar. You will be able to make the cuts at 90 degrees, 45 degrees or any other angle to suit your project.

Disk cutters, or angle grinders, come in different sizes. They start usually from 100 mm diameter wheels, or disks, 125 mm disks, up to 250 mm disks and cutting wheels.

The smaller disk cutters will do an excellent job in general steel welding and fabrication work.

Remember that you won't be able to grind brazing, or brass welding. The soft metal will clog the pores of the disk, and render it useless after only a short time.

When buying cutting disks and grinding disks, buy several. They won't last long, and you will be replacing them after a short time.

Grinding wheels usually start at around 3 mm thickness, up to 5 mm thick, while cutting wheels, or cutting disks, are usually no more than 2 mm thick.

When using angle grinders, wear a dust mask so that you don't breathe the material that is worn from the wheel, and use ear muffs that are adequate for the noise produced. The tool itself is noisy. When used to grind steel, it is even noisier. Think of your hearing and protect it. But more of the safety equipment later in this chapter.

Cut-off saws

If you intend doing a lot of steel work and welding, you might consider a cut-off saw. This is a saw with a special blade that will cut smaller pieces of steel, such as pipes, angle iron and the square hollow tubing and various thicknesses of flat bar that are often used in welding projects.

A properly equipped workshop will have other tools too, to make most jobs easier and faster, and give a wider scope to the workshop. The rest of the tools you will need are quite likely to be standard items in any home workshop.

Square and tape measure

To mark steel accurately for cutting, you will need a square—possibly one you use for your carpentry as there are of course no special ones for use with metalwork. One with 90° and 45° angles is essential. And a tape measure for measuring—a metal one, rather than a wooden ruler or fibreglass tape will be preferable. Steel can remain hot for quite some time after welding, and this, over time,

will cause the wooden ruler or a fibreglass tape measure to deteriorate rapidly.

Scribe

And to mark the steel before cutting it, a felt pen will be better than a pencil which is often difficult to use on steel, particularly on new, greasy metal. Steel chalk, really a piece of cut gypsum, will mark steel too. But use a scribe—a small instrument with a sharp point that will scratch the surface of steel. The mark will show during welding or cutting.

Paint the middle of the scribe with a bright coloured paint. Red will stand out on the workshop floor, and you will be able to find it amongst the off-cuts of steel lying around on the floor.

The sharp end of a small file will suffice until you find your scribe again. A file is made from hardened steel, and will scratch mild steel easily.

Clamps

You will need two or three clamps—strong enough to withstand the strong forces of buckling. They will keep the components in place while you are welding them together.

Electric drills

Most steel will be attached to something else with bolts, or you will be attaching wood to some of your projects (such as the wrought-iron table or the bench shown in the project section of this book), so you will need a drill, or drills, of adequate capacity.

For convenience, you will need a small hand drill, one that can take drill bits up to around 6 mm. These are light weight and are easy to use with one hand.

An electric drill and a drill set are essential for those projects where holes need to be drilled. Your budget, and the projects, will determine what size drill you buy. Quality will be worth the extra expense. Cheap brands won't last, and very soon you will have spent more money replacing the cheap drill bits than if you had bought a set of good quality ones.

If you're building a box trailer or other large projects, a 13 millimetre drill will let you do all the jobs you want to do. This is more expensive than a small drill, but is certainly worth the extra expense. The larger hand drills will last longer with a lot more use in the workshop. They take larger drill bits — up to 13 mm. Large drills are often rated at half-horsepower. In other words, they are powerful. If you use a slow revving half-horsepower electric drill with a 13 mm drill bit, be very careful. They have a tremendous amount of torque, or turning power, and can easily throw the operator if the drill bit catches on the steel. Expect to be picking yourself up off the workshop floor if this happens.

Welding helmet

Many new welding units come supplied with a couple of items you will need. The first is a welding helmet to shield you from the heat and the radiation of the arc. Use it at all times. It has a darkened screen for eye protection,

and no welding should be undertaken without using the helmet.

Modern welding helmets designed for arc welding have a filter that darkens the moment the arc is struck. The idea is that you are able to see the work until the moment you start welding. While these might sound like a good idea, I am not so sure they are one hundred percent effective. Some welders I have spoken to admit that after quite some time using them, they develop sore eyes — the same as they would expect if they inadvertently caught a glimpse of the arc. So if you do want one like this, then perhaps you might find benefit in closing your eyes for that brief moment when you first strike the arc.

There are special goggles that must be used for oxy welding. They provide effective protection against ultra-violet radiation. While some 'welders' use sun glasses to protect their eyes from the radiation, believing these will give them adequate protection, their good eyesight might not be retained as well as it otherwise could be.

Backing plate

An off-cut of steel plate, obtainable from any steel merchant, will be ideal for clamping the pieces of steel onto while you are welding them. Any off-cut of steel about 200 by 200 millimetre and 10 millimetre thick will help you keep your work straight. Clamp the pieces on to the plate and then weld them.

Stands or saw horses

One of the projects described in the project section of this book is saw horses. These are easy to make — cut two lengths of steel pipe, bend these in the middle, weld them both to a piece of flat bar and attach a piece of hardwood. Put on some rubber feet, and there's your first saw horse.

You will need at least two of them, possibly three to support the long lengths of steel, some of which will be eight or ten metres long. If you have only two saw horses to support the longer lengths of steel, you will find there is a lot of bowing and this will result in inaccurate cutting and welding. If the long length of steel is bowing in the middle and you are cutting vertically, the angle down will not be 90 degrees. At least if the steel lengths are straight, you can only blame yourself and your carelessness if the cuts and the welds are not as straight as you would have hoped for.

Pipe bender

A tool that isn't necessary, but is helpful for some projects outlined in this book, is a pipe bender. With one of these you can build farm gates. You can make a bull-bar for your car, or a tow bar, and you can put the pipe bender to many other uses. If you have one, you will certainly be able to use it, and make it pay its way.

It will take only a minute or two to bend a pipe at right angles. It could take you half an hour to cut, clamp, weld and grind a joint

to gain the same effect. Perhaps, if your needs are not ongoing, you might be able to hire one for a day or so to complete a particular job.

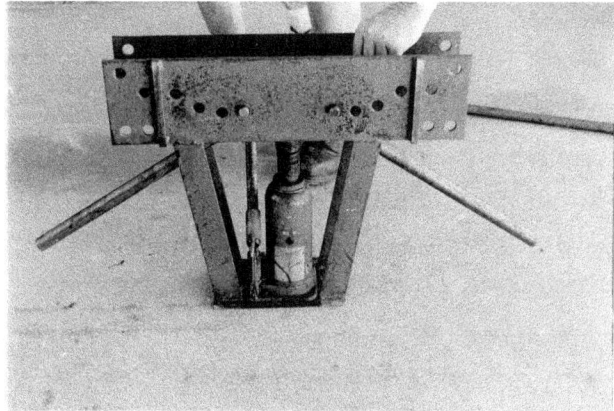

Files

A couple of files, one large, one small, will help to keep your work neat and tidy. They can be used to remove rough edges, from cutting and also small amounts of excess weld metal from joints — if you don't have a disk grinder.

A file will clean up roughness around cuts and welds. A coarse and a fine file will be sufficient, but to remove large amounts of weld metal to tidy up the welding and make it look professional, use grinding disks attached to the disk grinder or angle grinder.

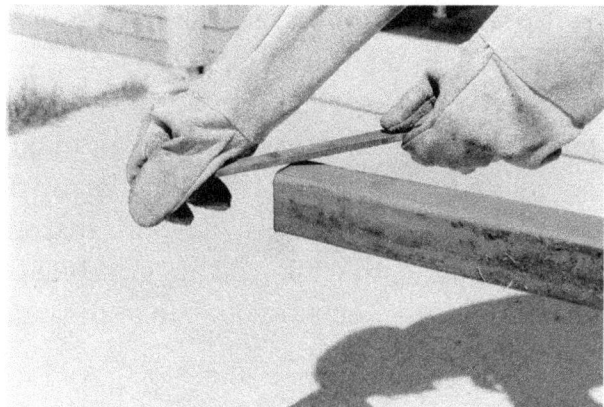

Wire brush

Most steel will come from the steel mills with a coating of grey, sooty material adhering to it. This is mill scale, and will rub off easily. If you brush down the steel with a wire brush after you have completed each project, and the areas you are going to weld, you will be able to remove most of it, so add a wire brush to your tool kit.

These wire brushes do wear out, so buy yourself one or two spares.

Welding pick

Also included with the welder should be a welding pick, a hammer-like tool with a pointed end and a flat edge at the other. This is used for chipping away the welding slag that is deposited over the weld metal.

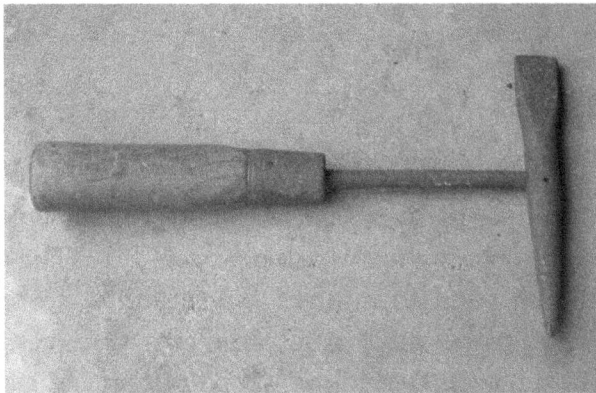

Dust masks

Don't breath in the dust from the grinding process. The cutting and grinding wheels have horrible materials in their composition, and the dust from these should not be inhaled. A dust mask of the right standard will prevent all or at least most of the dust particles lodging in your lungs. At least they will if you wear them correctly—that is, make sure they cover your mouth and your nose with no gaps either side, or at the top or bottom. In other words, make sure that all the air you breath while you are grinding or cutting the steel enters your lungs through your dust mask.

Ear muffs

Angle grinders are noisy tools to use, even when they are running with no load. This is because they rotate at such a high speed, and the motors used to turn the wheels are powerful. Add to that base noise level the sound of the grinding itself, and you have

noise that will be painful and damaging to your ears.

Ear muffs are rated for different applications, and different noise levels. Those to be used for grinding will have the highest rating, and will give you maximum ear protection. Like your eyes, you only will ever have one pair of ears to use through all your days ... as long as you protect them from the loud noises.

Safety goggles

When you cut steel with a power tool such as a cut-off saw or disk cutter, you will generate lots of red-hot sparks.

Those hot sparks can be thrown far from the steel, and once they get into your eyes after travelling at high speed, you can expect a few trips to see the ophthalmologist to repair the damage—if that is even possible. This is one injury you will not be able to fix by applying a band-aid. The only way is to prevent those hot sparks entering your eyes in the first place. Your eyes should be cared for so they last you your lifetime. Respect them. Protect them.

If you have an assistant nearby, make sure he or she is protected to the same level that you protect yourself. If you value your own eyes, you must value the eyesight of your off-sider too. They will appreciate it, and I am sure you will too if you realise they are at no greater risk of eye damage or injury than you are willing to subject yourself to.

Cleaning the steel

Wipe the metalwork clean with a cloth and plenty of turpentine.

To get the steel really clean, a wire brush isn't sufficient. It will still be greasy and dirty. Some old cloths and turpentine will ensure a clean, grease-free surface you can paint or, more correctly, prime with rust-inhibiting paint. And always use a good quality metal primer as well as a paint that is recommended for use on metal.

Rust inhibitors

All steel will rust, but some will rust faster than others. Steel needs oxygen and moisture to rust. Remove one of these two ingredients and the rusting will be minimal or absent. In warm, humid environments, steel will rust more quickly. In a salty environment, such as near the coast, especially if the steel will be kept within a few hundred metres of the ocean, expect rusting to be a significant problem.

While you can get all the steel items you make fully hot-dipped galvanised for permanent rust prevention, this is not always convenient. After sandblasting the whole item to remove paint, it must be sent off to the proper facilities that can handle hot-dipped galvanising processes.

An alternative is to use a metal primer that has rust inhibitors in it. These are usually based on zinc or chromium compounds.

Coating steel with an acrylic paint will not prevent rusting. It might be alright until you have been paid for the work you have done, but expect the owner of the job to be contacting you after a few weeks to complain that the rust is starting to show through the paint ... and demanding that you please go and paint the steel properly.

All steel will rust—the humidity in the air, even inside your home, will cause rusting unless it is primed all over. Primers will help protect the surface from rusting.

Buy quality tools

Always buy quality tools. The cost isn't much more than cheap lines. Cheap clamps, for example, will break or their threads will strip. Replacements cost more money. Electric drills that are too small for the heavy drilling you might do will soon burn out. Welding units that might seem cheap become more expensive if you can't buy spare parts for them.

Steel is so much heavier and harder than wood. The tools need to be tougher to withstand that extra use.

So, buy wisely the first time, and save your money.

From time to time you might realise that you might need an extra tool or two other than those I have mentioned here. But this list will certainly be enough to get you started in your welding pastime or career.

Proper clothing

For all welding operations, proper clothing is a must. This includes leather gauntlets, overalls that button to the neck, and leather boots. But there's more about the proper clothing to wear for your welding under the section Safe Welding.

Some additional tools you might need in your welding workshop

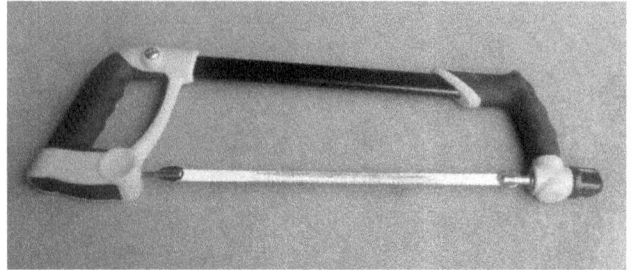

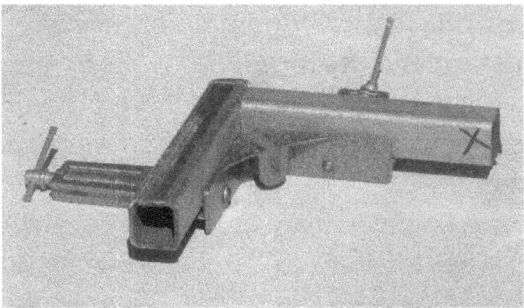

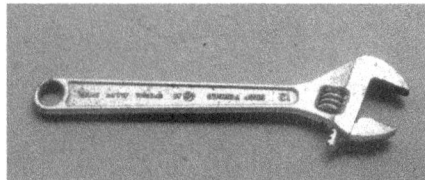

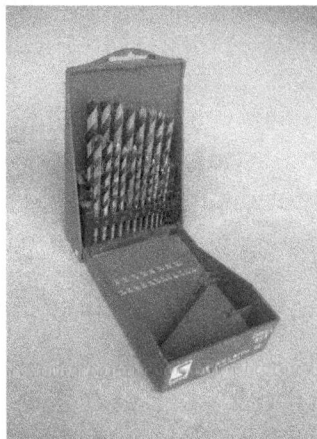

4 Learning to weld

To ensure the best, strongest welds possible, you must prepare the steel you are about to weld. There are no shortcuts to this, and the small amount of time you spend on preparing the surfaces will be rewarded years later with a weld that is as strong as a single piece of steel.

Sloppy work habits are easy to develop early in your career, so eliminate such practices before you even start. Remember, good workmanship takes almost the same time as sloppy workmanship does, but the results will be significantly different.

In this chapter, you will learn the correct way to weld most joints.

For many jobs, it might be possible to weld without much preparation. However, for thicker pieces of steel, proper preparation is essential. That means ensuring you leave the correct gap between the pieces of steel for weld metal penetration, or bevelling the edges to achieve the same purpose. For

Grinding a space in preparation for welding is one way to ensure a sufficient gap between the pieces of steel

heavier sections of steel, and for many repairs, such as repairing cast iron, you will need to grind an angle between the pieces, or each side of the repair.

Make sure the steel you are welding is clean, dry and free of paint, oils, rust, mill scale and other substances that will lead to impurities getting into the weld, thus weakening the joint. If you cut the steel with oxy-cutting, you must remove all the slag residue that is left from this process. Grinding using a disk grinder or angle grinder will rapidly take care of a lot of potential impurities. Finish off the grinding or cutting by cleaning the surfaces with a wire brush.

There are several types of joints that most welders will encounter in the early stages of welding.

Tack welds

When you weld pieces of steel together, if they are long, you might prefer to tack weld them together. This simply means short welds of around one to two centimetres spaced about 300 millimetres apart. These hold the steel together to make it easier for you to commence welding. Don't try welding one long length of steel plate to another long length of steel plate and hope that the distances at the end will match your expectations. They won't. Other forces, including distortion, or buckling, will creep into your work and cause a disaster.

For large pieces of steel, tack welds running either direction, and starting from both ends of the work, will be preferable.

Whenever you weld over a bead of weld metal, you must remove all weld slag and

31

mill scale from the site. Do not think that because you cleaned the site in the preparation stage, that it should still be clean. It won't be. Use a wire brush over the weld before re-welding it. If you are turning over the steel to weld from the other side, make

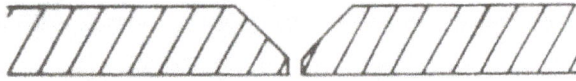

Bevel both sides, but leave 2 mm without bevelling to ensure maximum weld metal penetration

sure the joint does not contain any slag or other debris. Any impurities that get into the weld metal will weaken the whole weld. Avoid this to ensure a strong weld.

Butt joints

This is the simplest joint of all. It merely denotes two pieces of steel, usually less than three millimetres thick, with a gap of the same thickness as the welding electrode you will be using, or the same as the thickness of the pieces of steel. You might be able to get away with leaving a slightly wider gap between the steel as you become more proficient—but don't try this until you have had lots of welding practice. For the first run of weld metal in that space, do not weave the electrode from side to side. You will want to attain maximum weld metal penetration, and you will only succeed here by maintaining a steady hand while moving the electrode along the gap only.

Single vee butt joint

If the steel you are welding is more than three millimetres thick, you should bevel part of each surface. This opens up the joint so that weld metal can penetrate between the two surfaces, thus enabling the fusion of the steel by the welding rod. You can maintain a thin section that is not bevelled, rather than taking the bevels right to the full depth of the steel pieces. You will still need to leave a gap so that weld metal can penetrate the bottom

section of the joint. Usually a gap of around two millimetres should be sufficient, if you leave two millimetres that have not been bevelled.

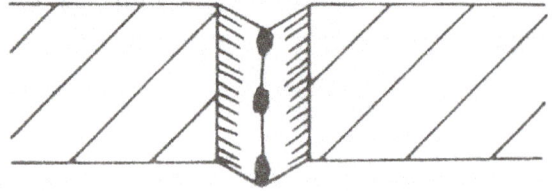

Tack welds will keep the pieces of steel together until they are fully welded

If you are welding a piece of steel not to the edge or the end of another piece of steel, you obviously will not be able to bevel both surfaces. In this case, you can bevel only one of the pieces of steel at an angle of 45°, but you can take the bevel right to the opposite edge.

Double vee butt joint

This is similar to the single vee butt joint, but you will bevel the edges on both sides of each piece, but leaving a thin section in the middle that is not bevelled. This type of joint is usually used on thicker steel that is harder to weld in a single pass on only one side.

Leave the mandatory gap between the unbevelled sections, and weld on alternate sides, turning over the pieces of steel between each pass of the electrode.

To fill the gap completely, use more than one run of weld metal over the joint.

Lap joint

For some applications, you might need to lap the two pieces of steel together. One piece of steel is placed over the other and welded

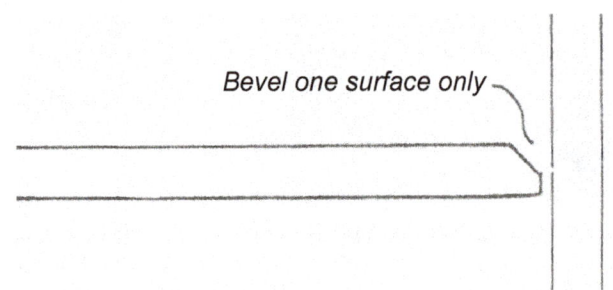

Bevel one surface only

along either one or both surfaces, turning over the steel to weld the second side where practical.

Fillet welds

You will be using a fillet weld often in your welding career, as many applications call for only this type of joint.

This one is simple, with no preparation such as grinding or bevelling.

One piece of steel is placed at an angle, such as a right angle or 90° to the other, and a run of weld metal (more if necessary) is run in the angle formed by the two pieces of steel.

Tee joints

This is an extension of the fillet weld, but performed on both sides of one of the pieces of steel. First a bead of weld metal is deposited on one side of the joint, and then the object is turned over (where practicable) and the same procedure carried out on the opposite side.

Downhand welds

You will often need to weld in the vertical downhill position. Here, you will start at the top of the joint and work your way slowly down along the length of the joint.

Sometimes you might need to apply a vertical up weld. Here, you should use a higher amperage than you would have used for the normal flat weld or the vertical down weld. You may find weaving the electrode from side to side beneficial to ensure a strong weld. Always keep the arc length as short as possible so the weld metal does not run away from the joint.

The vertical down weld is ideal for steel up to three millimetres thick. Weaving the electrode should not be necessary on plate of this thickness using the vertical down method.

For these positions of weld, practice will help ensure the correct arc length, the correct rate of travel, as long as the correct electrode is used. A smaller electrode might give a better result in the vertical positions.

For both vertical up and vertical down welding positions, the electrode should point slightly down.

The electrodes

Which electrode will you chose to weld your steel?

Your choice depends on several factors— what steels you are welding, and whether the two steels differ in composition.

As a general guide only ...

For mild steel, electrodes rated as E6012 or E6013 will be suitable.

Other electrodes are available if the two pieces of steel give a poor fit up, with a large or irregular gap that you can not rectify through proper preparation. Sometimes this does happen, and is unavoidable. Check to see which electrodes are available to you. Any welding supplier will be able to guide you in the correct electrode to use if the joint is out of the ordinary.

For cast iron, use an electrode that is designated as suitable for cast iron. An electrode intended for use on mild steel will not be suitable, as it will draw too much carbon from the cast iron, and weaken the whole component. If this happens to be an expensive engine block or some farm equipment that is very expensive to replace, don't select the cheap, easy option. Cheap is not cheap. Here, cheap electrodes will be very expensive in the long run (in fact it might not even be a very long run).

For stainless steel, use an electrode that is intended for use on stainless steel, and don't use anything else.

There's more about welding cast iron and stainless steel in later chapters.

For high alloy steels, and steels of dissimilar metals, and for those hard to weld jobs, there are welding electrodes that are designated as weld-all electrodes. These special electrodes will have an application in even the most difficult jobs such as car springs (a special steel), broken tools, shafts, and for welding dissimilar metals, such as welding mild steel to stainless steel.

For hard facing, making surfaces that are prone to wear and tear and abrasion, such as plough tines, hard facing electrodes should be used. These impart an extremely hard-wearing weld deposit on the edge or on the surface. These electrodes are used to resist wear on rock drills, earth moving and digging equipment, and even worn cam shafts.

There is more on hard-facing electrodes in a later chapter.

Thickness of electrodes

As a general guide only, use the following rough guide:

For steel up to 1.6 mm thick, the diameter of the electrode should be 1.6 to 2 mm diameter.

For steel up to 3 mm thick, the electrode size should be 2.0 to 2.5 mm diameter.

For steel over 3 mm thick, the electrode diameter should be 2.5 to 3.25 mm.

For steel above 5 mm thick, the electrode diameter should be 3.25 mm. For thicker electrodes you might need a much larger welder, one that delivers a much higher amperage, and these machines draw 415 volts at a high amperage. This sort of power is not available in the smaller workshop or around the house. You can do an admirable job even on thicker steel by depositing several runs of weld metal using a smaller diameter welding electrode.

About the electrodes

Welding electrodes consist of an inner metal rod, surrounded by a coating of flux.

The flux coating should cover the whole of the metal rod, except at the very tip where an arc is struck on the metal being welded. If there are breaks in the flux coating, the arc will be difficult to impossible to maintain, and the resulting weld will be very poor.

The coating provides a shield for the weld metal, and preserves it from oxidation by the atmosphere while the metal is still molten. This is why it is essential that the flux coating is not removed from a weld until the weld metal has cooled sufficiently. After that point, most of the flux will peel away from the weld easily.

The coating also helps provide a steady arc and provides a means for the current to flow from the electrode to the metal being welded.

The coating also provides a cleaning action on the metal. The slag, once formed, helps to produce a bead of weld metal of the correct contour.

Sometimes the coating contains additives that are deposited in special types of electrodes.

Starting to weld

This is the fun bit. It's what the whole welding process is all about. Don't rush the procedure, and remember that you won't become an expert in the first few minutes of welding. Good welding is an art, and for most, if not for all people, the process from amateur to professional welder can take some time to develop. Be patient. It will be worth it.

In your early days as a would-be welder, practice on old pieces of steel. Try deposition beads of weld metal on any old surface you can pick up. This is where scavenging on rubbish dumps might be worthwhile. What is trash to one person, might provide off-cuts and discarded steel objects that are just right for you to practice on.

Use a general purpose electrode, one of 3.25 mm diameter. If you are using old, discarded steel, make sure it is clean, free of paint, rust, oil, grease and other substances that could impart impurities into the weld. And if the steel you are practising on has been coated, make sure you remove every bit of paint. Old paints contained lead. Metal that has been primed usually contains zinc or chromium compounds, and their fumes should never be inhaled. See more about this aspect of welding under Safe Welding.

Position the practice piece of steel in a comfortable position so you can perform a downland welding position — that is, where you move the electrode from one side to the other. This is the easiest way to becoming proficient before tackling anything more complicated.

Connect the earth clamp to the steel, ensuring a good, tight fit so that electricity can pass from the lead, through the clamp, to the steel being welded. The circuit is completed through the electrode. A bad electrical connection will give a bad welding job.

Position of the welder

How you are positioned in relation to your work is important. You will want the travel of the electrode to be from left to right (or right to left), not away from or towards you. Make sure the electrode and the electrode holder are not obstructed by anything, including pieces of steel, or even protrusions of the work itself. Support the electrode lead if you can—even if this means placing it over your shoulder.

Striking the arc

The idea of striking and maintaining the arc is to hold the electrode close enough to the steel but not so close that it sticks to the metal, and not too far from it so that you get a lot of splatter and the arc stops. With a lot of practice, you will get the feel for it. And at the same time, listen to the sound of the arc. If it's noisy, it's probably too far from the base metal you are welding.

A long arc, that is, one where you are holding the tip of the electrode too far from the metal, will produce more heat than a shorter arc. The long arc will produce a loud crackling and spluttering noise. The result will be that the weld metal will be deposited in large, irregular blobs.

Because the arc is hotter with a long arc, and because it produces more heat, the weld bead deposited will be flattened.

For good quality welding, a short arc is essential, but not so short the electrode sticks to the metal or freezes to the base metal.

If your electrode does stick, give it a twist to break it free and strike the arc again.

An amperage that is set too low will result in an intermediate deposition of weld metal

Brush the tip of the electrode quickly over a short distance along the base metal until you get a continuous arc. This will be similar to your action when you strike a match on the side of the match box. Adjust the distance, and thus the length of the arc, and weave the electrode slowly from side to side so that the weld metal gradually builds up.

If you have started the arc correctly, allow the tip of the electrode to rest on the base metal and draw it along the metal. The electrode will be melting—that's the whole process of welding. And as the electrode melts, you will need to move it closer to the

In this example, the amperage was set too high for the thickness of the material being welded

metal as you run the electrode along the base metal. If you don't adjust the distance, continually bringing the tip of the electrode closer and closer to the metal, eventually the distance will be too great to carry the arc. If this happens while you are welding, strike the arc again and maintain it, this time at the correct distance from the metal.

Once you strike the arc, you will draw the electrode from the metal. If you draw it away too far, the arc will stop. Strike the arc again and try again until you can maintain the correct distance, and the correct rate of travel.

The angle at which you hold the electrode in relation to the steel you are welding is important. Aim for an angle of around 15 to 20° from the vertical, aiming the electrode at the joint, not anywhere else. The weld metal should be deposited on both pieces of metal evenly.

When you have gone a short distance along, stop and look at the result.

If the weld metal has formed in a large mass, it means you have moved the electrode too slowly. If the resulting deposition is spasmodic, it means that you have moved the electrode too fast, so that gaps appear in the deposition.

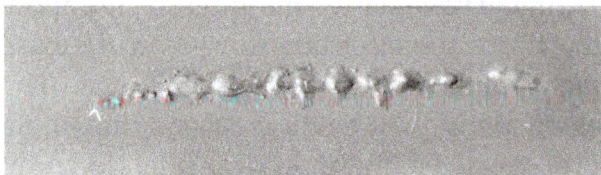

If the arc is too fast, you will get an uneven deposition of weld metal

After a short while of trial and error, you will be able to correct the distance of the electrode from the steel, and also check that your rate of travel is about correct.

At first, you might find that the tip of the electrode sticks to the metal. This indicates that you have not withdrawn the tip of the electrode from the metal once the arc has started.

Another reason the electrode will stick is because you have the welder set at too low an amperage, one where there is not enough current, and thus heat, to melt the electrode. Adjust the welder to increase the amperage.

Rate of travel

Once you have established the arc, the next important consideration is the rate of travel of the electrode. After practice, sometimes after lots and lots of practice, you will be able

An even deposition of weld metal is what you should strive for

to determine the correct rate of travel, which requires moving the electrode tip towards the molten pool at the same rate at which it is melting. At the same time, the electrode has to move along the metal to form the bead. Make sure you direct the electrode at the resulting weld metal pool, and at an angle of around 20°.

Make sure the rate of travel results in a well-formed bead. If the rate of travel is too fast, the bead will be narrow, perhaps strung out or broken into small globules.

If, on the other hand, the rate of travel is too slow, the weld metal piles up and the weld metal bead will be far too large. You will have to do a lot of grinding to remove the excess weld metal, and you will be wasting a lot of money on electrodes you will grind away.

Distortion

Distortion is the enemy of welders when they begin welding, and even sometimes more experienced welders. A lot of this distortion or warping can be eliminated by a simple practice.

As mentioned earlier in this chapter, tack welding the longer pieces together prior to welding the complete joint is advisable. The tack welds keep the job together until you can weld the joint fully.

The tack welds are intermittent, about one or two centimetres long spaced about 300 millimetres apart, but welded from different directions and from end to end.

If you weld two pieces of steel together, welding on only one side, you can guarantee you will end up with welding distortion.

Overcome this by one of two ways. The first is to weld equally on both sides of the weld, laying down one bead of weld on each side at a time before turning over the steel and welding on the opposite side.

The second method is to clamp the ends of the welded pieces firmly. This will place a strain on the welded joint, and on the clamps, so the backing plate needs to be a substantial thickness to prevent itself from buckling under the strain. The heat of the midday sun in summer in some areas of the world is enough to buckle railway lines. The intense head generated by welding is even more than the sun shining on the railway lines. So be aware of the tremendous force of distortion or bucking.

5 A Guide to quality welding

You have followed the directions in Chapter 4 on learning to weld, and hopefully you have now grasped the basics of welding.

This chapter could be regarded as the trouble-shooting chapter—what to do if your welds don't turn out the way they should.

Bad welds are a bit like poor building jobs—they're best covered up with a thick coat of paint. Bad welds are best avoided at the best of times; at worst, they can fail and, with large structures or heavy machinery, prove dangerous.

They're unsightly too—something that's hard for anyone to take pride in. That's where the coat of paint comes in handy to hide the less than professional quality of work.

Welding will substitute for that twisted-wire technology only if the welds are as strong as the twisted wire; a good weld should be at least as strong as the base metal that is being welded. Welds of this strength are easily attainable if proper attention is paid to their preparation. Proper welding practice will determine the success or otherwise of any weld. A good weld is strong, durable and permanent.

There is little point in using thick pieces of steel, for example, if the weld keeping them together is weak. Suppose you manufacture an item from steel five millimetres thick, but with a weld that is equivalent in strength to a piece of steel only three millimetres thick. An item made entirely from steel three millimetres thick, properly welded, will be as strong—and as useful—as one made from heavier and more expensive materials.

All good welding starts with the correct preparation.

Weld metal penetration

In the chapter on learning to weld, there are extensive instructions for ensuring full weld metal penetration. This means that when you weld two pieces of steel together, the weld metal that is deposited goes the full depth of the base metal. Anything less will result in a faulty or a weak weld. Please read the chapter on learning to weld again to ensure that your welds are as strong as it is possible to achieve.

What's the difference between good welding and bad welding? There's about two minutes difference between the two standards. Obviously, the answer is to take your time, and make sure the result is the best you are able to achieve.

Look at the causes of bad welds. All bad welds can be avoided, or at least minimised, by understanding their causes and knowing the procedures for good welds.

If using welding electrodes, make sure these are stored correctly, and make sure you handle them carefully. Don't get them wet, and don't break the coating by dropping them or stepping on them.

Arc welding electrodes consist of a metal core surrounded by a coating of flux. With careless handling, the flux can break away from the metal. Striking the arc can be rather difficult; maintaining a smooth arc is just about as difficult. The result of broken or deficient flux coating is a weld that has low strength and poor appearance.

If the flux coating is damaged, use up that portion with the damaged flux on scrap steel until solid flux coating is reached, or, better still, throw out the electrode and select one that's in good condition.

Incomplete weld metal penetration will result in poor welding strength. The strength of the weld is dependent, in part, on the depth of weld; if only the surface has been welded, or weld metal deposited only on the surface, then the strength of the weld is limited by the depth of the weld metal as well as the quality of that weld. Full penetration will ensure that the weld is at least as strong as the base metal itself.

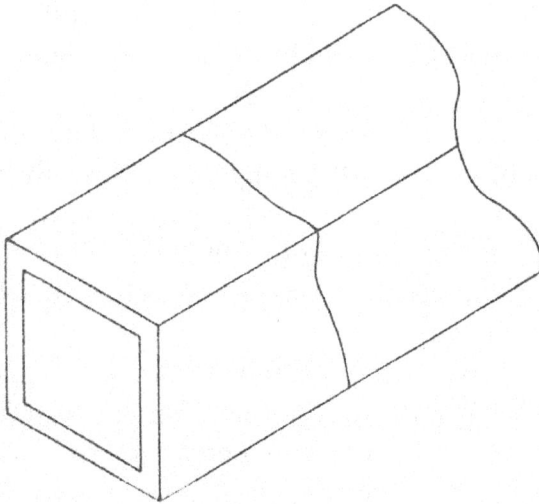

Whether new welds or repairs, the same preparation applies

Incomplete penetration may not always be obvious until a fracture of the weld occurs. Weld metal may hide any shortcomings in the work. The cause lies below the weld metal itself. While the prime cause of this weakness is often an insufficient gap between the two pieces of metal, other causes include using an electrode with too low an amperage, or even an electrode that is too large for the joint, or holding the electrode at an incorrect angle. The remedies for these causes should be obvious.

Bevel the edges

Full weld metal penetration is easy. If the parts being welded are up to three millimetres thick, bevelling of the edges won't really be necessary, but a space between the two components is essential. As a rough guide only, there should be a gap between the two surfaces approximately the thickness of the metal; that is, steel three millimetres thick should have a gap three millimetres wide; steel two millimetres thick, a gap two millimetres wide.

Leave enough metal (about three millimetres) so the electrode does not burn through the steel

Many applications will require metals much thicker than three millimetres. Then, tapering of the edges will be essential. This can be achieved by grinding each of the two surfaces at an angle of about 45° so that, together, they form a right angle.

If the metal is more than six millimetres thick, bevel both pieces, and from both sides

An incorrect profile, or angle, can severely affect the overall strength of a weld. If the angles are too wide, several runs of weld metal may be necessary to achieve full build up, resulting in wasted electrodes, a poor weld, and the chance of slag being incorporated in the weld metal. Stresses can build up too because of the use of excess weld metal and the heat generated by the unnecessary welding resulting in buckling.

Thin metals are very easy to burn right through; a piece of steel that is half a

For thicker pieces, build up the layers of weld metal so there is some over-fill that can be ground down later

millimetre thick, welded with a high amperage, soon won't be there at all.

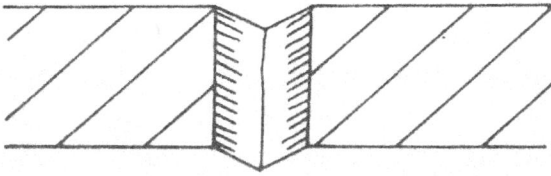

Bevel the edges for maximum weld metal penetration

It is often a temptation to push the two surfaces close together and to weld over the joint. This may look tidy, but seldom is full weld metal penetration achieved; the weld metal may be deposited as a thin bead about one millimetre thick over the joint; when this is ground down, there is barely any weld metal holding the two parts together. Although, especially with repairs, this may seem to be the logical, neatest and most practical way of bringing the parts together, it is, in reality, the weakest and poorest welding practice possible.

Structure of the material

Some welding operations will alter the crystalline structure of the steel. This structure may be altered with each successive run of weld metal; the first run may deposit metal of small crystalline structure; the second run may alter that structure to one of coarse grains. Instead of strengthening the joint by adding more weld metal, the process may indeed weaken the joint altogether.

After tack welding, make one run along the joint. If the run is too long, lay down the weld metal in stages

Buckling

The heat generated by welding processes causes distortion to the metal. This movement can be reduced, although never eliminated, by, where possible, bevelling the surfaces on both sides. Obviously this can't be done where access to either surface is restricted, but, where possible, and certainly for thicker materials, this should be undertaken.

This is the factor that will cause more unsightly welds than anything else. Steel that is straight can be easily thrown out of shape by welding. It's caused by the weld metal contracting on cooling. All metals contract at a set rate for a given drop in temperature. Weld metal that is deposited in the flat position when molten will soon shrink when it's cool. When it contracts, it pulls the base metal out of shape, unless the base material is securely clamped down. A welded precision component of some farm machinery that's to fit exactly in place may not, after being welded, fit into its hole. Distortion can, depending on the job being undertaken of course, be overcome by exaggerating the positions of the base metals being welded. In other words, don't weld the joint flat, but build into it a slight offsetting so that when cool, the contracted weld metal will pull the pieces of metal together in their correct, flat positions.

Distortions can sometimes be corrected by heating the weld and then beating it heavily with a hammer. This is a good remedy for removing the frustration caused by the distortion too.

Improper welding sequences can cause distortions, particularly in large sheets of

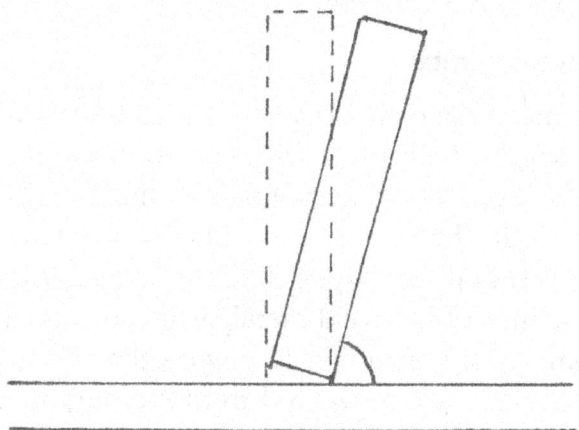

The welding process will distort the pieces of steel being welded. You can off-set this to some extent by aligning the pieces at an exaggerated angle before welding

steel. Use intermittent welding, and skip sections of the join, and step back. This is preferable to laying down one very long run of weld metal. Altering the direction in which weld metal is deposited will certainly help to overcome distortions, even if it can't be eliminated altogether.

A segment three millimetres thick should be left in the middle; the weld metal can easily fill this gap, and each successive run of weld metal deposited will gradually fill the rest of the gap from either side.

One run of weld metal applied to one side, followed by one run on the opposite side, the third run on the first side and so on until weld metal has been built up slightly higher than the original surface level of the metal will achieve an almost distortion-free weld. This alternating method is highly desirable if access is possible from both sides, but often it isn't. However, when it is possible to attack the job from both sides, the method involves welding a small run, perhaps 50 mm long on one side. This will pull one component out of alignment with the other. This will then be pulled back into its correct position (or close to it) by a similar amount by welding on the back of it.

Welding in different areas along both sides tends to eliminate most of the distortions, at least so that a neat job is obtained — one that is functionally strong and aesthetically pleasing.

Using clamps

Securing the components together against a strong backing plate will tend to minimise distortion, as well as holding the metals firmly in their right place. This is practical, but it does have its limitations, as the tendency of the weld metal, as it cools, is to contract significantly. Be aware that if the steel parts are prevented from moving, the weld metal may stretch with the result that the weld will have built into it a high degree of stress which may cause the weld to break at any time. Nevertheless, it's surprising how often this method is employed in welding

practices, so it must work okay, despite its possible long-term disadvantages.

Moisture

Using damp electrodes will probably result in a fiery arc — you'll recognise this symptom when it arises! The weld metal will be laid down spasmodically. And you'll recognise the excess splatter when the weld metal, instead of being laid down in a neat row, ends up all over the base metal.

Steam gets into the weld metal and explodes, sending the molten metal in all the wrong places. It just isn't possible to get a smooth, even flow of weld metal with damp electrodes.

Storing your welding electrodes to keep them dry doesn't mean just keeping them away from water.

The flux of most electrodes can absorb moisture from the air once their package is opened. Electrodes should be stored in heated cabinets once unwrapped. The cabinet only needs to be kept a few degrees warmer than outside temperature. This is because moisture from the air will not move from cold to warm conditions.

If you need to store lots of packets of welding electrodes, use an old refrigerator. Make your own electrode storage cabinet. It may seem strange to warm something in a refrigerator, but the cabinet is well insulated and can be easily adapted for storing electrodes. Drill a hole at the top for ventilation, feed through the flex for a light socket, and run a low-wattage light bulb of about ten to twenty watts. It won't cost much to run the unit, and will save much frustration when the electrodes weld the way they were intended.

Alternatively, line the inside of a wooden crate with aluminium foil, or turn a polystyrene box upside down over a sheet of plywood or chipboard. A low-wattage light bulb will work just as well in one of these storage units.

Dry surfaces

Moisture on a surface that is being welded will produce a weak joint. Moisture may not be apparent, but with machinery that has been left outside in all weathers, it can be on the back, as well as the front of the material being welded. Small bubbles generated by the steam become trapped as the weld metal is deposited. These bubbles mix with the molten metal, resulting in long-term problems and weaknesses.

Electrical contacts

Tight contact between the welder and each of the leads is essential. The result of having loose terminal connections will be the same as having grit under the earthing clamp. Intermittent electrical contact is assured, with intermittent welding too. Certainly this is not conducive to good welding procedures. The connections should be tight, but it isn't necessary to use a large wrench to tighten them. Smaller machines may have finger-grip heads on the terminals. Finger tightness is all that's needed.

A problem that's quite often overlooked, yet is common with arc welding, is improper electrical contact, particularly between the clamp and the base metal. A good contact here is essential. If the contact is poor, the arc will be intermittent or non-existent. The weld metal will be laid down in blobs instead of a neat, straight row. The clamp can look firmly attached to the metal, but any grit, even the size of fine sand, under the clamp can prevent electrical contact. The electric circuit is not completed, and no welding can take place. It's often useful when attaching a clamp to the metal, to clean the metal itself to remove grime, grit and other electrical insulating materials to allow good contact.

Electrodes

Proper electrodes for the job are essential. There are so many types on the market now that it's reasonable to assume that one was made for every situation anyone could think of. The 'general' electrodes, such as those rated E6012 or E6013, are just that – general

electrodes. They have their application in general fields, such as with mild steel fabrication. Some electrodes have their applications in different positions; some are good for overhead welds, others are not; others are intended for 'vertical down' or 'vertical up'; others aren't. Using one that's designed for downhand welding in an overhead position will give results that the manufacturer wouldn't be impressed with.

Use an electrode intended for the metal you are using – mild steel electrode for mild steel, 'special' electrode with 'special' steel – cast iron electrodes for cast iron, stainless steel electrodes for welding stainless steels, and so on. While many different electrodes will give at least some results on many different metals, their effectiveness won't necessarily be consistent. Ascertain the base metal you are working with, and select the electrode accordingly.

While it is implied that some electrodes have a 'universal' application, that term might be rather like some 'universal' threads – the term 'universal' means they won't fit very much at all.

Of course there are those 'specials' in electrodes, like some of those coming out of certain countries. They will look the same as any other, but (at least my experience has shown) they deposit metal sometimes, will freak out in the middle of a run, and they aren't as strong as better-known electrodes. They might be a quarter of the price of good quality electrodes, but they're not much good for anything!

Use the correct amperage

Success is assured (with electrode selection, at least) by not only using the correct electrode for the job, but using the correct size electrode, and with the machine set at the right amperage. Packets of electrodes will (usually) have the recommended amperage set out on them. As a general rule, the range is large, such as those for the 2.5 mm E6013, which suggests a current somewhere between 55-90 amps, or 90-135 amps for the

3.25 mm electrodes. On thick metals, the lowest recommended setting won't achieve much; on thin metal, the highest setting will probably burn right through the steel. It's best to select a current somewhere between the ranges, and raise or lower the amperage according to trial and error in a particular application, and according to your own competence of welding.

A thick electrode (such as 5.0 mm) will require a very high current; a small electrode such is 2.5 mm will be too thin to weld thick plate, such as 12 mm thick. Use electrode diameters according to common sense and your competence of welding. Practice will soon determine what's best for you and for a particular situation.

A low amperage with a thick electrode, or a high amperage with a thin electrode — that is, a current that's outside the recommended range for a particular electrode, will result in a welding job that's far from satisfactory. And it's at harvest time that weaknesses will manifest themselves. Again, mid-point between the recommended range is a good starting point, with an adjustment made either side of that current, if necessary.

If the amperage is too high, weld splatter will mess up the work, and the excessively hot arc will result in a poor quality weld.

Any operator will know when the current is too low for a particular electrode — the arc cannot be maintained except with great difficulty. The tip of the electrode will stick to the metal — it will melt just enough to melt it onto the base metal and there it will remain. With a low amperage, only poor weld metal penetration can be achieved — in other words, the weld metal won't flow through to the full thickness of the metal.

Arc length

You'll soon get the feel for the right arc length to use. It will come with practice. But too long an arc — that is, one where the tip of the electrode is held a long way back from the base metal being welded—will produce lots

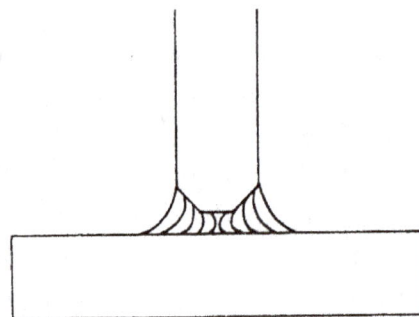

Always aim for a smooth, even weld

of heat. On thin pieces of metal, this may result in burning through—this despite the fact that the same setting, on the same metal, but with the correct length of arc maintained, will give a good weld. But you will be aware of the long arc; just listen to the excessive crackling, and look for the splatter and the blobs of weld metal.

Listen for the right arc length

In welding jobs, you can keep your arc at the correct length by listening for the sound the arc makes.

For example, the MIG dip transfer process makes sounds like the rattles of a machine-gun when the right length is reached (that is, when the arc voltage between the tip of the electrode and the job is correct for good welding without burn-through).

The MIG spray transfer process hisses like a leaky valve, while the general purpose range of stick electrode welders, a favourite with rural operators, sound like eggs crackling in a frying pan when using electrodes at the correct amperage and arc length.

The golden rule: too short an arc generates less heat and the electrode or wire can become fused to the job. Too long an arc produces too much heat, too much burn-through and reduced appearance and quality.

An arc that's too short will also become apparent. The electrode will become buried in the slag and the molten metal.

So when you are welding, keep both your eyes and your ears on the job.

Rate of travel

The speed at which the weld metal is deposited into the joint will determine its characteristics including its appearance and strength. If the rate of travel of the electrode is too fast, the weld metal will be spindly and intermittent; if too slow, the pool of weld metal will soon catch up with the tip of the electrode and prevent the arc from doing its job.

The electrode should be held at an angle of about 15-20° to the vertical, with the tip pointing towards the weld metal pool. A well-formed bead of molten metal should be formed.

Maintain an even deposition of weld metal by ensuring the rate of travel is even and smooth

Undercutting

This cause of poor welding and potential weakness is apparent on a close inspection of the weld. The bead of weld metal should slightly bulge above the base metal. With undercutting, the edge of the weld metal bead will be slightly below the level of the base metal, and it will be seen to have cut into the edges of the joint itself. The causes of this problem are several, their remedies easy; high amperage, too long an arc (causing too much heat), incorrect angle of the electrode, too large an electrode for the base metal, and incorrect deposition of weld metal, especially with wider joints where the electrode needs to be weaved back and forth. But sometimes weaving itself can cause undercutting.

Undercutting may not look like much of a problem in welding – perhaps just a slight deficiency of weld metal in a particular place, but it can be one of the more serious failures of welding. It not only signifies improper welding, but it indicates that insufficient weld metal has been deposited in the groove, resulting in a weak weld. Stresses can build up, too.

Avoid undercutting by using a lower amperage. Undercutting weakens the joint

Can it be welded?

There are of course other causes of welding failures, but there are also ways to overcome or at least minimise these.

To weld any metal correctly, the correct welding electrode is essential. Mild steel requires the use of mild steel electrodes. Hardened steel will require different electrodes.

A mild steel electrode used for welding hardened steel will result in a dismal failure. Certain components of steel, such as carbon, may be removed with the use of different electrodes, resulting in the remaining steel being given different properties. What may have started off as hardened steel, may now be steel that has had some of its carbon content reduced, and a mild steel electrode that has gained some of that carbon.

And with dissimilar metals, weaknesses can result by using the incorrect welding electrode or rod. A filler rod may bond securely to one metal, but not to another, although now there are many welding rods and electrodes that will weld together dissimilar metals. There are just so many electrodes and rods available now – almost one for every specific purpose. These are very useful rods and electrodes too, often enhancing the strength of the welds considerably, particularly in the case of machinery repairs. The trouble though is to

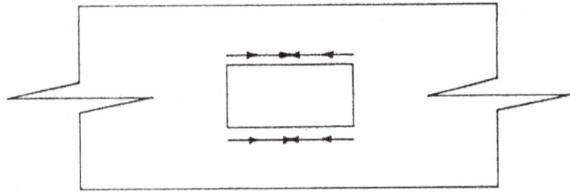

For larger pieces of steel, and for steel plate, stagger the welds and weld from different directions to minimise distortion and buckling

find the right combination of metal and electrode.

Manufacturers of the special electrodes, particularly those designed for metals of unknown composition, have overcome the problem of selection by producing special-purpose electrodes or rods and publishing good quality literature on their products.

Impurities in the weld

Just as water can cause problems with welding, the slag from the welding electrode may also impair the strength of a weld. Slag may be incorporated in a bead of weld metal; its presence is often associated with too low an amperage, or insufficient removal of slag from an earlier run of weld metal, or by using the wrong electrode angle, or an excess of rust or mill scale — that flaking coating that is present on most new black steels.

Slag sometimes builds up in the weld metal if the electrode is weaved from side to side too much. Keep the weaving to a minimum and chances are that slag inclusions will be minimal too. The slag, like water, has no tensile strength whatsoever, and its inclusion in a weld can be the source of potential cracking and failure.

Slag can also built up and weaken the weld tremendously by preventing the weld metal from penetrating the full thickness of the base metal. This often happens if the gap between the surfaces is inadequate, and especially if the amperage is too low. The use of a wrong electrode can cause slag to be incorporated into a weld, such as when using an electrode that is suitable for downhand

welding, in a vertical up, or overhead position.

Whatever the cause of its presence, slag must be removed, perhaps by grinding or cutting, and replaced by a run of weld metal from a small electrode (such as a 2.5 mm electrode), using a high amperage.

Fusion of the metals

Sometimes portions of weld metal do not fuse with the base metal, particularly with electric welding. This may be the result of a small electrode being used at low current, producing too little heat, particularly if a large, thick piece of steel is being welded. The correct size electrode, at the correct amperage, should overcome this cause of weakness. An incorrect electrode angle will result in the same type of problem. The angle should, for downhand welding, be held at about 15° to 20° from the vertical. Different positions, such as vertical down, or overhead welding, will require the use of different angles.

If the rate of travel of the electrode is too fast the result can be poor or incomplete fusion between base metal and weld metal. The rate should be sufficient to maintain the arc near the well-formed molten pool of weld metal. If the rate of travel is too fast, the bead will be narrow and strung out or even broken up into small segments, resulting in a poor quality weak weld. If the rate of travel is too slow, weld metal accumulates and becomes too large.

Lack of fusion

This is a problem that usually manifests itself when the repairs are back in place on the machinery. Again, harvest time is a good time to locate poor-fusion welds!

They're caused by the deposit of too much weld metal without any action being taken to direct the welding electrode at the base metal itself. This problem can be overcome by using the correct rate of travel, the correct amperage and correctly using the electrode.

Cracking

Cracks in welds can occur at almost any time — for example if the base metal was clamped too tightly as it was being welded, preventing any 'give'; it can be caused by using damp electrodes, or too high a current, or by slag entrapment, or by using too large an electrode for the base metal, or too slow a rate of travel, or too low a current. And many other causes. Often the crack can be extremely small. If tack welds are not sufficient for the job, they can crack, and here experience will show that the cracks can barely be seen. Cracks can develop in any weld. The cracks will usually be thin and often inconspicuous. Even too slow a rate of travel can lead to cracking.

Really, good welding isn't at all as difficult to achieve as it's made out to be. Your welding certainly will improve the more you weld, so don't expect perfect welds the first time you try.

6 Welding with safety

We want all our readers to stay alive and in good health long enough to complete the welding projects in this book and to enjoy their pastime or their training. A few basic rules of safety will lead to continued good health, and an operator and a property still intact.

Most machinery is safe — until someone has an accident with it. Welding equipment, both electric and gas, is about as safe as any other piece of machinery, provided it is used correctly. It's not the welding equipment that's unsafe, it's the operator who makes it dangerous. And it's not only how a welder is used, but also where it's used that makes it dangerous.

You can weld safely if you follow a few basic rules. If you don't follow even the basic rules, then welding can be a dangerous occupation for you.

Get it right the first time, by doing the welding properly. It will save you time and much pain. You will be dealing with mains electricity. For small welders, that means using 240 volt mains power supply and often even higher voltages. If you are using larger welding units, the welder will probably be drawing 415 volts. The usual safety

This is a most dangerous work area. Note the water, the clutter, the steel pieces in the working space, and the electrical cords that are easy to trip over

precautions just won't be enough if you're using your welding appliance outside, particularly in wet weather.

Perhaps the most important component of welding is you — the operator. Your safety is even more important than that of the equipment. So, you will need special protection. The protection here comes from three factors.

Welding in wet conditions

The first is electrical safety. Other than the rules listed earlier, a common fault is that some people insist on using electric welding equipment in wet, or even moist, foggy conditions. Water will help conduct electricity much more easily than if your skin and clothing are dry. On a dry day, you may not feel an electric shock if you accidentally touch the work. But if your gloves are wet, or if your clothing is damp from mist, you will feel more than a gentle electric shock!

Before very long, you will feel mild electric shocks through your damp gauntlets or overalls. The time to stop welding is before the steel, the ground, and your clothing get wet, not after.

Wear the correct clothing

Clothing is obviously important. First, good leather gauntlets are a must. If you weld without them, you won't do it again! They will protect your hands from the very intense ultraviolet rays from the arc. This arc can cause radiation burns. Even if it doesn't, your welder will throw off sparks. These sparks are really small molten globules of metal. And they're hot! So gloves, or gauntlets, protect your hands.

Some people who begin to weld don't appreciate the extremely high temperatures associated with welding. The arc itself from an electric welder is sufficient to melt steel. It is around 6000° Celsius — the same temperature as the surface of the sun. Gas welding equipment produces a slightly lower temperature than the arc, but nevertheless sufficiently high (about 3000° Celsius) to melt most metals. Those temperatures on bare skin are hot! These hot sparks are the cause of another serious hazard, particularly where there are combustible materials around.

Protection against fires

The sparks are thrown in all directions, and they can spontaneously start a fire in material in the workshop, and particularly in a field of dry grass. With mobile welders that are now so frequently found on rural properties, fires can be started inadvertently by welding equipment throwing sparks some distance from the machine. It could be some time before the flames are noticed — certainly enough time for a fire to get a hold in the dried grass. A thousand burned out hectares are a costly mistake, but mistakes like these can easily be avoided by ensuring that ALL flammable material is removed from within a reasonable distance of the welder.

Sometimes straw, and bales of hay are stored close to a welding area — a sure way of setting fire to the workshop and possibly the house too. Straw on the floor, fallen from the vehicle the last time it was taken in for repairs, is a fire hazard.

If flammable materials cannot be taken out of range of stray sparks, then take the welder out of the range of the material.

Sparks from cutting steel using gas equipment can fly a considerable distance too, and remain unnoticed until the flames get a hold.

Make sure you are fully protected, with the right clothing, including leather gauntlets

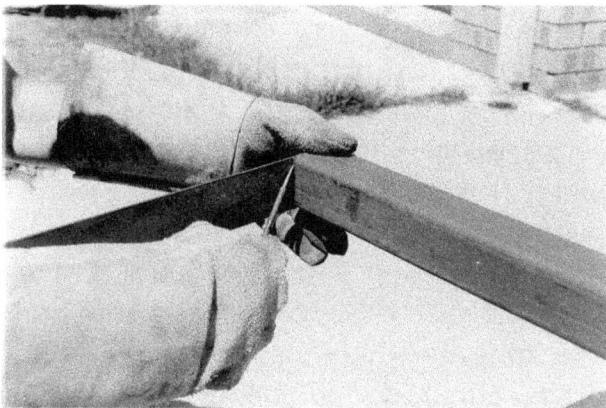

Leather gauntlets protect the welder from hot sparks and heat

But don't despair. You will not suffer any of these problems if you take sensible precautions, protect yourself, and treat electricity with respect, and think of your skin as something that will be going around with you for many years.

And now for the ways that you can avoid these threats to your life — and property. Let's look first at electric welding.

Electricity

Many electric welders run on 240 volts, while some of the larger machines operate on higher voltages, such as 415 volts. Even so, the voltage can be lethal, whether it is derived from the mains, or from another power source such as a generator.

Extension leads

Unless you have an adequately set up workshop, you probably will need to use a long extension lead, and here too there can be problems. Most of the cheap extension cords are lightweight cords, capable of carrying no more than 10 amps. Many of the welding units run on 15 amps, so the lead will not be able to carry the heavy current that the welding unit will draw. The result is that the extension cord, particularly if it is long, will create too much resistance and will overheat. This is dangerous as it will cause the insulation around the cord to melt and create another danger. This also places a strain on the power facilities of your home.

At least match up the rating of the extension lead used with that of the appliance, and make sure that the connections and the insulation are in good repair, with no frayed ends, breaks in the insulation, or damage generally.

If you are drawing 15 amps from a 10 amp power supply, then you will blow numerous fuses. However, if you replace the fuses with heavier fuse wire, then you are strengthening the part of the circuit that is designed to be weak (that is, the fuse) and create a fire hazard elsewhere in the house. The welding unit you use MUST NOT exceed the rating of the power supply from which it is operating. It won't cost very much to have an electrician install an outside power point adequate for the current and the voltage drawn by the welder.

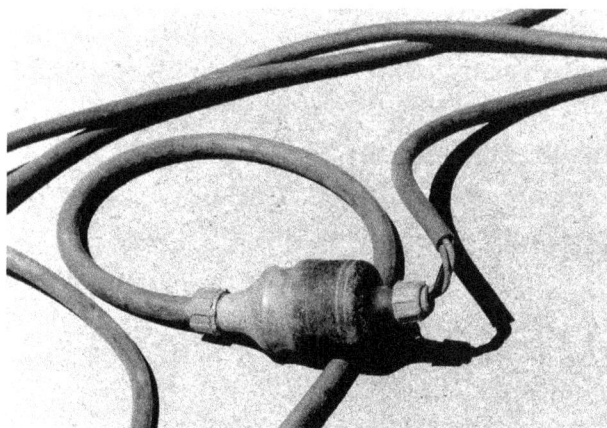

Straighten out power leads in the work area

Even the leads from the welder to the electrode holder, or from the welder to the work clamp, should be in good condition, with no frayed insulation, and tight fittings where the leads clamp to the welder.

Some plugs don't come out of wall sockets or extension cord plugs easily.

Make sure all insulation on leads and plugs is adequate

51

Always switch off the power to the unit before you attempt to remove a plug. This sounds basic, almost childish advice, but even experienced workers don't always obey the rules of safety. Pull one plug from another by pulling on the plug, or plugs, not the cord. Eventually, constant tugging on the leads will loosen the wires within the plug, creating a short circuit and dangerous sparks, or it may possibly burn your hands—or worse. If one wire (and often only one wire is sufficient) touches your skin, it will pass 240 volts through your body.

On the welder itself, there is another potential danger. This is from the work and electrode leads. These are the leads that carry as much as 150 amps. That current, converted to heat, can mean serious burning.

If you accidentally touch one of the output leads against the other, you can expect a large blue spark—after all, that is all electric welding is—a large spark that will melt metals together.

Through continual use, the insulation around the output leads weakens and frays. This can be dangerous because a short circuit here is the same as crossing together the two output leads.

Safe work area

The state of the welding site, if it is not tidy, can pose a hazard. Clutter, and steel over the work area floor, jagged pieces of metal above ground level, can be a threat to the well-being of people on the site. It is easy to trip over lengths of steel that are in the way. Keep the site neat and tidy, and remove any material you don't need immediately, and watch those extension leads—they're easy to trip over.

Dangerous places

There are plenty of places where you can do your welding, but there are a few places where you shouldn't weld. Or, if you do, then you may not be making all the projects in this book.

Sheds can be very dangerous to those who don't check the contents of tins on the shelves or in cupboards. Often there are containers of solvents, many of which are highly flammable. There are paints; there are paint strippers; there are cans of lawnmower fuel and probably a drum of petrol. Twenty litres of petrol will drive your car a long way. The same amount of fuel near a welder will drive your shed, and you, even further! So either remove all flammable materials from your shed, or better still, work outside. Close the door to your workshop so sparks don't go inside unnoticed and start a fire.

Keep the work area tidy at all times and remove obstacles that anyone can trip over

But why work inside a shed? If you're welding during the day, and the ground is dry, the light is much better outside where there is less risk of inhaling the fumes during the welding process. If you weld in an enclosed shed and look at the air, you will see more smoke than you would see over any huge, dirty city. Welding creates fumes; these are best kept out of your lungs. Over a long period, there could be the possibility of some temporary (or even permanent) lung damage.

Farm practices often include using disused fuel drums for purposes other than those for which they were intended. Admittedly, an unused fuel drum can make a splendid feeding trough, or some other item that the farmer ingeniously puts it to.

Whole 44-gallon drums, still with the top on and smelling strongly of petrol or kerosene fumes are potential bombs containing enough power to send them high into the sky, and the welder himself into sudden shock. Drums like these are extremely dangerous to weld. Avoid doing so! However, if they have been open for some time with all traces of fuel gone, with no risk whatsoever from explosion, then that may be different. Only the operator can decide if they really are safe to weld.

Most of the metal objects you will weld will be steel. But the steel objects you MUST NOT weld are fuel tanks, no matter how expensive they are to replace. It is very difficult to get all the fumes out of a petrol tank. And only a drop or two of petrol left in the tank, mixed with the right amount of air, is needed to make the tank explode. You won't be given any warning; an explosion from a fuel tank is instantaneous, and violent.

Flammable materials aren't limited to liquids; old mattresses, wooden boxes, cardboard, clothing, all of which are found in sheds, will be a potential fire risk.

Total fire ban days

In summer, we often experience days of high temperatures and very low humidity. The fire service will most likely impose a total fire ban over a region, or over a whole state if the conditions demand such action. This means that no fires will be lit or maintained in the open on such days. A welder, even an electric welder, will be deemed to constitute a fire in the open. So don't try welding in the open on such days. And on such days, be very careful if you decide to weld just inside your workroom doorway. Sparks from the welder can be thrown out through the door, setting fire to the immediate area, or beyond. Expect police action to be taken in those circumstances, and expect the full wrath of the fire chief to come down on you when he realises you were the cause of the fire he and his crew had to put out. Sometimes they lack a sense of humour.

Health risks

Actually there are advantages in working out in the open while you are welding, the main one being lots of fresh air. Welding processes, particularly electric welding, give off smoke and fumes. In a confined space, such as in a closed workshop, the fumes build up to an uncomfortable level. While manufacturers of welding electrodes don't always say that the fumes are dangerous, it is reasonable to expect them not to be safe either, if they are inhaled in large quantities.

Also given off in the welding process are zinc fumes from galvanised steel that is frequently used in farm welding; the steel used to make farm gates, and welded mesh is often galvanised. The heat of welding is enough to vaporise the zinc, or at least to create smoke containing zinc compounds. In a confined space, these fumes are hazardous to your health. Limited ventilation in the work area may not be enough to ensure the continued good health of the operator. The more open the space, the better.

Old pieces of steel are a good stand-by on properties, especially on those properties that are some distance from a steel supplier. For convenience, old steel lying around the property will often suffice just as well as new material will. However, if the steel has been previously painted, burning paints will create more health risks. Some of the older paints contained lead, while many primers used to prevent rusting contain chromium and zinc compounds. Both these materials are toxic if inhaled. Even modern acrylic paints can become toxic if they are burned. Any previously painted surfaces that you are about to weld must be cleaned down to the bare metal to remove all traces of paints and primers. Removal of all paints, primers and grease from the heat zone is recommended. That includes the area of steel that is not only welded, but the area of material that will nevertheless get rather hot through the welding process.

Use correct clothing

Having considered some of the things you shouldn't do, and where you shouldn't do them, don't overlook the most important risk of welding—the risk to yourself, and to your off-sider if you have an assistant helping you.

If you wear shorts while you're welding, you must be immune to pain. Overalls are necessary for full body protection. First, from the arc, and secondly from the molten metal and sparks that can burn you.

Sturdy overalls keep sparks from the operator, but only if they are done up fully. This means having even the top button at the neck done up. Too often overalls are worn partly undone—if they are worn at all. Pockets too should be done up where possible, as sparks frequently find their way into open pockets and start the overalls smouldering.

Those sparks have a habit of finding their way through small openings in your clothing. There's nothing more painful than feeling a red hot piece of metal rolling down the inside of your shirt against your skin.

Sparks seem to enjoy finding their way into footwear. If you wear thick socks, then often the sparks have cooled down sufficiently before they reach your skin. If you are wearing only thin socks, then the sparks will burn through immediately and cause the discomfort of yet another burn. And of course don't forget to protect your feet. Steel is heavy. A 10-metre length of angle iron dropped on your foot is uncomfortable, and so is a foot that's in plaster. If you can buy a pair of steel-capped work boots, then wear them. They will protect your feet. If your leg is in plaster, you'll still have one foot to hop around on.

Boots are preferable to shoes, but nothing, surely, could be more painful than wearing thongs or open sandals when welding. Yet this is done. Those people must have such a high tolerance to pain, nothing would wound them.

Gauntlets keep the hands and the lower arms free from painful burns. Thick leather takes a lot more battering from hot metals than bare skin ever could. Old cows are tough compared to our tender flesh!

Hot steel that has just been welded can be picked up by mistake before it has cooled sufficiently for it to be handled comfortably. If you pick up the same steel when you are wearing gauntlets, then the pain and the burns you receive will be far less.

But gauntlets and overalls do more than protect the operator from hot sparks. They are essential, as is the correct helmet or goggles, to protect the skin from the harmful ultraviolet rays emitted, particularly from the arc and to a lesser extent from the flame of gas welding appliances.

Radiation

Most arc welding units will come with a kit that includes a helmet. If not, you must buy one. If you buy a cheap welding unit, then at least buy a good quality helmet. This will protect your face and neck, and, even more importantly, your eyes, from radiation and sparks.

The ultraviolet rays are in the UV-B part of the electromagnetic spectrum, the rays that cause severe skin burning (similar to severe sun burning). That's why correct eye protection is essential too. The higher the amperage used in arc welding, the greater the intensity of UV rays. The darkened glass filters in the welding helmet must be suited to the range of electrodes and amperages being used.

In the front of the helmet there is a small window. If you look through it, you won't see much. It is designed that way to protect your eyes from the intense light and UV that would otherwise burn them, causing permanent eye damage, and possibly blindness.

Don't compromise on your safety, particularly your eyesight. Don't remove any of the filters from the helmet. They're there for a very good reason. If you need to replace the filters at any stage in the life of the helmet, then replace them with a filter recommended for the work you are doing, and not with one that is sub-standard.

The eyes in particular are very sensitive to these dangerous ultraviolet rays. Lack of protection, even briefly, will possibly cause lasting ill-effects. Even a flash from an arc, caught by accident can cause sore eyes. Staring at the arc is definitely dangerous.

Sturdy eye protection is inexpensive compared with the ophthalmologist's bills but make sure you have an adequate safety margin. Don't even consider using cheap plastic goggles as they may not give you the protection you need from fast-moving red-hot pieces of metal.

Occasionally a person can be seen welding, wearing sunglasses. Even for gas welding, these are not adequate, and provide insufficient eye protection. And as for these glasses for arc welding …!

Oxy-welding equipment has one additional danger. You are handling flammable gases, often liquid petroleum gas or acetylene. Either of these gases will be combined with compressed oxygen to give the intense heat required to melt steel. Respect that heat. It will melt almost anything the flame comes in contact with. So keep it away from the cylinders of compressed gases. The flame may extend further from the end of the blowtorch than you realise, as it isn't always possible to see the full length of the flame, particularly in bright sunlight.

Sparks while grinding

The next stage after welding is the finishing off, and this usually involves grinding down the excess weld metal. Here, too, are some inherent dangers which can, and should, be avoided. Most of the problems from grinding lead to eye damage! However, proper eye protection will eliminate these injuries, and again, don't forget your off-sider. Those sparks from the grinding wheel or the angle grinder are not only hot and sharp, but they are also travelling very fast. They can move well beyond the grinding wheel and cause a lot of personal injury and suffering.

The dangers don't come only from the welder and the electricity. You will have to use a grinding wheel to finish off your projects. This completes the job and is a necessary part of welding. But if you are using any form of grinder, whether it is an angle grinder, a grinding wheel attached to an electric drill, or a bench-mounted grinder, there is always a danger to your eyes from sparks thrown off from the grinding wheel.

These sparks in your eyes can be extremely painful. They are red hot, they can also cause temporary or permanent eye damage. Eye protection is necessary. Don't grind anything without adequate protection. If you value your eyesight, buy adequate eye protection that meets with the relevant level of safety standard.

No doubt you will be working on some, or all, of these projects with other people. Welding is ideal for involving your family and friends—they get almost as much enjoyment out of making things as you do and they provide a ready source of assistance. But you have an obligation to protect them as well as protecting yourself.

Ear protection

The noise caused by grinding steel is painful to listen to for even a short time. Grinding emits a high-pitched sound that is very loud and painful. If you don't wear ear protection at such times, you won't hear much in the near future. Ear damage is caused by being near loud noises for even a short time. Loud noises over long periods will in the end lead to permanent hearing loss. Even the noise emitted by the angle grinder when it is not in contact with the metal is very loud. That, on top of the noise of the grinding, will hasten the demise of your hearing very quickly. The ear protection you wear should meet the safety standards when used under conditions such as grinding. Ear protection comes in a range of standards. You will need to wear protection of the highest standard when you are grinding steel using an angle grinder or cutting steel using an disk cutter or a cut-off saw.

Respect your assistant

Just as hot sparks find their way some distance from the welding process, the ultra-violet rays will be dangerous some distance from the arc. If the operator is prepared to protect himself, then he should also ensure — in fact demand — that his off-sider is similarly protected. He has an obligation to ensure that all people around him are safe.

It is quite common to see the off-sider turning his head around on command, believing that he will not receive any ultra-violet radiation. This is not true. If he is not fully protected, then he is liable to the same risks as is the operator. Ultraviolet can also be reflected from surfaces, such as the bright walls of a shed. They will be the UV-B rays that damage eyesight.

Children are particularly susceptible to eye damage, because of their curiosity that compels them to stare at the arc. An arc can cause eye damage even from behind a gauze door, or a window. Children should NEVER be encouraged or allowed to look at a welder

Always, without exception, make sure your off-sider is fully protected when in the welding area

being operated unless they have the correct eye protection, as well as being clothed correctly.

Your insurance scheme won't provide for massive medical bills and compensation.

If working with steel, then they should have a pair of leather gloves and overalls for protection the same as you do.

If you're not prepared to protect any helpers then you should work entirely alone.

With care, foresight, and a sensible approach to yourself and those working with you, all of the dangers can be eliminated so that your welding can be safe welding.

Safety first in welding

Power supply: ensure the welder is plugged into a correctly earthed power point of correct amperage for the machine.

Cords: keep all leads in good order and avoid using long extension leads.

Moisture: do not weld in damp conditions.

Fuses: if your welder blows a fuse, do not substitute a higher rating fuse. You may need a higher rated circuit. Consult your electrician.

Fire: Welding generates large amounts of heat and an electric arc. Ensure before welding that your work area is clear of flammable materials, with paints and thinners closed tight and out of the way of sparks.

Ventilate the area to remove fumes from the welding process.

Burns: Steel retains the heat for long periods. Always wear leather gloves and protective clothing to prevent burns.

Arc flash: The welding arc gives off radiation similar to the sun. Eye damage can occur if you watch the arc without adequate eye protection. Skin burns similar to sunburn can occur to unprotected areas of skin. Always use a head shield and wear protective clothing, gloves and footwear (sturdy boots).

Fumes are given off when welding. Ensure the work area is well ventilated.

Children are always fascinated by welding. In the interests of their safety, take precautions to avoid their contact with your welding equipment. Make sure children are not in a position where they can see the arc.

Safety equipment and advice are available from your welding suppliers. Seek out the manufacturer's safety guides and purchase the correct equipment.

7 Ordering and cutting

The steel you will use for making your projects is sold in different lengths according to cross-section. It might be solid bar or rolled hollow section (abbreviated to RHS), angle iron, rods, flat bar, pipes or almost anything else you can think of.

Your steel merchant will cut pieces for you if you require only a small piece of one particular size, so you won't have a surplus of offcuts you might not use for quite some time. There is usually a charge for cutting, so it is often more economical if you order whole lengths of steel and cut them to size yourself if you require reasonable lengths. Before you order, check with the steel merchant the lengths of the different pieces you will need.

By knowing the lengths of stock steel, you should be able to estimate your total requirements fairly accurately. This will not only save you frequent trips to the steel merchant to buy more steel as you progress with your project, but will also save you the cost of having a large amount of scrap steel over at the end of each project.

Don't forget to rummage through your own stock supply of surplus steel, commonly called offcuts. You might be surprised at how many suitable pieces there are in the scrap box or under the work table.

Before cutting any length of steel, spend a few minutes minimising wastage by working out which pieces for each project will come from a particular length. Calculate, and then cut for economy. You'll be surprised how little steel you have over, after you've completed several projects.

Quite often, if you are using 45° cuts, you can minimise wastage and cutting by turning over one piece—the next 45° mitre cut is already there. You will, of course need to make a similar angle cut the other end, but remember that the mitre cut for the next piece is already in place merely by turning over the steel.

If you are making several mitre cuts (say at 45°, make sure the angle is always the right way. If it is not and you have to correct the angle, then the piece will be shorter than you had planned, which might mean wastage.

After working out the lengths, and before you actually start cutting, heed the advice given by most tradesmen 'check twice but cut once'. This can save a lot of wrongly cut pieces that will be of little use to you. I like to start with the longest pieces I will need, and then going to the smallest pieces. For example, if you have an eight-metre length of angle iron, and your longest piece is only five metres, that leaves three metres over. From that three-metre length you now have, see which pieces you can cut from this length. Juggle around the numbers so you have the best fit. There will be three metres over, from which you could cut two pieces at one metre, two pieces at 450 mm, leaving you with only a 100 mm length of scrap steel. Not bad from an eight-metre length that you started with!

Cutting the steel

Read Section 14 A guide to cutting steel. It will make this aspect of your work so much easier.

If, for example, you are using a hacksaw, then select a hacksaw blade that is appropriate to the steel you are cutting. The higher the number of teeth per inch (this figure is still quoted in the Imperial system of measurement) the finer the cutting teeth on the saw blade. Blades with higher numbers of teeth are more suitable for thinner metals, lower number of teeth are more suitable for thicker metals.

For most of the projects here, such as cutting RHS, the heavier flat bars and pipes, eighteen teeth per inch will be best. Keep the blades with twenty-four teeth or more for very thin metals, and for the non-ferrous metals of your other projects.

Don't overlook the use of cutting wheels attached to disk cutters or disk grinders. Apart from the noise and the dust they create, these can be an efficient means of cutting a lot of steel easily and quickly.

After you have cut the steel with the hacksaw or cutting disk, there may be a rough edge. A cut finger may be the first time you become aware of it! Avoid this sort of mishap by running a file over the edge of each piece of steel you cut.

You will have measured the steel and marked where to cut it. If you are cutting six or eight metre lengths of stock steel, you should find it convenient to rest the length along two, or preferably three, saw-horses or other supports. Instructions are given in this book for making saw-horses for you to rest long pieces of steel on while you cut them and weld some sections. Most welders find it easier to cut pieces of steel if the end that is being cut off is supported level.

The weight of the overhang will pull down on the end, and will make cutting through the rest more difficult, and you may not be able to achieve the desired angle. Of course, if the overhang is only 100 mm or so, it won't be necessary to support the overhang. Use your discretion here.

Supporting the steel will ensure that the saw blade doesn't flex or break, and the angle of the cut will be the angle you intended it to be. You will also have fewer problems cutting the steel with disk cutters if the cut-off section is level.

8 What can you make

The types of items you can make once you have learned the basics of welding will surprise you. The range of things you will want to make will be limited only by your imagination.

Whether you are learning welding as a hobby, or as part of your vocational training, I am sure you will get a lot of satisfaction out of everything you do with metal.

When people start to weld, they won't want to build a bus the very first day, even if that is their ultimate goal. Often people come into welding (particularly as amateurs) with the sole purpose of building their dream yacht. And what an admirable goal that is! Most people are envious of the yachts they see in any harbour or near the coastline while they are on holidays, and realise that other people have taken their adventurous holidays to a much higher lever. Instead of sitting in a camping ground, they are sailing the Pacific to the islands of enchantment and excitement.

But ... whatever your ultimate goal, most people start off welding small objects, and they build up, using their experience, to that ultimate project, or that ultimate dream they have held for so long.

So what can you weld? What is it possible for you to make?

Well, if you are a home owner, you can make double wrought-iron driveway gates. They look superb, with their scrolls and their twisted pieces adding something exquisite to the project. If you don't need double driveway gates, there is usually a need for smaller gates—such as those at the side of the house, or dividing off some of the garden.

Display your garden with a decorative arch

Some of the interesting projects listed in this book, with full instructions for you to follow, include a bird feeder tree that will attract colourful birds to your garden.

Some house owners spend a lot of money on elaborate letterboxes, just to hold their mail each day. But why not make a decorative wrought-iron letterbox stand? Personalise it with your house number, and incorporate some timber work in it, just a bit to add contrast to the project, and you will have a letterbox stand you can be truly proud of.

Some businesses, such as shops, have a need for decorative signs. One advertising antiques, such as the sign shown here will be something you can be proud of.

Or if you are a professional person, you can construct a signpost that will point your clients your way. Here, Dr Squiggles is pointing his patients to his surgery. Why not point your customers to your shop or to your business?

Make your business stand out with a unique sign

House numbers can be ordinary, especially those you buy from a hardware store where the back peels off the number leaving a sticky surface that is attached to a surface. How boring! Why not advertise your house number with an attractive wrought-iron house number? I am sure with a little imagination, you can design a frame, and the numbers for your own house, based on the construction methods depicted in this book.

If security is an issue in your urban environment, you can weld a security screen that even the most hardened criminal will have trouble attacking and entering your workshop and depriving you of your workshop tools. Don't let them get away with anything! Protect your property with a security screen over the window.

Firewood is a great way to keep warm in winter, where open fires and slow combustion stoves are permitted to be used (unfortunately some shire councils, and even some cities, have prohibited the use of such heating devices because of the pollution they generate). But if you do have an open fire, or a slow combustion stove, a rack to support the logs for a few days just outside your door will make life easier for you each evening.

Look around your house. Do you see a need for anything that you could construct? Then draw a diagram of how you would like it to look, and set to work and build it.

These are only some of the items you can construct from steel around the house. But what about around the farm? Many city people own a small acreage not too far away that they like to escape to with their family over weekends. And why not? The country provides a great lifestyle, even if it is only for a couple of days each week, or for annual holidays.

On such a property, you can make cattle grids to keep your cattle in, or your neighbour's cattle out so they don't eat all your pasture. There are feeders that will hold grain, or hay, so animals can eat the bales of

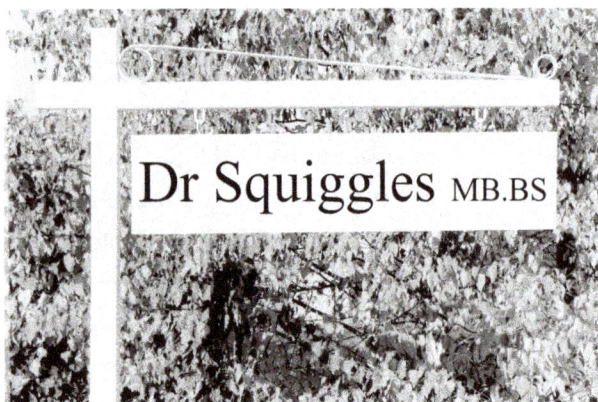

Direct your clients to your business

Build a comfortable garden bench

hay during hard times. These days, those times of drought seem to be all too frequent, so by buying hay and giving the cattle or sheep a place that they know will hold their feed will be to your advantage as well as that of the animals.

If you have a few acres, you will need a

A balustrade around a dangerous verandah can improve safety and functionality

box trailer. Never underestimate the value of such a vehicle. They can be used to carry rocks, soil, feed, fertiliser and hardware back to the house. There are instructions in this book on how to build a box trailer. You can build your trailer and construct a cage from mesh to carry large items, or even the odd farm animal such as sheep or a couple of goats.

A cattle ramp will enable you to load your cows onto a truck with ease. Follow the instructions here, and you will have that aid to make your life on the land a little easier.

Laying out the farm fence, especially if you are using barbed wire, can be a painful

A chain fence can enhance many gardens

experience. Here you will find instructions on building a roller that will let you lay out the wire netting and that barbed wire so that you are spared most of the sharp points,

You will need gates. Make them. Many properties, especially those that were subdivided many decades ago, did not have standard width entrances. You can make your own farm gates to whatever width you required without modifying the distances between fence posts.

A welder, even on a small rural holding, will often overcome the need for that good old standby on farms—twisted wire technology. We have all seen it in action. Often if you can't find something, a piece of fencing wire wrapped around a fence post or a gate will suffice. But sometimes it won't. So a welder on a farm will be essential to repair those broken items.

A garden trellis for your favourite plants will be thought of highly

Build a letterbox stand

Make your own wrought-iron gates and personalise them

If you are on your small holding in the country, you will be working with steel mesh to make not only farm gates, but hay feeders, trellises and many other items that you will wonder how you managed to do without for so long. Well, now is your chance to stop wondering and make all those items you need.

Welders are good too for returning life to old steel objects. Wrought iron around the house, with pieces missing, can now be repaired. Broken gates can be repaired. Benches that are not safe to sit on can be rendered safe once again. Leaking stainless steel vats, and stainless steel tanks, can be repaired or even built from scratch.

This book can give instructions for only a small range of uses for welders, and a small number of projects the average person can make.

How good is your imagination? Then put your creativity to use and see what you can come up with.

9 Welding repairs

A welder is one means whereby a farmer or home owner can not only manufacture items they need, but carry out some emergency repairs when machinery breaks. The machinery can be repaired and be back in service in a short time, perhaps within an hour or so—certainly in far less time than if replacement parts have to be ordered, or obtained from overseas. Many properties are isolated, sometimes a day's drive from a large town. Not that distance is all that important—the supplier may not have the replacement part needed to get the machinery back into service anyway. A grain crop won't wait for weeks for harvesting, and pickers still need to be paid, whether they are picking fruit or not; the excuse that some piece of machinery has broken down won't necessarily be accepted by the workers.

Any machinery can break—and it will always break when it is being used, never when it is idle in the shed.

Welding repairs to most machinery are inexpensive and (sometimes) easy with the right equipment. They will cost dollars to perform, compared to hundreds or perhaps thousands of dollars for replacement parts.

A break in any equipment is due to either faulty materials, such as a weakness in the metal itself, or to metal fatigue, which can be brought on by vibration or stresses.

Any repair must be at least as strong as the original component. If the machinery broke once, it will undoubtedly break again at the same place if the repairs are inadequate. Faulty repairs are time-consuming, and the repair may fail again at a critical time, causing either injury to people, or damage to other machinery.

One of the problems encountered in repairing steel is that not all steels are identical in their composition. They all look alike, but their appearances can be deceptive. The composition of any steel may not be known to the welder carrying out those repairs. And the electrodes used must be compatible with the metal being welded. A mild steel electrode used to repair a high tensile steel, for example, will eventually fail.

Manufacturers of welding maintenance electrodes have produced electrodes that will weld strongly all steels, regardless of their compositions, as well as welding together steels of dissimilar compositions.

Preparation

Any good repair starts with the correct preparation, so that the thickness of the weld is comparable to that of the base material, that is, the weld metal must penetrate to the full depth of the base material. However, obtaining full weld metal penetration is not always easy.

Ideally, the equipment being repaired should be welded from both sides, particularly when thicker components are being repaired. In practice, this is seldom possible, as the repair can be carried out only on one side. Steel pipes and enclosed sections are items that can be repaired from only one side.

The metal around the repair can be removed either by grinding, or by the careful use of an oxy torch so the edges around the repair are tapered at about 90° to allow full penetration of the weld metal. Don't remove so much metal that the components being welded are pulled out of alignment during the welding process. The edges should be tapered so the original material is no more than three millimetres thick, and there is a gap of three millimetres between the two pieces of metal to allow full weld metal penetration. Allowing for the correct space is repeated throughout this book, because that is so important. If you do not leave sufficient space between the pieces of steel being welded, then you will not be able to attain proper and strong welds.

Tack weld the two pieces of metal together, using a small amount of weld. For repairs, perhaps about five millimetres long and 50 mm apart deposited in alternative directions will suffice. This will keep the pieces of steel in their correct position even during the welding process, and ensure that distortion is kept to a minimum. Tack welding makes the repair job so much easier, and the correct alignment of the components is maintained.

Run a bead of weld along the joint. A small electrode (2.5 millimetres) will ensure a good, even and strong weld. The weld metal should fill the joint.

Build up the weld metal with successive runs in narrow beads, rather than one wide-sweeping deposit of weld metal, to ensure strength of the overall weld. Laying down the weld metal in short segments (about 50 mm long) rather than a continuous long run will be preferable for most applications to minimise distortion.

The number of runs needed to repair a particular fault will of course depend on the thickness of the original material being repaired.

Finishing off

Grind down the excess weld metal that protrudes above the base metal. Always wear suitable eye protection when using any grinding wheel or angle grinder.

The machinery should now be as strong, if not stronger, than it was originally, provided the appropriate maintenance electrodes were used.

Sometimes it is possible to tackle a welding problem from both sides, such as with open channel, angle irons, beams, or other structures that are open.

While the methods of welding will be similar, the preparation will be different in that a double vee should be ground or gouged around the fracture. The first run of weld metal will fill the gap between the two sections; subsequent runs can be laid down first on one side, and then on the opposite side. Excess weld metal will be removed by grinding. There is more information about the correct preparation in Section 5 - A guide to quality welding. Please re-read that section so that your welding repairs are strong enough to maintain the equipment or machinery in a working and safe condition.

Repairs like these can often be carried out in a few hours; delays while the necessary electrodes are purchased from the nearest town, or ordered through the mail (as they often need to be) add to the time that machinery is out of action. A delay in getting the machinery back into service can be disastrous. A piece of useful machinery is one that works — machinery lying idle in the shed waiting to be repaired isn't worth all that much. Be prepared, and have a packet of the necessary electrodes on hand for when the machinery does break down. The Boy Scouts' motto applies quite well to all of us!

10 Twisting flat bar

An alternative to using square steel bar in some projects, such as in wrought-iron gates and other ornamental work you create, is to use flat bar. Even for a gate or handrail, you can create a very attractive style by using twisted flat bar for the verticals. This decoration can be used in many other projects to add interest. By using twisted flat bar, you can minimise on cost and on weight.

Measure, then cut the length of flat bar you need. The flat bar can be twisted as often as you wish within reason. It is easier to work in this way than the square bar. If you are putting in only one twist for each piece, cut the flat bar to the required length. Determine the portion you want twisted and mark it clearly the same distance near each end.

Clamp the flat bar in a vice at one of the marks.

Put an adjustable spanner about 25 mm from the vice and give the spanner one quarter of a turn. Turn the bar around and put it in the vice at the other mark.

Now, with the spanner again 25 mm from the vice, twist the bar in the opposite direction.

If, however, you want the bar twisted along its full length, or along most of its length, clamp one end of the bar in a vice a short distance from one end, and place the adjustable spanner the same distance from the opposite end. Any twist you apply like this will centre itself between the spanner and the vice. You can put in as many twists within this distance as you wish, but remember that beyond a certain number, you will weaken the steel, and the bar may start to buckle. So, keep the twists to a reasonable number of turns.

If you want to twist the whole length of flat bar, you will have to allow a little extra for that part that is held in the vice, and the part held in the adjustable spanner. You will cut off the ends to fit the space you wish to fill.

11 Twisting square bars

You will be able to make very attractive wrought iron work by using twisted square bars, such as for the vertical bars on some types of wrought-iron gates.

The whole bar need not be twisted, only the middle portion of about half or two-thirds of the length. Both ends can be left straight—that is, without the twist.

The maximum thickness you will be able to work without difficulty, and without the use of heat would be 10 mm square. Heavier 12 mm square steel bar is too difficult to twist without using special equipment. The type of equipment needed to twist bars heavier than 10 mm square would be prohibitive for a small workshop in its early stages of establishment or for a handy person working from their garage.

Measure the length of bar you need and cut it to size. Determine the portion that you want twisted, and mark this clearly at both ends. Your vice should be sturdy, as the force you will be exerting on the steel as you twist it is far greater than that required for twisting flat bar.

If your project requires several bars to be twisted in the same way, cut them all, check that they are all of the correct length, and mark them all where you want to twist them. This way, the twists will all be consistent.

Clamp one end of the bar in a vice at the first mark.

Place a large adjustable spanner at the second mark, and turn the spanner from half to one complete turn. The bigger the spanner you use, the easier it will be for you to twist the steel. Make sure you keep the steel bar straight at all times. It will tend to bend, but you can overcome the natural tendency to some extent by straightening it as you proceed with the twisting.

If your project, such as a gate, requires more than one bar to be used, make sure you give each bar the same number of turns and in the same direction.

Over a length of about one metre, you should be able to twist the bar one full turn without difficulty, but this of course depends on the anchorage points for the vice, and on the length of the spanner you use. If the vice you are trying to use is too small, or if it is bolted to a flimsy particle board workbench top, it just won't hold together. And if you tried to do the same amount of twisting of bar using a small 150 mm spanner, again, you will find it just won't work. Go for a heavy vice, and a large spanner to make the work easier and more successful.

12 Scroll tool

This is a very simple tool which is used to make the decorative scrolls and patterns in wrought iron work. With a tool as simple as this, steel bar up to 20 mm wide and 3 mm thick can be curved with little effort. You won't need to apply heat to make the scrolls, either.

If you like ornamental work, this tool can be one of the most useful and time-saving items in your tool kit. With only a little practice, you'll be able to make several scrolls in a minute.

The tool comprises an off-cut of steel pipe with an outside diameter of 70 mm for the larger scrolls, and a piece of pipe with an outside diameter of about 35 mm for the smaller end of the scrolls.

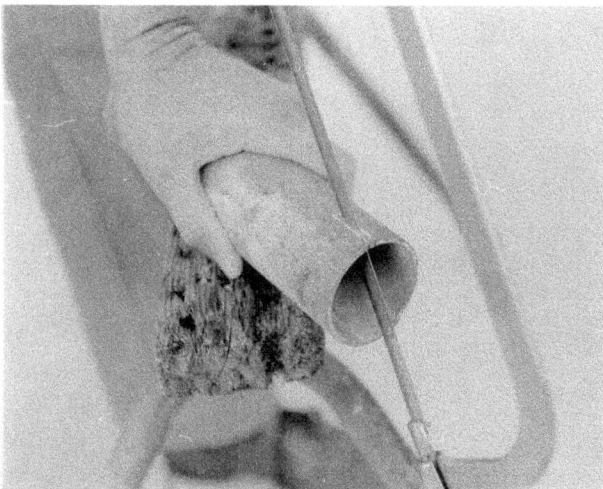

Insert the point of a strong screw driver into the slot and push the screw driver down to bend the pipe so one side of the cut is slightly lower than the other.

Weld a short piece of flat bar, about 100 mm long on to the side of the pipe opposite the slot but at the other end of the pipe. This will prevent the pipe from turning around as you are making the scrolls.

This tool can be clamped on to any workbench, saw horse or other convenient work area. I prefer to work from a saw horse, as it is possible to work from behind the tool and manage the work easily.

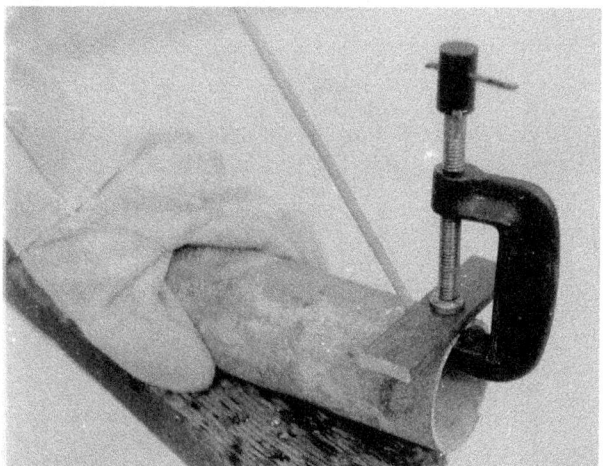

To make this simple tool, cut a piece of pipe about 150 mm long.

At one end, cut a slot with a hacksaw, 30 mm long and about 3 mm wide. Remove the thin piece between the cuts to leave a narrow gap. You could cut the groove with a 3 mm disk in a disk cutter.

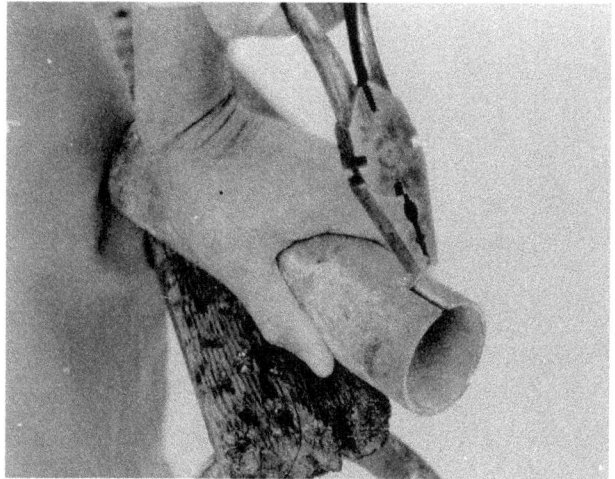

13 Scrolls

You have made the scroll forming tool from off-cuts of pipe. Now clamp the tool firmly to a saw horse or other convenient place.

Determine the length of steel you will need for each section by wrapping a flexible tape measure around the outside of each scroll former or scroll tool, and add these two lengths to the distance between where the scrolls will be welded to your project.

Cut the steel to the correct length, and round off each end of the flat bar to make it neat, rather than leaving a square end.

Insert a few millimetres of the flat bar into the slot. No more than three or four millimetres should be sufficient — it should

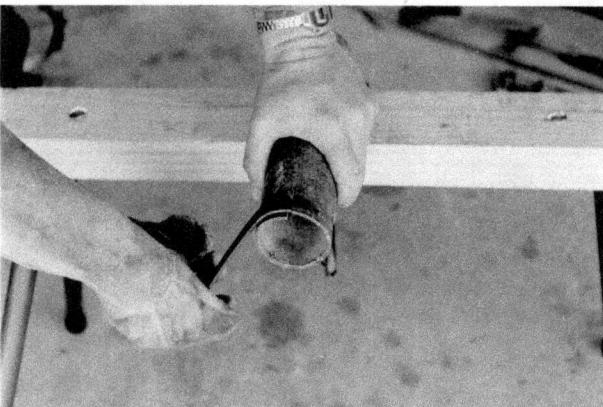

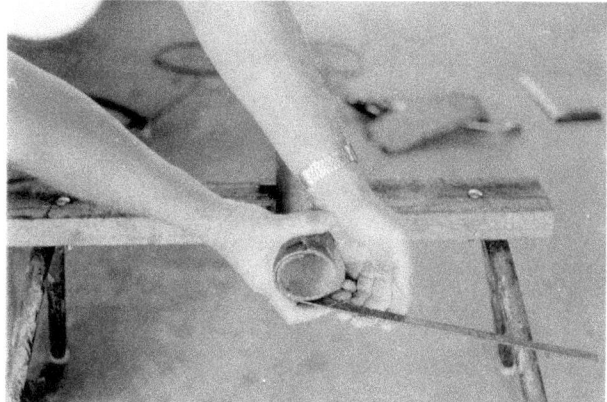

not slip out of the scroll former as you turn the steel to form the scrolls.

Wrap the steel around the tool, bringing it in tightly all the way around. Don't let go of the tension on the steel until you have completed the loop. Stop when you have

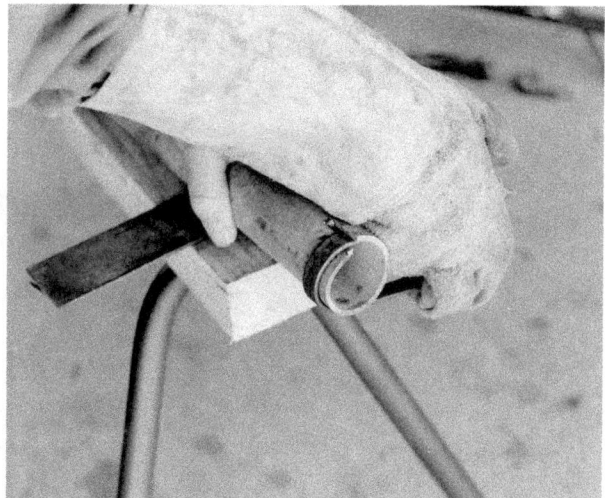

brought the bar back over itself — that is, directly over the slot in the tool.

Often a half-scroll is an attractive addition to a gate, these being arranged in a diamond pattern or a series of half-diamond patterns set between the vertical bars.

If your design calls for half-scrolls, you can make the curves in the same way as you would for the full scroll, but stop opposite the slot instead of bringing the flat bar all the way around the tool and over itself again.

Keep the first half-scroll as a reference piece. As you make each subsequent one, check the length of it against the reference and adjust if necessary until they are all the same length.

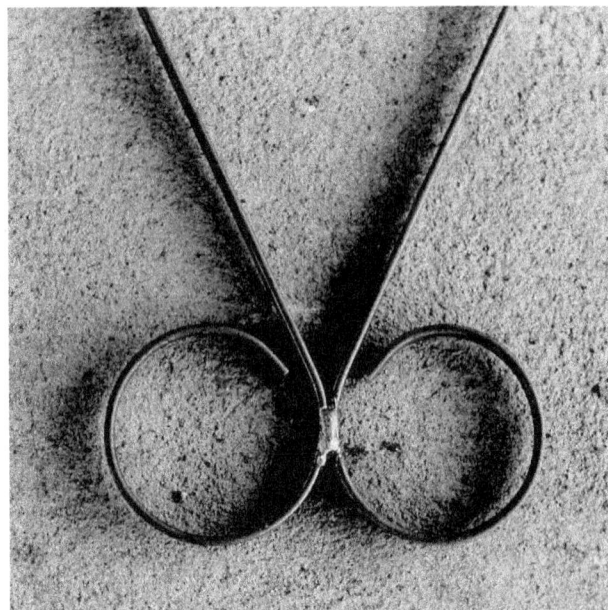

14 A guide to cutting steel

It's easy to cut steel, despite its hardness. The most difficult part, maybe, is to choose the right method to use. Here are several ways, with each giving different results.

First, there's the hacksaw, a special, low-cost saw that uses interchangeable blades; the saw is designed to cut most metals except some of the toughest, such as hardened steel, spring steel, stainless steel and some of the metals even harder than steel.

Hacksaws are great where patience is freely available, but nevertheless they have their place on the farm or in the home workshop whenever thin pieces and small pieces of metal need to be cut. They're great too for cuts where a neat, straight edge is required. That's most of the time anyway, and perhaps a hacksaw might be considered first whatever cutting jobs you undertake. Hacksaw blades are interchangeable – small teeth (24 teeth to the inch) for fine work or thin metals such as thin sheet steel or galvanised drain pipe, and brass tubing and copper pipes. Then there are the blades with larger teeth and fewer of them – perhaps only 18 teeth per inch. These cut through mild steel quickly and easily. Burred edges left can be removed with a few strokes of a file.

These metal-cutting saws are great too for pipes, such as 25 mm or 50 mm galvanised pipe used for irrigation and farm gates. Or a better method here might be to buy a pipe cutter – a special tool with a wheel that digs into the pipe as the tool is rotated a number of times around the pipe, each revolution needing a tightening of the wheel. The cut is always neat and even. These pipe (or tube) cutters are suitable for soft pipe too, such as copper or brass tubing. But if you have one, keep the cutting wheel well oiled to prevent rusting, and to make the job of cutting simpler.

Disk cutters

Most workshops will have disk cutters or angle grinders and, hopefully, even metal cut-off saws. All these tools use thin disks that are intended for cutting through steel cleanly and efficiently. Be warned – they all make a lot of noise, so make sure you wear suitable protection to preserve your hearing – ear muffs or similar that meet high standards. Cutting by this means will damage your hearing – permanently too – if you don't take this precaution.

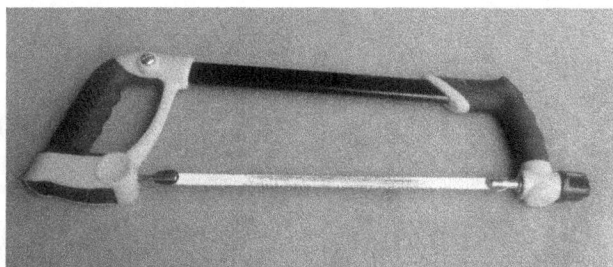

These disk cutters are ideally suited to cutting pipes, sheet steel and even flat bar and steel rods.

The order of choice of tools for cutting steel would be:

- for very small pieces of steel — the hacksaw;
- for larger pieces such as pipes and flat bar — the disk cutter or cut-off saw;
- for large pieces of steel such as railway lines and car bodies — electric cutting and oxy cutting.

Electric cutting

Often though, work requires cutting of more extensive lumps of steel than thin, small pieces. But that's no great problem. The proper application of the right tool and right method will make short work of even railway lines. Try that with a hacksaw!

If you have either an electric welder or a gas welder (and many workshops have one, or should have either) then cutting isn't difficult. Take the arc method for example. Unfortunately the results obtained using the electric welder are similar to cutting a fresh loaf of farm-baked bread with a chainsaw. It can be done, but ...

The cut can be far from neat, the correct bevel hard to obtain, and where possible this method should be used more as a method of cutting up old steel and car bodies for scrap rather than as a method of shaping material to go into a newly manufactured implement. Cutting with an electric welder is really a matter of gouging; the electrode simply melts the steel and forces the molten metal away from the 'cut' — or tear.

Special gouging and cutting electrodes are available for this job, removing metal quickly. These electrodes create an intense localised heat, and then force the molten metal away from the cut.

These gouging electrodes are ideally suitable in pre-welding applications, such as cutting an appropriate groove to enable proper weld metal penetration essential for a strong weld. They're good too for removing cracks from metal sections, such as in farm machinery and at the same time preparing the equipment for welding in the normal way. But ... before buying a packet of gouging electrodes, ensure that your welder has the capacity to use them. Even the 3.25 mm electrode will require a current not attainable from some of the smaller machines.

Ignore the current settings marked on your welding machine. For the cutting electrodes those just won't apply. Use the settings recommended on the electrode manufacturer's packet.

Or, if you don't have these gouging and cutting electrodes, you may be able to get away with using a hot electrode — that is, one that requires a high welding amperage, and using that at a very high setting, far higher than you would use for any welding application. You might have to set the welder at its maximum, or near maximum setting for anything like the results you are after, but make sure you don't overheat the electrode. As a general guide, use the maximum setting for the next gauge electrode up from the one you are using.

You will need to direct the tip of the electrode so the point faces towards the cut being made. You will have to weave the electrode up and down. As the arc length is increased, greater heat is available to the steel to melt it. As the electrode tip is weaved closer to the steel, the electrode forces the molten pool of metal out of the cut.

There are practical limits to cutting steel by this means. The thickness of steel that can be cut using an ordinary electrode is merely determined by the capacity of the welder. Many machines have a maximum amperage of under 150 amps, and the heat available from these might not be sufficient to cut very thick pieces of steel. But certainly for cutting up old car bodies lying around, or cutting most other structures around the house or farm, there should be no problems. You should naturally expect to get the best results from the correct cutting electrodes though.

Square holes

If you've ever tried to drill holes through hardened steel, such as railway line or spring steel, you might have got through many drill bits before you realised the futility of this silly exercise. The gouging method is often satisfactory for putting holes into tough steel where drilling or punching them is not practicable. Unlike the cutting method where the electrode is weaved back and forth, the arc is started, then concentrated on one spot where the hole should be, until the metal surrounding the arc becomes molten. When that is achieved, the tip of the electrode is dipped quickly into the pool of molten metal and forced right through the metal. The results will be crude, but quicker than drilling. The hole can then of course be enlarged or shaped if necessary (for example if a square hole is needed). Hopefully the results obtained will be covered up and out of sight, because they certainly won't be neat and tidy.

Carbon arc

The carbon arc can come in useful for perhaps not so much cutting, but heating the steel sufficiently to go ahead with punching those odd holes in hardened steel. The carbon arc apparatus comprises two special electrodes held close together and close to the work. The equipment should be available from most welding suppliers. The carbon arc can be operated from any standard electrode holder, one tip connected to the work lead, the other to the electrode terminal. The heat will be localised. The current needed for this type of work is much lower than that required for the gouging electrodes, and will be within the capabilities of nearly all electric welders.

Gas cutting

Most trades people realise the tremendous benefits of cutting (and gouging) using gas cutting equipment, which is really only a modification of the gas welding apparatus normally available in workshops. It's quick, quite accurate, neat, and, when finished, the job is ready (usually) for a quick grind down to polish up the work in preparation for welding. Cutting with gas has far more advantages than disadvantages.

Gas cutting equipment is, basically, gas bottles (oxygen in one, and either acetylene or a liquefied petroleum gas in the other), and the blowtorch with interchangeable cutting nozzles, and provision for a jet of oxygen to force the molten metal away from the cut. Simple — provided the nozzle matches the thickness of steel being cut, and the gas pressures are regulated correctly.

Don't expect to do a lot of cutting over a weekend and at the same time limit your capacity to one bottle of oxygen. Gas consumption, particularly that of oxygen, is very high when cutting. So, be prepared for lots of trips into town. Cutting plate 12 millimetres thick might require an average-sized oxygen bottle (one cubic metre) about every twenty minutes.

Safety

Cutting metals out in the field, particularly with gas cutting, but also with electric equipment, could give you the exercise you need. Be ready to stomp out the little fires you start as you cremate your last summer reserves of dry feed or what once resembled a lawn before that drought began. Remember, when cutting with gas, those sparks are hot, and fast, and they can travel quite a way from where you are working, particularly if the cuts you are making are horizontal. When they land somewhere in your last paddock of feed, they will still be red hot—certainly hot enough to start a small grass fire. Or lots of them. So keep a good look out for small spot fires. And be prepared for your foot exercise.

Take care also on what you cut up when you have your cutting urge. The same precautions apply to welding too, and to electric cutting: don't cut (or weld) any container that has held fuel, particularly petrol, and don't cut from inside a tank or storage container. Fumes can build up inside a restricted area and become a health hazard. Fumes from the cutting itself won't be good for your health either. Anyway, it's just as easy to work from the outside of any container or tank. Remember that a great deal of heat is involved in cutting steel.

Often old steel is coated in paints, grease, and other compounds that can give off toxic fumes and other nasties when heated or burned. Keep upwind of any fumes from cutting and avoid breathing the fumes as much as possible. These precautions are obvious, but somewhere, someone no doubt will ignore even the most basic rules of safety.

And of course use the correct cutting or welding goggles or face shield at all times. They will protect your eyes from the harmful radiation (UV rays) and from flying sparks. And with electric cutting, a proper welding helmet is required, as well as full protective clothing.

Preparation

When you are about to begin cutting with gas, purge the hoses for a few seconds to rid them of any mixture of gases that could have accumulated along their lengths.

To light up the blowtorch, adjust the regulators to the required settings. To use excessive gas pressure can damage the regulators; too much gas can be expensive and wasteful. Turn on the acetylene tap (on the blowtorch) first, light the gas using a flint lighter and adjust the level of flame so it is orange, with most of the soot gone from it.

Then turn on the oxygen tap (on the blowtorch) slowly, and adjust the flame so that the inner cone of the flame becomes clear and blue. Ideally, for cutting most steels, you will be seeking a neutral flame—that is, equal volumes of acetylene and oxygen. The same neutral flame should persist even when the cutting oxygen lever or switch is depressed.

When closing down the gas cutting system, first turn off the taps at the torch (oxygen first, then the acetylene). This is satisfactory if a brief halt is needed during the operations. For a pause of more than a few minutes, turn off the gas supplies at the regulators. And, when you have finished the cutting altogether, turn off the gas supplies at the bottles.

Just as you would clean the surface if you were welding the metal, give the surface a quick clean with a wire brush to remove rust, dirt and grease if present.

Pre-heat to redness the edge of the steel you are intending to cut—an area about 25 to 50 mm back from the edge in the direction of the cut is sufficient. Then, when you consider that the edge is hot enough, hold the inner cone of the pre-heating flames (they're the small flames around the outer rim of the nozzle) just above the steel. Then press the cutting oxygen lever or switch and move the torch slowly ahead. Sparks will penetrate through the plate, indicating that effective cutting is taking place. Without those sparks as an indicator, go back to the edge and pre-heat further. The flame might be cutting only partly through thick steel, hence no sparks will emerge from the other side.

With practice, you get the feel for the correct rate of travel, or cutting speed.

Appearances

A correctly cut piece of steel (that is, one where the gas pressures, rate of travel, and nozzle sizes were all correct) will have a sharp edge all around, and the end of the cut will have a smooth surface with very little in the way of visible drag lines. These will be almost vertical if they are visible at all. The surface should have a thin coating of oxide adhering to it, but, if you have cut the metal correctly, this coating will be easily removed. It will actually look right—clean and neat.

However, if the speed of cutting is too slow, the top edge will appear melted and rounded, with prominent gouge marks over the cut surface. Too great a heat build-up will cause molten metal to be deposited in the cut; this material will be hard to remove, as it will have fused itself to the metal.

Another cause of bad cutting is too fast a cutting speed. The flame will cut the metal successfully, and the overall result will not be as severe as it will be with the other problems just discussed. Most noticeably, the drag lines will appear to curve in the direction of travel.

You may find that the speed is too fast anyway because the torch will suddenly stop cutting altogether. But that's no real difficulty. Go back to the edge where the cut stopped, and pre-heat again. Next time, slow down the cutting speed.

Poor cuts can be caused by incorrect distances of the flame from the work. You must regulate this at all times by keeping the tip of the flames barely above the steel.

Poor cutting may also result from slag or a small amount of molten metal blocking one or more of the gas jets, particularly the pre-heat jets. Remember, every one of those pre-heat flames will be needed for effective cutting. If they become blocked at any time, simply remove the cutting nozzle from the blowtorch when it is cool, remove the blockage, then re-assemble the blowtorch again.

You may need to cut a hole somewhere in a section of the metal, not necessarily at the edge of the metal, but towards the middle of it. In that case, pre-heat a small portion within the section being cut out, and proceed to travel the flame towards the edge of the proposed cut.

15 Distortion

Distortion will be present with all forms of welding. If you are lucky, in many cases it is so small that it is barely noticeable. In other cases allowance has to be made for buckling and distortion before welding commences. Here is a brief outline of what causes it, and the ways it can be minimised, or at least so its effects can be significantly reduced.

The cause of distortion

Distortion is caused by contraction of the weld metal from the molten state to atmospheric temperature. As the steel and the weld metal cool, they contract, pulling any adjoining steel along with it.

Different rates of expansion and contraction between the weld metal and the steel adjacent to the weld will show up as buckling and distortion.

Cool zone   Hot zone   Cool zone

Another problem can arise in welding large steel plates which are often used in farm work—or more especially, that yacht

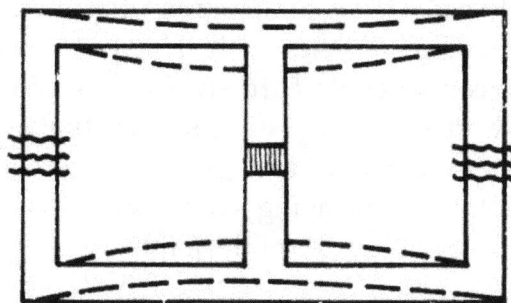

On cooling, contraction will cause tension

most of us dream of owning. A plate can be put in the correct place. Once welding starts, distortion will pull it out of that position. It may have moved so much that its position now bears little resemblance to its original location. This can often result in a steel plate that is so badly buckled that nothing can be done with it. Cut it out and replace it with a new piece of steel, because nothing will fix the problem. You won't be able to straighten it.

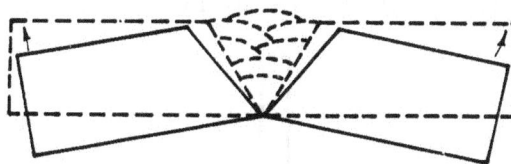

As the weld metal cools, it will realign the steel to a more level shape. Exaggeration of the base metal will help achieve this

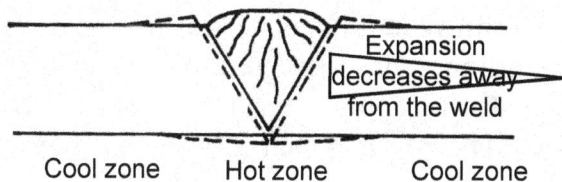

For large areas such as plate, tack welding is the logical answer. These are small beads of weld metal placed short distances apart, about 300 mm or so, and only a centimetre or two long, just to keep the two components

The dotted line shows the effect if no pre-heating is applied to the steel

81

together until they are fully welded. If distortion has become apparent at this stage, the tack welds can be broken or cut out and

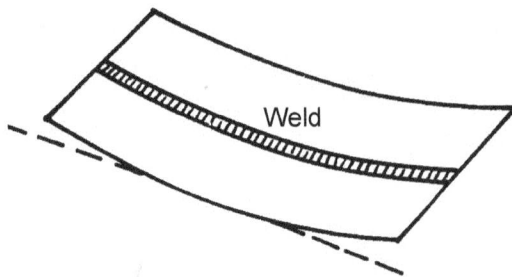

The effects of welding in long runs

the material realigned.

Distortion can also be minimised on plates by staggering the welds and performing them in alternative directions, a process that involves welding small sections then reversing the direction on another part of the job. One small distortion in one part will tend to cancel that from another direction (well, at least in theory!).

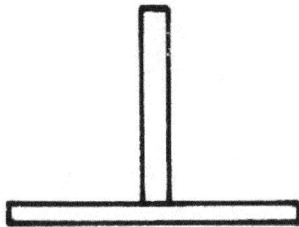

This is the desired final alignment of steel

Contraction of weld metal

Molten steel contracts by about 11 per cent in volume on cooling to room temperature. This means that the molten weld metal would contract in all directions. In a welded joint, the metal fuses to the side of the joint but it cannot contract freely. Cooling causes the weld metal to distort, so that the weld metal itself has to stretch if it is to overcome the effect of shrinking volume and still be attached to the edge of the joint.

Cracking of the weld

If the restraint is great, as for example in a heavy section of plate, the weld metal may

Distortion if the joint is welded on only one side

crack. Even in cases where the weld metal does not crack, there will still be stresses locked up in the structure. If the joint material is relatively weak, for example, a butt joint in steel 2.0 mm thick, the contracting weld metal may cause the sheet to become distorted.

Expansion and contraction of parent metal

While welding is proceeding, a relatively small volume of the adjacent plate material is heated to a very high temperature and it expands in all directions. It is able to do this freely at right angles to the surface of the plate through the weld. But when it expands across the weld or along the weld, it meets considerable resistance. For continued expansion to occur, it has to deform because the metal adjacent to the weld is at a high temperature and hence rather soft. By expanding, it has to overcome the resistance against the cooler, harder metal further away. The result is that it tends to bulge in any direction, in any place, that it can.

When the weld area begins to cool, the weld metal and the base steel attempt to contract as much as it expanded. Never assume the steel or the weld will resume its former shape. The contraction of the new shape exerts a strong pull on adjacent metal.

Several things can then begin to happen. The metal in the weld area is stretched and the steel may be pulled out of shape by the powerful forces of contraction leading to distortion. When this happens, stresses will remain in the steel.

Overcoming distortion effects

The good news is that all is not lost. There are several methods of minimising the effects of distortion.

Preening is one such method. It is done by hammering the weld while it is still hot (and hence rather soft compared with the rest of the steel). The weld metal is flattened slightly. Because of this, the stresses are reduced further. The effect of preening is rather shallow and it is not advisable on multi layers of weld.

Distribution of stresses need to be considered. Distortion may be reduced by selecting a welding sequence which will distribute the stresses so that to at least some degree they tend to cancel each other out.

Choice of a suitable welding sequence is probably the most effective method of overcoming distortion. Keep in mind that the opposite is also true – an unsuitable sequence may exaggerate it. On a large welding project where space permits, simultaneous welding of both sides of a joint by two welders can successfully help to eliminate distortion.

Restraint of parts can to some extent help minimise distortion. Forcible restraint of the components being welded is often used to prevent distortion. Jigs and tack welds are just a couple of methods used to achieve the desired result. If, however, the components being welded are restrained too tightly, the weld might crack. This could be a hairline crack that goes unnoticed.

Presetting the steel at an exaggerated angle is often a useful technique in minimising the effects of distortion. From past experience or by trial and error it might be possible to determine approximately how much distortion will take place in a given welded structure. By correctly presetting the components to be welded, stresses caused by contraction can be made to pull the parts into correct alignment.

Preheating, if possible, can be effective in achieving the desired results. Suitable preheating of parts of the structure other than the area to be welded can sometimes be used to reduce uneven contraction, and hence distortion. By removing the heating source as soon as welding is completed, the sections hopefully will contract at a similar rate, thus reducing distortion.

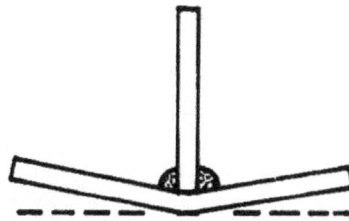

Possible distortion when the joint is welded on both sides

16 Welding galvanised steel

Galvanised steel is easily and satisfactorily welded using the the most common welding techniques. The best part of manual and semi-manual welding processes is that they provide quite a high degree of flexibility.

With manual welding, external heat sources are applied to make the weld using the common welding electrodes.

Unfortunately, the quality of manual welding of galvanised steel is mainly determined by the competence of the operator. In other words, get some practice and learn to weld properly before you tackle galvanised steel welding. But no special skills are necessary although minor variations in the techniques are required to achieve satisfactory results. If you follow this advice, your welds of galvanised steel should be strong, neat and just the way you intended that they should be.

Excellent results can and usually are obtained by using shielded gas welding techniques, but that type of welding is not covered in this book. So let us stick to the manual metal arc welding method.

Arc welding is recommended for welding galvanised steel thicker than 1.6 mm. Thinner than that, you should go to shielded gas welding. Thin metals are hard to weld with a metal arc method because of the potential to burn through the steel. It can be done, but get plenty of practice welding thin metals first.

Generally, the procedure using the manual metal arc welding is the same as it is for welding uncoated (or shiny or black) steel, with a few additional points you should consider.

For welding galvanised steel, the welding electrode should be applied a little more slowly than with the whipping action you have already learned, which moves the electrode forward along the seam in the direction of progression and then back into the molten pool of metal.

Use a short welding arc (it is cooler in all positions) to give you better control of the weld metal. It prevents intermittent excess weld metal penetration and undercutting (often caused by too much heat, hence the advice to keep the arc as short as possible).

The zinc coating should be completely burned off before the beading process. After you have achieved this, welding will be no different from welding uncoated steel.

Weaving, as well as multiple weld beads, or runs of electrode, should be avoided. Heat input into the joint should be kept to a minimum to avoid unnecessary damage to the adjacent galvanised layer.

Use slightly wider gaps — perhaps up to 2.5 mm or 3 mm in butt joint to give complete weld metal penetration.

The most important consideration in welding galvanised steel is the safety and health of the operator. Ensure that you have adequate ventilation. Consider using a respirator if you can. Don't weld galvanised steel (or any other steel) in a confined area. Work outside whenever possible, or ensure that you have extractor fans powerful enough to remove fumes.

Zinc has a much lower melting point than steel, so on applying the welding rod, the heat will be sufficient to volatilise the zinc. These fumes are not healthy to breath in, hence the advice to weld galvanised steel outside, or use a powerful extractor fan.

On cooling, the residual zinc will form a coating of white zinc oxide. This is easily removed using a wire brush. All traces of the oxide should be removed before welding. If any of it gets into the weld, it will impart almost zero strength to the weld.

Once you have welded galvanised steel, you must re-coat the area around the weld, and the weld metal itself. If you don't do this, then there is no obvious reason for using galvanised steel in the first place with its extra cost.

Electrodes for welding galvanised steel

Generally, most electrodes used for metal fabrication are suitable for welding galvanised steel. In other words, unlike when welding materials such as stainless steel where special electrodes are required, no special manual arc welding rods are required.

Galvanised steel can be welded in all positions, but as with most welding fabrication, flat and vertical welding are easiest to carry out on galvanised steel.

If you intend welding a lot of galvanised steel, consult your welding distributor. Some welding electrodes with a different flux composition and different properties might give a slightly better result and help prevent slag intrusion and undercutting, but these problems are generally eliminated by careful and proper welding procedures.

If these procedures are considered when welding galvanised steel, the operator can avoid just about all other problems that could arise. Fracture toughness will be the same as for welding uncoated steel. Fracture strength (that is, the strength of the weld itself) should be no different from that obtained by welding non-coated steel.

Porosity of the weld will be a problem if proper procedures are not followed. If they are followed, then porosity should not be too great a problem.

Weld damage

Severe damage can occur to the galvanised coating on many steels. Lengths of steel rubbing together on the back of the truck or utility, rough handling, using galvanised steel for supporting rough materials such as bricks, gravel and other substances, can severely damage or remove the protective coating. This might not even include the area of coating removed by the welding process itself.

Coating the steel

Whether the galvanised coating has been removed by rough handling, abrasion or by the welding process, adequate protection must be given to the uncoated steel.

The easiest and the most commonly used protection is by the application of two coats of zinc-rich paints. These are generally quick drying, and the second coat can be applied after a few minutes.

If you are coating the welds, make sure you remove all the slag from the weld. Use the welding, or chipping, hammer, followed by wire brushing. Applying the paint by brush results in a more satisfactory protective layer than could be achieved by spraying the metal.

Galvanising bars are another satisfactory method of restoring the protective coating to areas of uncoated steel, but these are not easily applied to large area. The galvanising bars are zinc compounds that are melted over the weld metal. But the galvanising bar metal should be applied only after the metal has been thoroughly cleaned back to bare, shiny metal. Remove all dirt, slag and other impurities from the surface and the joint. As long as the surface to be treated in this way is sufficiently hot (over about 315°C) the zinc bar will melt and run along the uncoated area. The alloy bar melts on contact with the hot surface and coats the damaged or unprotected area. A small wire brush can be used to more easily spread the molten zinc bar.

17 Welding stainless steel

Shiny welds in stainless steel are what you should aim for.

Stainless steel is finding its way more and more into the rural scene, particularly in the dairying and related industries in both large and small operations. Stainless steel is unique amongst steels in that it resists rusting and corrosion.

The composition of stainless steel, mainly its chromium content, gives it this unique property. This same composition can make it difficult to work with. This steel depends for its corrosion resistance on an extremely thin film of chromium oxide which forms on the surface when it is exposed to air or oxygen. This film of oxide is resistant to most chemical actions, and has the ability to 'heal the wound' if the surface is scraped or scratched at all.

The minimum chromium content, before steel can be classed as stainless, must be more than about 12 per cent, but can range up to around 30 per cent. Other metals, such as nickel, may also be present.

There are three main groups of stainless steel; the martensitic, which are air-hardened steels and are hard and brittle; the ferritic, which are not really easy to work, and those in the austenitic 300 group, which are most often used, particularly for agriculture and food production.

There's nothing magical about welding stainless steel. It's mainly knowing how to do it, and understanding the material you are working with. Most important of all it is having the right materials on hand to work with. This section will point you in the right direction to satisfying all these requirements.

Cutting stainless steels

Unlike ordinary steel that oxidises readily in the presence of oxygen, stainless steel cannot be properly cut with oxy cutting equipment. Stainless steel is brittle and hard. This makes cutting even the thinnest sheets with shears or tin snips rather difficult too. A cutting electrode that will provided excellent results, even on thin sheets or pipes is available. The cutting electrode can be used in any AC or DC electric welder. It cuts cleanly without build-up of fused material around or below the cut.

Welding stainless steel

Most welding electrodes such as mild steel electrodes cannot be used at all on stainless steel. When welding stainless steel that is used in food preparation, it is **essential** to ensure that the welding rod, electrode or solder does not contain nasties such as cadmium or lead. These rods, electrodes or solders have a place in other welding applications, but if they are used in contact with food, the wrath of the health departments will be upon you.

Some stainless steels such as those in the martensitic and ferritic groups require pre-heat treatment where the temperature of the base metal has to be raised considerably before welding, and cooled slowly after welding. In the austenitic group, the stainless steel most commonly used in rural and food production situations, no heat treatment is needed, either before or after welding. Thankfully, the steel in this last group is also the easiest to weld.

Many of the problems in welding stainless steel come from changes in the metal composition when the steel is subjected to heat. When they are heated to about 800° Celsius, some of the carbon in the steel combines with the chromium to form chromium carbides. The chromium can no longer provide the corrosion or rust resistance that it did. The use of correct electrodes or rods will alleviate this problem.

Another problem encountered with the heating of austenitic stainless steel involves a behaviour different to that normally encountered when welding mild steels. The expansion rate in stainless steel is different, and the expansion is not gradual over a large area. Consequently, irregular expansion occurs—better known as buckling. Electric and gas welding can be used to repair stainless steel. Both give good performance under most situations provided the correct welding electrode or rod is used.

Surface preparation

Cleaning the area to be welded is essential. as it is with all welding operations. With stainless steel though, emery paper of very fine grade will ensure adequate fusion. Avoid wire-bushing the area except with a stainless steel wire brush.

Oxy-welding

Thicker stainless steel, usually those above about 3 mm can be welded with an arc welder. Those thin sheets that any welder is likely to encounter are often too thin for arc welding, and so oxy welding for soldering must be adopted. Because they are so thin, little preparation is necessary as far as bevelling the edges is concerned. Butt joints where the two edges are side by side is all that's needed.

The welding rod should be dipped into the correct flux. Flux should not be applied to the surface of the base metal in the immediate area of the weld.

On larger surfaces, tack welding along the length of the join will be advisable to keep the article in the shape it's supposed to be in.

Distortions caused by heat will change the shape of any steel object permanently.

The flame of the torch should be as small as possible. It should heat the base metal near the weld and the rod but not much more than that. The flame should be neutral or slightly reducing, which means that it will have a slight excess of acetylene. The instructions supplied with the rods will point the operator in the right direction here. Those guidelines should help any operator to achieve a good, solid weld.

Striking the arc

If arc welding is to be used, then any electric welder of either AC or DC polarity will work well. Keep the arc short. A long arc, where the tip of the electrode is a long way from the base metal, will cause chromium losses as well as increase the temperature of the arc itself, something that should be avoided especially if the steel is thin. Although a short arc is necessary, it is also necessary to ensure that the tip of the electrode does not touch the base metal being welded or repaired. Somewhere in between these extremes will more than suffice. Use the lowest amperage necessary and no more. A series of short welds is recommended after tack welding the components together. This will give a better weld simply by minimising distortion and keeping the heat to a minimum

Seldom is thick stainless steel used in general applications. If it is, such as for shafts, then on those rare occasions, the edges should be bevelled to an angle of between 45° and 60° to open the join up for maximum weld metal penetration

Particularly important in items used for food preparation is the avoidance of areas where bacteria and other little bugs can accumulate. Poor welds that give hollows and holes should be most definitely avoided. This can mostly be prevented by proper welding methods and by using the correct electrodes, rods, or solders.

A wide range of welding rods, electrodes and solders are available for the fabrication and repair of stainless steel. However, a thought-out selection of rods or electrodes will reduce the number of different ones needed to be kept on hand for those emergency repairs—perhaps one or two to cover a whole range of jobs, rather than a different one for every job.

So, what's available to do the job?

Welding products

Most stainless steel electrodes will weld or repair many steels of different compositions, particular those in the 300 series stainless steels. These electrodes have a low carbon content, minimising not only those carbide problems, but oxide formation as well. They are good for welding thin sheet too. Welders who have tried to weld thin sheets of mild steel will appreciate this quality. It's less prone to burning more holes than are being mended. Such welding electrodes are handy for eliminating bacteria breeding grounds as the weld will be of a low profile, smooth and without those cavities and crevices that bacteria and bugs find so attractive.

Some rods that can be used on just about any stainless steel can be applied with an oxy torch. They are used in conjunction with flux. The alloy is melted in a reducing flame from the torch (that is, one with slightly more acetylene). Such rods control the carbon content of the repair or weld, so at least part of the problems of welding will be eliminated. They are quite suitable and safe to use in the food industry too.

A low-temperature silver solder type of alloy is good for use in food production areas, because it doesn't contain anything horrible such as lead, antimony, cadmium or any of the other nasties. When applied correctly, these solders are quite strong, and will tolerate a lot of wear and tear and tossing around. Solders can be applied with a soldering iron, which is actually preferable to the use of an oxy torch. With a melting point of just over 220° Celsius, the heat from a soldering iron is sufficient.

The low melting point's added features are that the solders will flow through even the narrowest of areas, making them useful in repairing cracks in stainless steel, and for repairs in areas where proper preparation is impossible to accomplish. Their strength ensures that joins made with this silver solder will take quite a knocking. Its low melting point and ease of application make this solder very useful on very thin containers—those of the type more likely to be found in general situations.

Sources of electrodes

Most welding suppliers will have a reasonable supply of suitable electrodes and solders to weld stainless steel. New products are coming on to the market all the time, so it is not possible to include details or name all products here.

18 Working with mesh

Mesh can be welded, and that is by far the easiest and the strongest way to attach it to framing when making items on the farm, and for some items for around the home, such as side gates and trellises. While mesh will have applications for the general fabrication around the home, most uses will be on the farm — for cattle grids, farm gates, hay feeders and more. It is easy to cut, shape and, because each vertical strand of the mesh is welded to each horizontal strand, mesh forms a very strong material. It will need bracing, otherwise it will be too floppy for most applications.

Using the various welded meshes that are available today can be likened to filling big holes with a lot of little ones. Mesh is versatile, durable, inexpensive, practical and easy to use. Manufacturers produce a wide range of meshes. These are readily available to farmers through their rural suppliers and many of the larger hardware stores.

Galvanised mesh

Mesh is available in black, that is, untreated. On a farm, this may have limited applications as it rusts over time. The most practical mesh to use is galvanised mesh, particularly where it is to be used on structures such as silos, gates, and truck or trailer sides. Galvanised mesh may be a little more expensive than black, but the extra cost is well worth it because it won't rust.

Mesh is supplied for a wide range of applications. It ranges in size from small spaces and small rods, to large spaces with thick rods. Each will have a range of uses. It is supplied cut ready for gates, as gate infills, and often it is available in long rolls, such as 30 m rolls that you are able to cut yourself. If you have a number of applications, the long rolls will reduce a lot of wastage.

Here is a small selection of ideas where you can use mesh. Of course, the number of applications is probably limited by one's imagination. It depends on the sizes of the mesh available too. As a rough guide, the following may be helpful:

Standard farm gates: 6.3 mm @ 100 mm x 6.3 mm @ 200 mm

Heavy cattle gates: 10 mm @ 100 mm x 10 mm @ 200 mm

Sheep and pig enclosures: 8 mm @ 100 mm x 8 mm @ 200 mm

Utility and trailer sides: 5 mm @ 50 mm x 5 mm @ 75 mm

And for every other application, most rural suppliers could advise you on the most suitable types of mesh for a particular need you might have. And there are many!

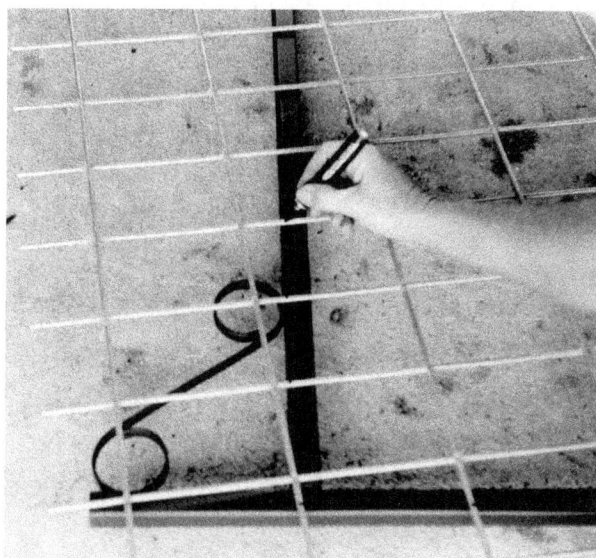

Mark the mesh with a felt pen for cutting

Clamp the mesh in place to make welding easier

Marking the mesh

A felt pen will mark easily on mesh, particularly galvanised mesh. Felt pens are often waterproof, so the mark that is made won't rub off.

The mesh is marked all around where cuts are to be made. Perhaps a warning is in order at this stage if you don't want to be skewered like a barbecue chicken. Mesh that has been rolled up, such as the 30 m rolls of farm gate infill mesh, will tend to roll up again unless the mesh is treated with caution, and a heavy weight used to keep down the loose end after the cut is made. Watch out for your face and particularly your eyes. If this does happen, it will occur without warning, and will be very swift!

Cutting

Cutting the mesh is easy. It is unlikely that the sheet of mesh purchased for a particular purpose will be the exact size required. Gate infills might be one of the few exceptions— they are supplied to fit standard farm gates. But even gate infill mesh can be supplied in long rolls, and this indeed is a very practical way of buying it. For most purposes, however, the mesh will need to be pruned a little here and there, particularly at the corners of gates.

Small bolt cutters are ideal for this purpose as long as they are heavy enough for your particular thickness of mesh. The result of using cutters is that the end of each strand is clean and straight, and is then ready for welding or attaching with no further preparation. If you are removing a short piece of the mesh, an end for example, using bolt cutters, make sure no one and no animal is in front of it. The cutting will result in a projectile with a high velocity.

Cut the mesh to the correct size using small bolt cutters

Primitive methods, such as using a cold chisel or a hacksaw work after a fashion, although cutting the mesh with a saw can use up a lot of blades and patience.

Shaping

Shaping any unbraced mesh is simply a matter of rolling it and curving it or bending it around the frame to which it is to be attached. Until attachment, it is flexible and co-operates well with the worker. The strength and rigidity come after attachment to the frame, such as the tubular pipe of a gate frame.

Attachment

There are several methods of attaching mesh to a steel frame, but possibly the least expensive and easiest method is simply to weld it to the frame. This method is permanent, too, although small metal clips that can be curved around the mesh and the frame are available, and can no doubt be

Weld the mesh to the frame with the electrode set at at about 30 amps higher than normal to remove the galvanising layer

supplied by most rural suppliers, particularly those supplying the mesh.

Special care needs to be given to welding galvanised steel.

Warning

As the welding processes give off zinc fumes which won't exactly improve a person's health or complexion, the welder should always make sure that the work area is well ventilated. Working outside with a breeze blowing is ideal. Any welding, but particularly welding galvanised steel in an enclosed area such as in a workshop, can be harmful to your health.

Removing zinc

The zinc coating should be removed from the steel. This is to achieve a strong weld. The heat from the welding is usually enough to remove enough of the zinc coating to ensure an adequate weld. Lay the weld metal down in two short runs. The first run will be sufficient to melt the zinc and form a zinc oxide that can be immediately brushed off using a wire brush.

The next run will be laid down slowly to ensure deposition of sufficient weld metal to attain a strong weld.

The usual electrodes you are familiar with, such as those rated E6012 or E6013 will suffice. A hotter arc than usual is required initially to burn away the zinc—an increase of about 30 amps for a 2.5 mm welding electrode will help, as will a longer and hotter arc. This can be obtained by holding the end of the electrode further away from the metal than usual.

Recoating

If galvanised mesh or steel has been used, the welding process will have removed the rust protection in the immediate area of the weld. Anyway, the weld metal that has been deposited will rust. The whole weld area must therefore be re-treated to prevent rusting. This will include any area of the zinc coating that has been affected by the heat of the welding.

The simplest method, and one that is generally used on farm gates and trailer sides, is the application of a cold-galvanising paint. These are expensive, but then, so is rusting over time. This is merely painted over the welded area, over the mesh and steel framing and under the mesh where the brush can reach. The paint dries quickly, and the item is serviceable within a few minutes. One coat of paint applied to the metal will give sufficient protection for most purposes for the life of the gate.

In addition to cold galvanising paints and metal primers, there are available specially formulated metal galvanising bars. There are even powders that can be applied and heated to melt them so they bond to the metal. This method of re-applying a coating to prevent rust will be about as permanent and as effective as was the original galvanising process itself.

Where to weld

Depending on what is being made from the mesh, welding can be done on one side only. In many cases, this is the only practical way to weld it. However, with some applications, such as gates, where access can be easily obtained, welding on both sides is recommended. Once welding has been completed on one side of the gate, the area on the opposite side of each weld should be cleaned with a wire brush. The zinc oxide will easily find its way under the mesh to that side. The mesh can then be welded to the frame opposite each of the previous welds.

It is highly unlikely that mesh will need to be welded to the frame along its entire length. Intermittent welds, 25 mm long and spaced about 300 mm apart will suffice. Even at these distances, the welds should be sufficient to keep any farmer happy, and any sheep that wants to escape, unhappy.

The result is a structure, such as a gate, with mesh that won't wave in the breeze or sag under modest weights.

Framing

The frame to which the mesh will be attached should be strong enough for the purpose. With so many applications possible, a full range of frame sizes that could be recommended is rather difficult.

As a rough guide, the frame used for the standard farm gate is 25 mm internal diameter, or about 32 mm outside diameter. That is sufficient to withstand sheep and the occasional cow banging itself against it. However, discretion will prevent a few bent frames. If you have an angry bull, use heavier pipe for the frame, and heavier mesh.

Joining ends of mesh

Like most materials we work with, the mesh will often be too short. This presents no problems as it can be welded satisfactorily.

For economy, it is practical to use a couple of shorter pieces and join them together. The free ends of the mesh can be welded, either with verticals back to back, or if this is not possible, then the free ends can be welded together.

If the free ends are placed side by side, that is fine, but, as the rods comprising the mesh are 6 mm or more thick, one piece of mesh will be displaced by this amount. To keep the two pieces of mesh in line, the free ends of the mesh need to be bent slightly — no more than the thickness of the mesh. This is done by applying an adjustable spanner over the rods and bending each one slightly in turn. The free ends of the rods will bend easily. The two free ends of the mesh will be

parallel, and can be welded together, using a 2.5 mm electrode.

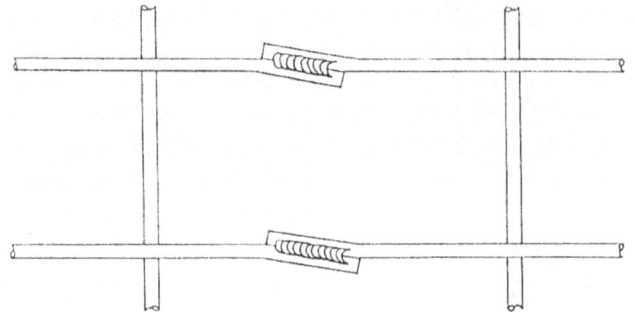

Bend the free ends of the mesh by half the thickness of the mesh so that, together, the joint is no wider than one rod of mesh

Rough edges

Care should be taken during any fabrication to ensure that no sharp edges protrude. This is especially relevant where the structure is to be used for animals. Prize Angora goats don't appreciate having tufts of hair pulled out just before show day, and neither do their owners!

Because mesh is so versatile, it will have widespread applications in many other situations; a bit of thought will soon discover other uses to which it can be put. Just some of them include storage bins, trellises, machinery guards and cages. But a good imagination will certainly extend this list. Because mesh is relatively inexpensive, and it is easy to work with, perhaps it could be

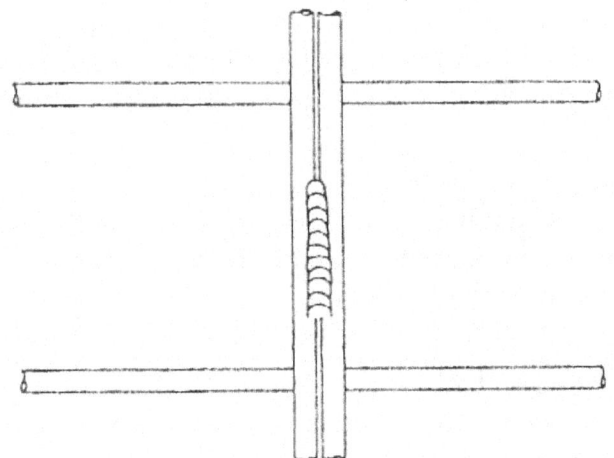

Use 25 mm weld beads spaced at 300 mm intervals along the length of the joint

considered before many other materials. After all, a lot of little holes can soon fill up one big one.

But just because this section is all about working with mesh, don't limit your project to just this subject. Even after you have completed the trellis or some of the other projects in this book, consider whether you can enhance its appearance further by adding the last bits to finish off the project so it becomes an aesthetically pleasing showpiece for your garden. In this trellis, for example, two scrolls were added from the ends of the two overhangs to the frame. While they do not necessarily make the frame or structure stronger, such add-ons contribute something to the trellis to make its appearance more pleasing.

While two scrolls here finish off the trellis satisfactorily, always consider other ways you could add to the project you have just completed. After all, a little imagination will go a long way.

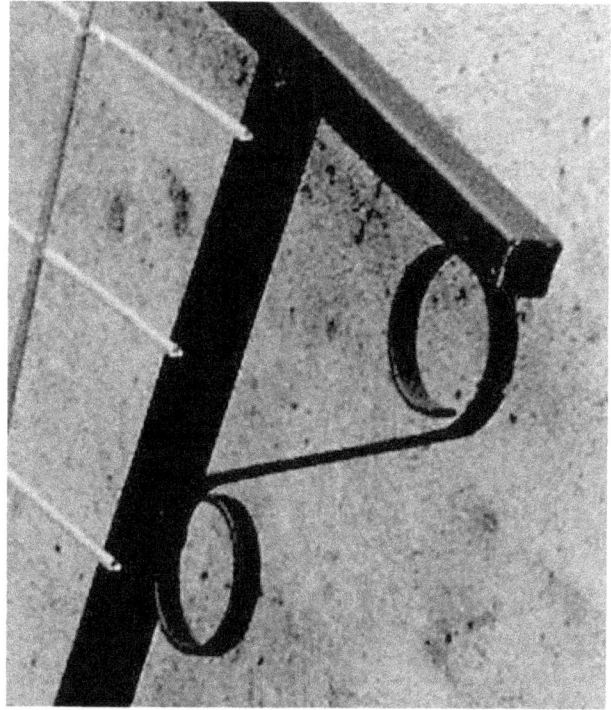

19 Repairing cast iron

Cast iron is a splendid material, with unique properties; its flow characteristics when molten enable it to be cast into many useful items, such as engine blocks, engine heads, flywheels and housings. It can even be machined. Many items, such as engine blocks of tractors and motor cars, and other machinery, including engine heads, housings for gears and pumps and many more, are made from cast iron. All are liable to cracking. The cost of replacing these items is high. A replacement engine block for a large tractor can be several thousand dollars; that for large machinery such as bulldozers, perhaps much more.

It is indeed a splendid material — until it cracks.

The characteristics of cast iron are due to its composition — a high carbon content, sometimes as much as 4.5%, compared to steel's carbon content of under 1%. It is this carbon content that gives the metal its brittleness.

Many years ago, the usual method of repairing cast iron was to use gas welding. This involved dismantling the item completely, preheating it for many hours, welding the fracture, then cooling it for a long time — often for days, sometimes for a week or more so it cooled slowly.

The cost of this procedure was exorbitant, and often impractical. Consequently, cast iron items weren't repaired, or they weren't repaired properly.

A lot of machinery used is now obsolete, and replacement parts may not be readily available.

Not only the cost of those replacement parts needs to be considered, but also the time the machinery is out of service can mean the difference between a crop that is harvested in time, or a crop that is ruined. Many farm activities may cease if machinery is inoperative for weeks while a replacement head or block for a tractor is obtained — if indeed it can be. This is an inefficient way to run a farm!

The logical solution is to repair the damaged machinery and have it running again within hours for perhaps only a few dollars.

Special welding electrodes are now available so that repairs to cast iron are fast and economical. The welds will be as strong, if not stronger, than the original item. These special electrodes are so easy to use in all positions.

If ordinary mild steel electrodes are used to repair cast iron, stresses are created because of the different rates of contraction and flexibility of the cast iron and the mild steel. If the welds hold for a time, this should be no indication that they will hold forever. They won't. Only the correct electrodes developed for use on cast iron should be used.

Using the correct electrodes for cast iron in most cases eliminates the need to dismantle the machinery. It may not be necessary even to remove the engine from the tractor. An engine head can be removed, repaired, machined and replaced, often without further dismantling.

Because of the size of some items, such as engine blocks of large machinery, preheating and subsequent slow cooling may not be practical on a farm. This is where electric welding now has many advantages and should be considered wherever possible.

Preparation

As with all welding, the surfaces must be clean. The strength of any weld is dependent on the quality of the weld and cleaning certainly improves the chances of obtaining a strong and satisfactory weld.

Cast iron machinery components will most likely have a coating of oil, grease or other organic matter adhering to them. This can be effectively removed with a suitable solvent. Alternatively, the oil can be burnt off using an oxidising flame from an oxy torch, followed by a brushing with a wire brush.

Removing water

Water can be a problem with some components, particularly when water jackets or water pumps are welded. Water may seep through the crack as the weld metal is deposited, raising impurities to the weld area. Bubbles caused by steam mixing with the molten weld metal may result in a weak weld. All moisture therefore must be removed from the area being repaired. **Mild** preheating with an oxy torch will do this effectively. Excessive heat must not be applied locally, as other cracks would develop. Of course, if an engine is being repaired *in situ*, the coolant should be drained from the cooling system, the area to be welded thoroughly dried perhaps by the gentle action of a flame. But be careful not to apply too much heat because you could extend the crack or cause a new crack to develop in the cast iron.

Isolating the crack

If the crack is localised, that is, it does not extend from one end of the casting to the other, it is necessary to ensure that the crack does stop right there. Cracks in cast iron can frequently be extended through stresses. Even as one end of it is being welded, it can grow at the other end. This can be overcome so the repair doesn't become a disaster, by drilling a small hole at each end of the crack and right through the casting. The crack will stop at each of the two holes.

An area around the crack must be gouged out for proper penetration of the weld metal.

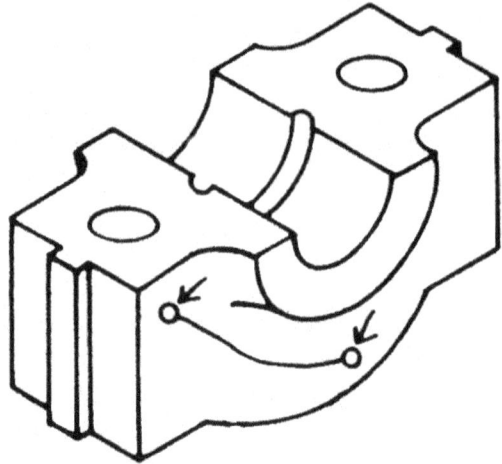

Drill a small hole at each end of the crack to prevent its spread. Gouge out the material from either side of the crack for proper weld metal penetration

Welding the metal

As the carbon content of cast iron is so high, improper welding procedures produce carbides of iron which are extremely hard and abrasion-resistant. If the repair needs to be machined, such as after an engine head has been repaired, the formation of these carbides can be a problem, and their formation must be prevented. Correct procedures will ensure that the formation of these carbides is negligible.

Strike the arc on the cast iron. The weld should begin at one end of the crack and run up to, but not over, the drilled hole at the end of the crack.

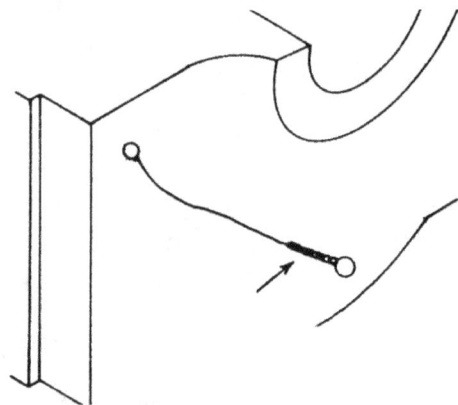

Weld only a small area of the crack about 20 to 30 mm at a time to prevent overheating of the cast iron. The first run should stop at the drilled hole

Then run a similar amount of weld metal which will terminate at the previous run.

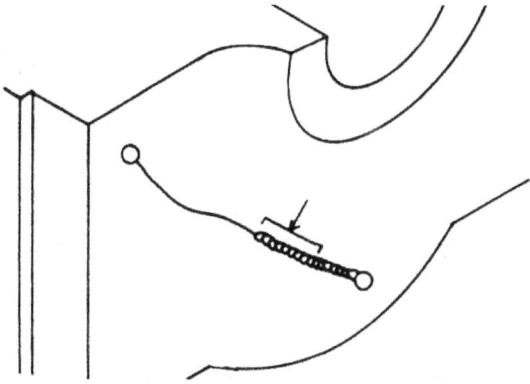

The second run of weld metal should end at the first run

Cooling the weld

The rest of the crack, no matter how long, should be filled by applying short runs no more than 20–30 millimetres of weld metal at any one time. Allow the casting and the weld metal to cool between each application to keep the temperature and the stresses of the cast iron as low as possible. To do this, use the lowest amperage possible to keep heat to a minimum. See the electrode manufacturer's guide for recommended amperage settings.

After the crack has been welded, allow the cast iron to cool as slowly as possible.

Weld the stop holes last – they will serve their worthwhile function until the very end.

It is tempting to cool items rapidly with water. The same treatment applied to cast iron will cause cracking, and must not be attempted.

Of course, now that the part has been repaired, check if possible for the cause of the failure. Cracking in cast iron will have a cause – it could be stress, overheating, differential heating, freezing, vibration or some other cause. It makes sense to take steps to reduce the number of repair jobs in the future.

Electrodes

The electrodes used to repair cast iron are specialised items and they must be ordered. Delays in the delivery service and in the processing of your order must be considered.

Cast iron can crack at any time. It is wise to order the electrodes before you need them, not after, and have a packet of them ready. Remember that a crop that needs harvesting won't wait for your electrodes to be delivered.

Check the Internet for electrodes that are suitable for welding cast iron. As it is anticipated this book will be sold and used in many countries around the world, it is not possible to give manufacturer details of appropriate products.

20 Pipes

This section discusses pipes, with a guide to their uses.

Pipe. It's rigid, strong and lightweight. And it's easy to work with, to cut and to weld. It's used for irrigation systems, for shed frames and roof trusses. In fact, it can be used for almost any structural work.

It can be cut, bent, but it can never be straightened. It withstands considerable pressures, such as with spraying equipment, and has a very high load bearing capacity. Welded with other pieces of pipe or steel, its strength is increased considerably.

There's a pipe size to suit almost any job on the farm and around the home. Pipe is available in a variety of dimensions, from outside thicknesses of just over 12 millimetres to those of over 150 mm. Wall thickness ranges from just over two mm for the smaller diameter pipes, to around five or six mm for those of large diameters.

It's possible to use pipe, welded in various combinations, to fabricate any number of other items on the farm, such as making the frames for machinery sheds, or frames for animal pens and cages, roof trusses, frames for greenhouses, and lots, lots more. Around the home, it can be used for constructing the frames of garages and sheds, and for making roof trusses.

Cutting

Cutting pipe is easy. A power hacksaw is ideally suited to this job, giving a clean cut perpendicular to the length of the pipe. This in itself makes working with the cut lengths easier. However, there is a dearth of power hacksaws around; a hand operated one will suffice, even though the cut might be a bit wonky. Angle grinders with steel-cutting disks will cut through sections easily and quickly, but not necessarily quietly. So will steel-cutting circular saws. Again, not necessarily silently.

Bending

Pipe can be bent when necessary. Pipe benders will generally take sizes up to 50 mm outside diameter, and these can be bent at least to right angles if required without wall collapse. Pipe can also be bent using heat. The flame of the oxy torch will be needed here. But don't heat-bend galvanised pipe as you will create dangerous fumes of zinc.

With thin-walled pipe such as vehicle exhaust pipe, it is necessary to heat one side of the pipe, the whole length being secured tightly. Gradually, the end can be bent in the desired direction. Bulges in the side wall of the pipe will appear, and these should be encouraged using the flame. Perhaps a series of bulges will facilitate this task more readily. Sometimes, though, the results with heat bending are unsightly. Unless you can bury these results, they might be best avoided.

Try the mitre cut instead. That's cutting through the pipe at 45° — two angles of 45° together will make the right angle you require. Leave a gap of about three millimetres, weld, and your right angle is completed.

Or you can use pipe of different diameters — one size with an internal diameter just slightly larger than the outside diameter of the other; make the angle in the thicker pipe and re-weld, insert the smaller diameter pipe into the angle you have formed, and weld.

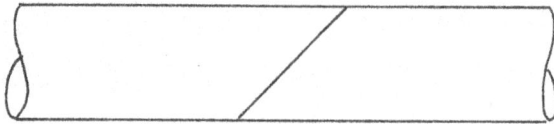

Cut the pipe at 45°

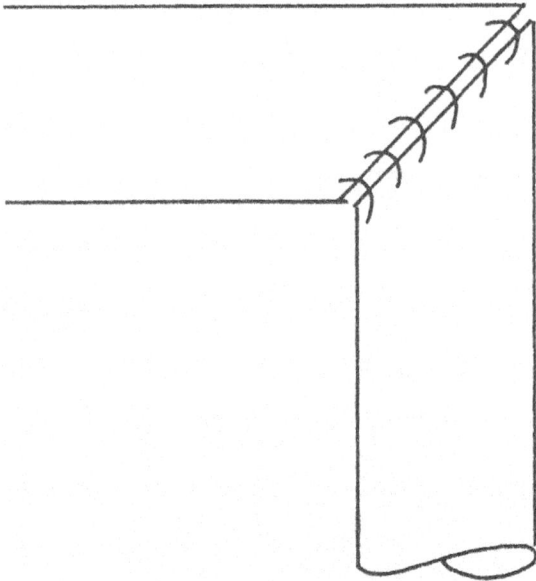

Complete the right angle by welding the joint

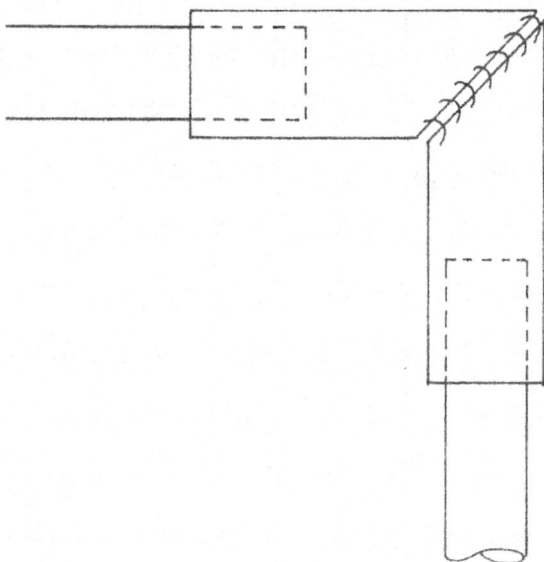

You are never restricted to using pipes of only one diameter

Welding

Galvanised pipe may present problems, both to your own health, and to the strength of the weld. First, avoid breathing the fumes if you are welding galvanised steel. They're not very nice. And try to remove as much zinc as possible from around the area to be welded. Zinc in the form of zinc oxide will get into the weld metal and weaken it. Repairs in the field after a storm has blown down your shed can be an inconvenience.

Tee joints

For irrigation systems, the liquids will need to flow through all the pipes. Perhaps special adapters for joining pipes at different angles are available from your local supplier. If they are, use them. They'll save you a lot of time and work. If they're not available, read on.

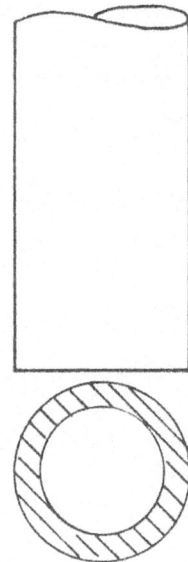

Watch out for the large gap you might have to weld unless you shape the end

With structures like pressure sprays, it may be necessary to form tee joints. These tee joins are easy to achieve. One section is formed to fit reasonably snugly over the side wall of the adjoining pipe, and the two are welded together. Unless the end is shaped properly, a huge gap will appear. This will have to be filled with a lot of weld metal, with possibly a disastrous amount of buckling at the same time, which is liable to pull the whole structure out of alignment.

Shape the end as shown in the diagram. Trim the end of the second pipe to fit over this hole. Get the two pipes to fit together reasonably well and weld them. In this same way, it is possible to adapt a small-bore pipe to a larger-bore pipe and make the liquid flow where it should go. Leave a gap of about the thickness of the welding electrode for full weld metal penetration, then weld around the pipe.

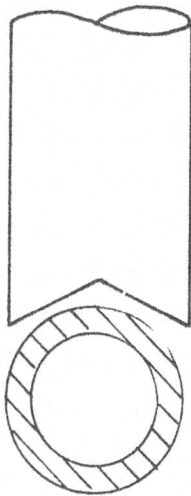

To ensure best fit when welding two ends of pipe together, clamp them to the inside of a piece of angle iron

Shape the end of the pipe for a better fit before welding the joint

Reducing tees may be an option, too. So much the better. But if they're not, or you can't wait for your stockist to order them for you, this method will be as good as any you can get.

Joining two lengths of pipe

All steel is either too long or too short. That's guaranteed by Murphy's Law! If the pipe is too short, sections may be welded together using a butt joint where the two lengths of pipe are welded together end to end. A gap the thickness of the electrode is left between the two ends, and the pipes simply welded. It's often best to weld a portion of the circumference, about a quarter of the way around, turn the two pipes over, and weld diagonally opposite the first weld for the

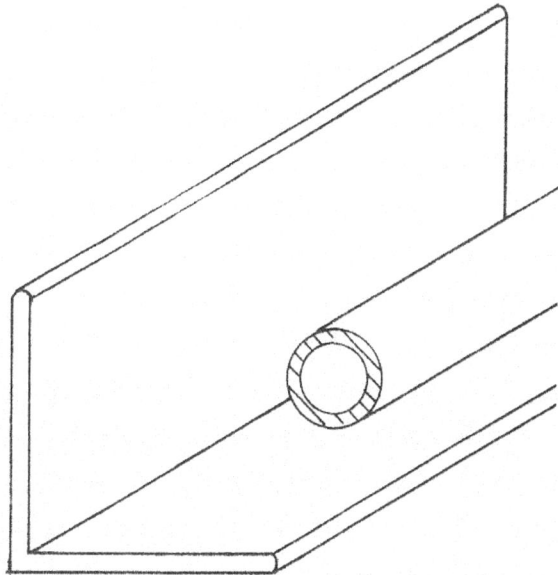

same distance, then fill the two remaining quarters with weld metal.

Keeping the two lengths straight, or even getting them to line up exactly can be a problem sometimes, but this is easily overcome by supporting the lengths in a more or less straight line, clamping first one end of a pipe into the corner of a piece of angle iron, and then clamping the pipe on two different sides to pull it firmly into the corner of the angle iron. Next, clamp the end of the second length you are joining in the same way. Leave the mandatory gap, weld, and turn. If you are turning the pipes over for easy access, ensure that after you have welded part of the way around, you allow for the build-up of weld metal. This, raised above the surface of the pipe, can throw out the whole alignment. You may need to grind off the excess weld metal at this stage before proceeding to complete the weld.

Spray nozzles

Of course, special applications of pipe will need special attachments. Spray systems for example will need fine spray nozzles fitted to the pipe. These, if they are the screw-in type, will need holes the right size drilled in the correct place in the wall of the pipe. The wall of the pipe will take a thread easily. The holes are threaded using a tap and dye set, and the spray nozzles screwed into position. Mark out the location of the points, drill the holes all in line, or at the desired angles, and finish the job as just described.

Brackets

In the farm workshop, pipe can be used for supporting engines as they are hoisted out of trucks, cars and the tractor. Pipe of sufficient strength can be welded to flat plate and the plates mounted to walls, posts, or other suitable points of attachment. Or pipes can be welded to a flat plate for bolting onto concrete. A run of weld metal is applied

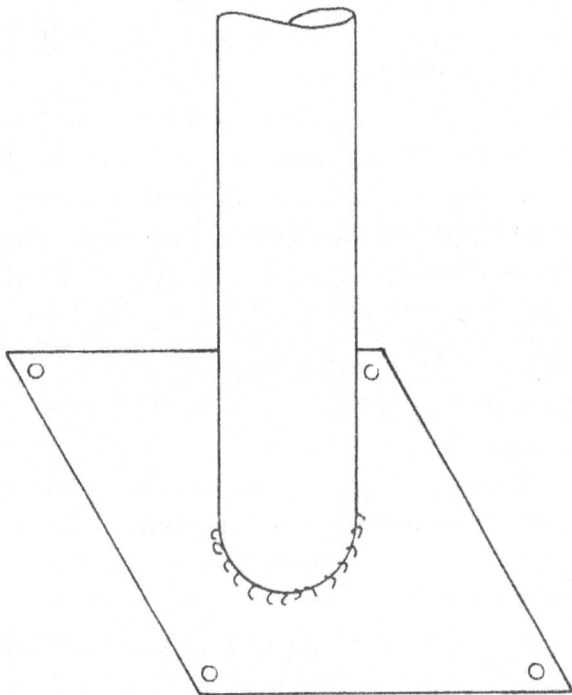

around the full circumference of the pipe. If the end of the pipe is at exactly 90° and sufficient strength is attained by welding around the outside of the pipe rather than allowing proper weld metal penetration, this will give a much easier and neater weld. But make sure the result is as strong as you need for the particular application.

Trusses

The real benefit of pipe comes when it is used in combination with other steel fixtures, such as cross bracing that is used as reinforcement. For example, a length of pipe six metres long, 20 mm internal diameter, flexes when unsupported. Use two pieces of similar pipe the same length, welded together, with half a dozen cross braces, and you have a roof truss of tremendous strength. Cross bracing should be sufficient not only to strengthen the rigidity of the pipes, but also to support the load being carried. And if you are constructing roof trusses, this is more than just the weight of the steel roof itself. Consider at the same time the force of a strong wind blowing down on to the roof.

Apply a run of weld metal to the full circumference of the pipe

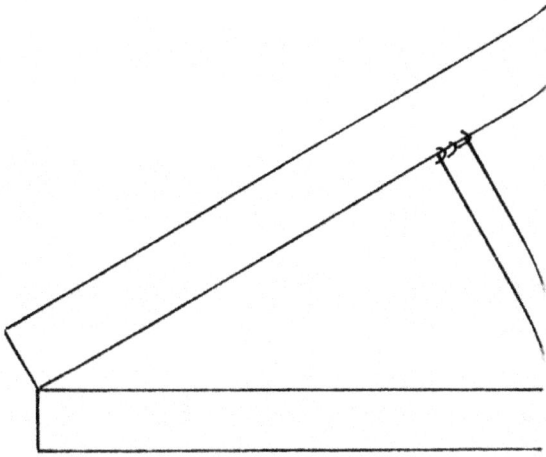

That's equivalent to a force of perhaps several tonnes applied to the roof. In a cold climate, consider the weight of snow accumulating on the roof.

Pipe is an ideal structural material for building roof trusses and shed frames. Local councils will have determined minimum requirements for frames and other building components, and will no doubt upset your plans. Check with your appropriate authorities before building anything such as a garage or machinery shed to ascertain what they need. This is easier than demolishing your handiwork because it does not comply with their minimum requirements.

Steel pipe will come into its own in roofs: the pitch of the roof can be made to suit any

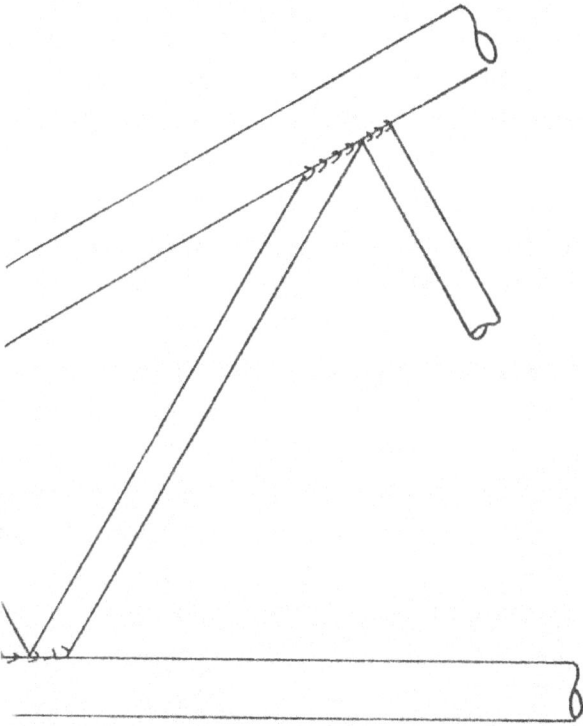

Determine the pitch of the roof and cut the pipes to the right length

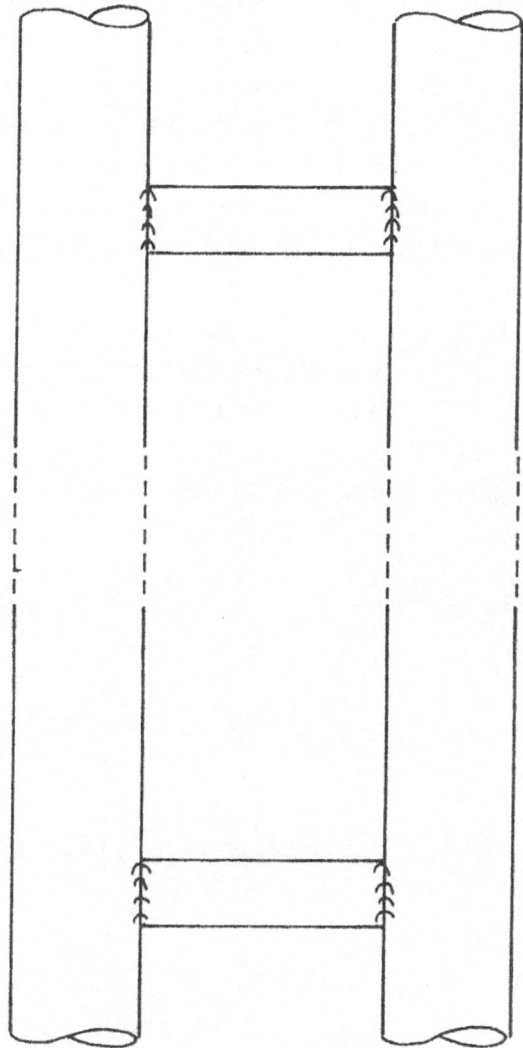

A frame for a shed will be incredibly strong if it is constructed from two parallel lengths of pipe welded together with cross pieces

purpose, and the strength of the trusses adjusted accordingly. Roof trusses made from pipe need bracing, but the bracing need not necessarily be the same diameter material that is used to make the spans.

First, determine the length required, taking into account overhang for eaves. Then determine the pitch—that is, the height of the rise. Cut the pipes accordingly, lay them out in the correct position on a flat surface, and begin welding the struts in place. These will not be straight up and down—there's not all that much strength in the overall structure with that configuration. The struts should be angled as shown in the diagram.

For small roofs with a span of about three or four metres, and carrying only modest loads such as those for small tool sheds with a metal roof, pipe of about 20 mm diameter should suffice. For larger roof spans, check the requirements with your shire engineer. Minimum requirements will apply in most shires. The council's engineer will give you the requirements you will need to follow. But nevertheless check those winds in your local area.

To attach the roof on to the trusses, pieces of flat bar, perhaps 50 mm by 3 mm and about 100 mm long, can be welded to the top pipe and at right angles to it. A hole through the flat bar for a bolt will allow roofing timber, possibly 100 millimetres by 50

millimetres hardwood, to be simply bolted across the roof. The metal roof is then secured to the timber.

Shed frames

Pipe is excellent for building the frames of sheds too. Here, particularly for sheds not much larger than a small tool shed, two pipes, with a minimum diameter of about 20 mm internal diameter, 75–100 mm apart, separated by braces, will provide a frame of exceptional strength. Compress the ends of the braces slightly to facilitate fit-up. These frame members are set into the ground in concrete, and the shed built around them. Flat bar can also be welded to the outer pipe to accommodate 100 mm by 50 mm timber for securing the cladding. And don't forget that those steel roof trusses can be attached to the steel frames of the shed you have just made.

21 Making steel stronger

Steel has many attributes—it is durable, readily available, and it can be worked with ease. It is also strong. But regardless of this last property, steel can be made even stronger.

Star posts used for fencing, which are much more rigid than three thin pieces of steel on their own, indicate the strength attainable from steel. The H-beams used in high-rise buildings achieve strength and rigidity without the weight of a solid mass of steel. A length of flat bar three millimetres thick and more than six metres long has almost no rigidity—carry it by its centre and both ends will trail on the ground. Yet angle iron will keep more or less its original shape without excessive bending. Because of its special shape, angle iron is far stronger than two pieces of flat bar.

Creative people are very practical, often because of necessity. Through their innovation, all sorts of inventions are possible on the spur of the moment. Adaptability of ideas to various situations is one of the secrets of success. By strengthening this already practical material, one can build countless strong but lightweight structures. Farmers are often confronted with situations when machinery parts bend through excessive or incorrect use. Perhaps it is difficult to bend thick pieces of steel? Then make a goose neck for a tow bar, for example, from thinner, easily worked materials. Or strengthen a special tine of a plough, or make a light weight device for lifting heavy objects such as bee hives.

Making a goose neck

Take that goose neck on a tow bar. Bending steel 12 mm thick and 50 mm wide to the required shape would require either a lot of heating with an oxy torch, or a special press. Think, instead, of using thinner steel, perhaps only 6 mm thick. That's relatively easy to bend to the right shape: hold one end firmly in a vice, which at the same time gives the required straight edge, and the steel can be easily bent by using a couple of large adjustable spanners.

The goose neck constructed from 6 mm steel on its own will lack the strength required to do its job, but a narrow piece of steel, again only 5 or 6 mm thick, can be welded to each side of the bent steel. When welded properly, the goose neck will be just about as strong as one made from 12 mm steel. Certainly it will be adequate for a light weight trailer on the farm (but it might not be adequate if towing a heavy trailer along a public road). And steel 6 mm thick is probably more readily available than steel 12 mm thick anyway. Cut it and shape it. Bevel the edges for welding. After welding, trim the excess steel if desired. All of this might

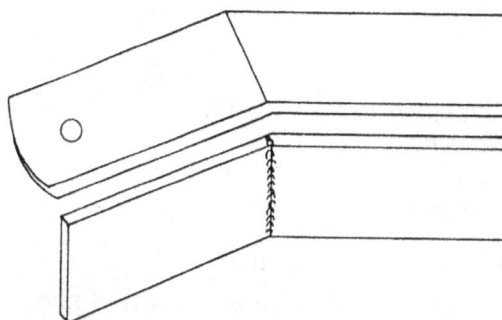

Two pieces of steel welded together are stronger than they are on their own

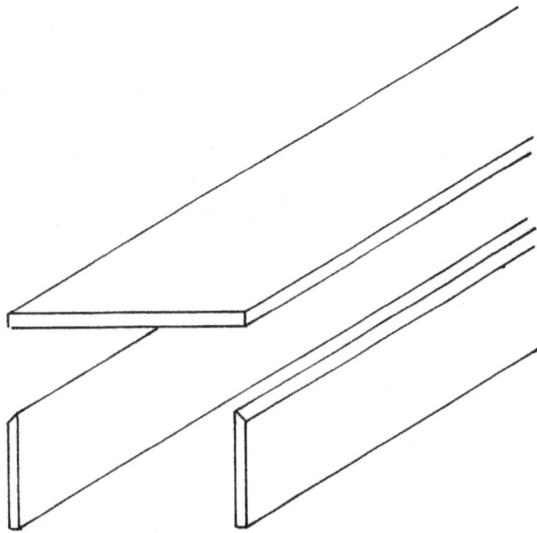

This configuration of flat bar will give a structure of immense strength

mean a little more work but if the proper machinery to bend it is not available, then at least by this means the goose neck is there, adequate and strong, when you want it. That's the benefit of being innovative with a welder.

The tee configuration

A tee configuration will be far stronger than a flat length of steel, even hardened steel. A reinforcing strip welded to the back of the steel (such as a tine) will generally give the additional strength required. Rocks and rough use will find difficulty in bending such a tine as this. Alternatively, the reinforcing can be welded in front of the curve.

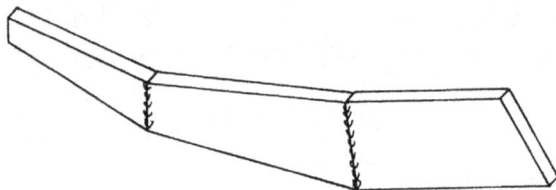

The strengthening plate can be a composite of several smaller pieces

Using the correct electrode

Some implements are made of a special composition, creating a hardened steel. Use steel of similar composition if possible for the reinforcement. Use the correct electrodes. Welding steels of different compositions will

require special electrodes which can sometimes accommodate steels of different, and unknown, composition. The correct electrode will ensure maximum strength consistent with that attainable from the implement you are reinforcing or building.

Welding a tee

How does one weld up a tee? It's simple. To the piece of steel that needs strengthening, cut a piece of flat bar the correct length, bevel the edges to attain maximum weld metal penetration. Tack weld together first then fully weld all around

That's alright if the device you are making is straight. A flat bar will already have the correct configuration to fit neatly into position. Suppose the device were curved? There's no problem in strengthening a curved piece of steel either. If the reinforcing piece can be bent reasonably easily (although often it won't be), simply curve it to the required shape, and weld.

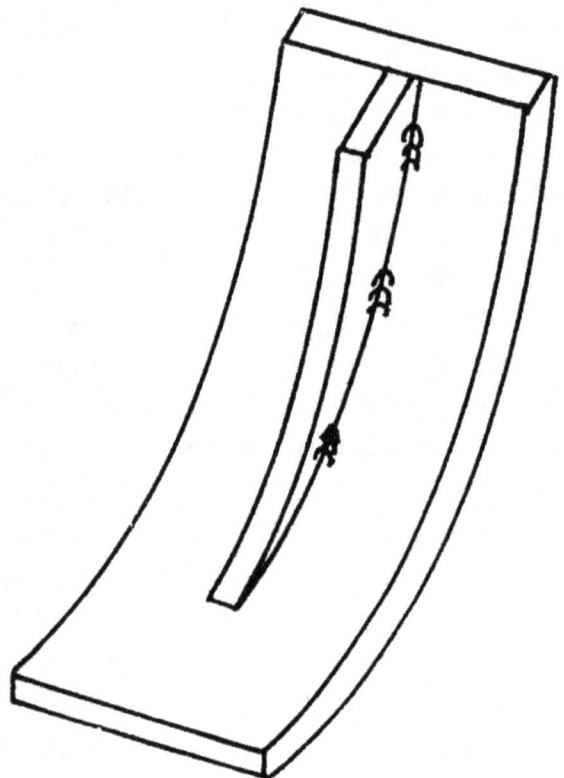

Welding the strengthening plate on the inside of the curve results in a strong structure

108

But what if the piece to be reinforced is at an angle? The reinforcing piece will need the same configuration. Suppose the piece has a bend in it at 30°. Cut two pieces of steel for reinforcing, bevel the ends to attain complete weld metal penetration, clamp and then weld these together to the required configuration.

If the piece to be reinforced is curved, this again should present no problem, as long as steel sufficiently wide is available. Draw an outline of the device to be strengthened on a sheet of steel plate or flat bar of sufficient width. Move the object along 50 mm and draw another outline. With an oxy-torch, cut along these two outlines. Clean up around the jagged edges, bevel the inner edge if necessary, and weld.

The amount of bracing usually depends on the strengthening required, the length of the object being reinforced. The longer the object, the more bracing that will be required is the general rule, and the type of work the object is intended for. Personal judgment can be the best bet here, although in most cases, bracing 50 mm wide and 5 or 6 mm thick will do the job. Don't overdo it. If steel only 25 mm wide will be satisfactory, then use it.

The bracing doesn't necessarily need to fit snugly against the reinforced steel along its entire length. A practical solution might

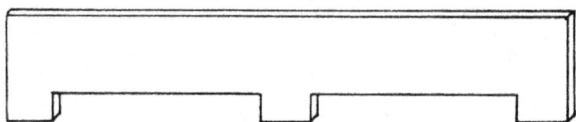

For most applications, welding around the entire bracing is not required

mean an M configuration, or a series of Ms — scalloped out and welded only in those points where contact is made. These points, when welded securely, are great when large, flat sheets of steel, such as steel plate, need a fair amount of stiffening. Although large, flat sheets of thin steel on their own are flexible, curving them to make a tank or small silo induces a high degree of rigidity into them, often without the need for further bracing.

So ascertain if the tank will stand by its own strength alone. If not ...

Making rigid frames for silos

On a farm, large curved frames, or ribs, may be needed from time to time, such as when large tanks or silos are being built. Special rolling equipment will curve these ribs; alternatively, a boiler maker will be able to carry out this type of work. On farms that are off the map, neither of these options will be available. Still no problem. Lay out flat a sheet of steel 3 mm, or even 5 mm thick, make a template of the frames, and mark their outline on the sheet of steel. Cut these with the oxy torch, and clean up the edge by grinding off the irregularities from the cut. The size of steel sheet you buy for these will depend on what you want to cut from it. Sheets are available in sizes from about 1800 by 900 mm to 1200 by 6000 mm. Buy the size sheet from which you can get all the ribs.

The curved ribs will have very little rigidity on their own, and you may well ask how on earth are these flimsy things going to keep the even larger sheets of steel that form the silo or tank in shape? Welded directly onto the inside of the tank, they will be as rigid as you want them to be.

If further strengthening to these frames is required, then flat bar 40 mm by 3 mm, or 50 mm by 3 mm welded to the inside of each rib will ensure that they cannot be bent. The 3 mm thick flat bar is easy to curve and work with. It is very flexible and here again you will probably develop more doubts about the success of your whole structure. It can be easily curved around the inside of the rib and welded intermittently (for example 25 mm runs of weld metal each 100 mm apart) to form a rather peculiar and curved tee shape. Just make sure that the flat bar fits snugly against the rib — clamp the two pieces of steel together and weld them with welds about 25 mm spaced out evenly. These, in turn, are welded to the inside of the round tank.

Once the first rib has been braced in this way, it will be easy to see other applications for this type of reinforcing—like the frame of a bull bar on the front of a vehicle, made from rather thin (not flimsy) strips of flat bar. Nevertheless, the frame comprising an H-section is tremendously strong.

Lightweight H-section

There are frames you can make up, ranging from those on the bull bar to anything else the practical farmer will want, like a lifting arm to load bee hives. Here, steel made into an H-configuration will have amazing strength.

Cut and weld the centre piece of the H to the required shape. Any reasonable shape can be obtained. Make sure the reinforcing piece of flat bar is a little longer than the length of the centre piece—it not only has to go on both sides, but over the top and, if necessary all around. Then wrap the flat bar (40 mm by 3 mm is usually ample) around the outside. Centre the steel within the bracing as you go, and tack-weld it intermittently. Again, 25 mm at 100 mm intervals is usually sufficient for reasonable strength. It's often a good idea to clamp the flat bar tightly to the centre piece to achieve a close fit—too much slack between the pieces could mean that a weakness is built into the structure, causing bowing and possible collapse. But that's only more likely to happen if there are very large gaps between the pieces. Once it has been tack welded, weld the structure fully for maximum strength.

The end of the centre piece can be curved to improve appearance and to facilitate a neat fit up. Cut the end neatly, either with an oxy torch or by a series of cuts and remove the roughness using a grinder (you must be wearing adequate eye and ear protection). The flat bar will then drape neatly over the whole frame.

So, it is easy to make a strong medium even stronger, isn't it?

22 Hard-facing surfaces

This chapter will show you how you can keep a sharp edge on things.

Almost every business is interested in cutting costs and saving money. Likewise, almost every businessman is keen to reduce expenses to lift his profits.

One way in which farmers and operators of heavy equipment can reduce expenditure is by minimising the replacement of parts that wear out.

The wear on those parts of machinery, such as plough disks and rock hammers that are subject to continuous abrasion can be minimised by the application of hard-facing material deposited on the leading edge by using an electric welder. The abrasive-resistant material deposited during the process reduces wear, sometimes as much as ten times. In other words, one set of expensive plough disks that have been treated will outlast ten replacement sets. What a saving!

The components can be prevented from wearing down through use. But once worn they can be built up again with the deposit of hardened material, bringing the parts up to the equivalent of new.

By using the same hard-facing electrodes, even a blunt edge can be made sharp and kept that way.

A cutting edge, for example, especially after it has been misused repeatedly and severely blunted, can have a new cutting edge applied. The implement will remain sharp for much longer than if it were merely sharpened again and again.

Almost any equipment that needs to be kept sharp can be treated this way.

Let's look at the applications of the hard-facing electrodes. It is assumed that the methods will be carried out using an electric welder. Other treatments are available for use with oxy welding equipment, but these will not be dealt with here because of the specialised equipment needed that is found only in well-equipped workshops.

The correct amperages may vary from brand to brand of electrodes used. The amperage used should be that recommended by the electrode manufacturer.

First, though, let's consider preventing wear from abrasion.

The surface to be treated must be cleaned of all dirt, rust, paint and other impurities.

Bring the surface to be treated to a shiny metallic finish. Usually a wire brush or grinder will do the job admirably.

The molten electrodes will run easily as they are applied, this being encouraged by applying the metal to the surface sloping at about 30° or so to the horizontal.

Two or three runs of the hard-facing metal may be necessary for maximum prolonged life of the equipment.

The first run should be along the outer edge of the equipment being treated. This

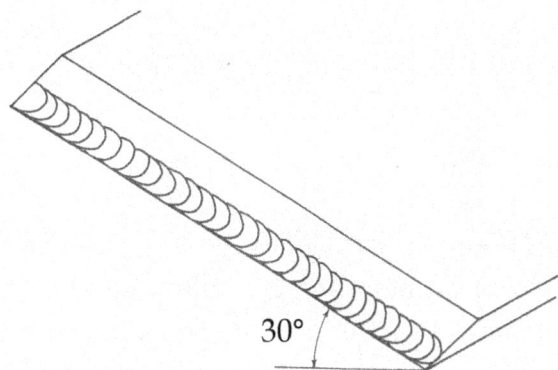

30°

first run will leave a very thin layer of material deposited along the edge, perhaps no more than one millimetre thick.

The second layer should be put directly over the first, but with some overlap, so that the material extends away from the edge of the implement. Apply by weaving the electrode from side to side.

The treatment should be completed over the entire edge or surface that is liable to severe abrasion.

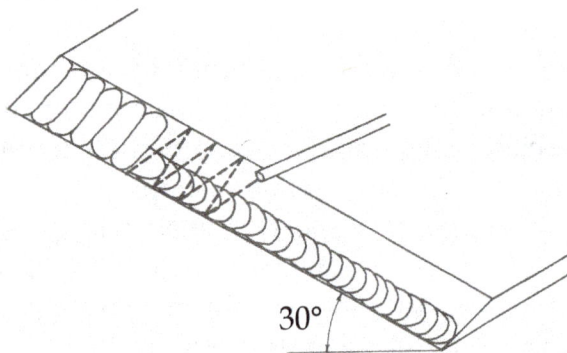

Turn the implement over and treat the opposite side similarly.

Most equipment, such as plough disks, treated this way won't need to be sharpened after this treatment.

With much use, even the hardened faces of equipment will wear. This is where more money can be saved. Instead of replacing the now worn parts with new ones at this stage, they can be thoroughly cleaned and a further deposit of hard-facing material applied along the edge to bring the implements back to their original shape and size.

If the component has been neglected, it will be too severe and it won't be possible to build up the material sufficiently. It's always wise to check the parts regularly and treat them before they become too worn. Save them, and you will save considerable time and costs.

There are also some edges (even those on axes) that need to be maintained in a sharpened condition for proper working efficiency.

Considerable time can be saved by applying a sharp edge and ensuring the edge stays sharp for a long, long time.

Let's now consider a cutting edge that's been worn down.

The edge to which the hard-facing material is to be applied should be ground down (if it isn't already so blunt) so the width of the edge is at least three mm wide, although worn edges can sometimes exceed this measurement.

The surface having the treatment must be clean and shining, and free of paint and rust. Grind the edge or use a wire brush.

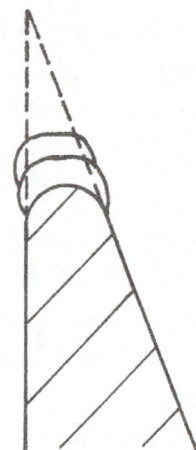

The first run of hard-facing material is deposited along the length of the edge, from one corner to the next, the metal deposited so it runs easily by holding the equipment at about 30° to the horizontal. Remove the slag and apply a second run. Build up the edge in successive runs.

After the metal has cooled sufficiently, the excess can be ground down if necessary either by using a grinding wheel or an angle grinder.

Grind the material until the edge is as sharp as you require it.

The new edge should outlive ten or more untreated edges before it needs sharpening again.

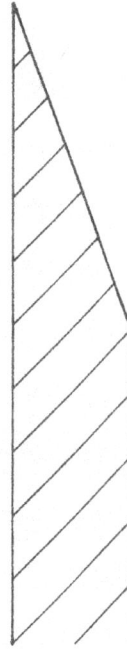

23 A guide to bending steel

That old stand-by of twisted wire technology often used on farms is possibly the best known application of bent steel. While wire is easy to bend, and often does an admirable job, not all steel can be bent with so little difficulty. Some of the hardened steels or spring steels bend only a small amount before breaking suddenly. They can be bent using heat.

Thin steel rods only 6 mm in diameter can be bent easily, the peg formed from them used to hold wire netting in place around fruit trees in the way tent pegs hold a tent securely in a wind. Hardened steel rods, however, should be heated with an oxy torch to allow easy bending to tent-peg shape. The heat may alter the properties of steel, or change its crystalline structure. Cooling hot steel quickly can also change the physical properties of the metal.

So if you need to bend soft rods, even up to ten or twelve mm diameter, then there's no problem as far as the steel is concerned. But all steel, whether it be rods or flat bar, pipe or square tubing, will have a maximum radius or angle through which it can be turned without affecting those physical

A gas flame is ideal for bending thin tubing, such as exhaust pipes of vehicles

properties. Beyond that natural limit, the crystalline structure of the metal changes, and the result could be a fracture, or at the least, a weakness. But sometimes a weakness is not really significant, particularly if no load is to he applied to the steel. At other times, a weakness can be significant.

So for any metal other than thin, mild steel rod, heat to red heat that portion where the bend is to be made, and bend the metal slowly to the desired configuration. Allow the rod to cool slowly. While the heat may affect the general strength of the rod, the peg can nevertheless be hammered in to even hard ground to hold that netting securely in place. Cutting that rod, by the way, is easy. Use a hacksaw or use bolt cutters if they are available, but be careful not to aim the off-cuts towards anyone or at an animal. Those sharp ends can depart from the bolt cutters very fast!

Some rods, such as concrete reinforcing rods, can be cold-bent as long as the means to do so is available, such as proper machinery, or muscle strength. On a farm, it is unlikely that the proper machinery to bend this type of rod would be available, so muscle power provides an alternative. Secure one end (the long end) of the rod, then slip a narrow-diameter pipe over the other end. This gives the leverage required. Simply bend the rod around an off-cut of pipe of suitable diameter, and remove the lever.

Thicker rod can be bent similarly. Heat the area right through until a deep redness is attained, then bend the rod slowly. With thicker materials, allow more time for the heat to penetrate to the centre of the rod.

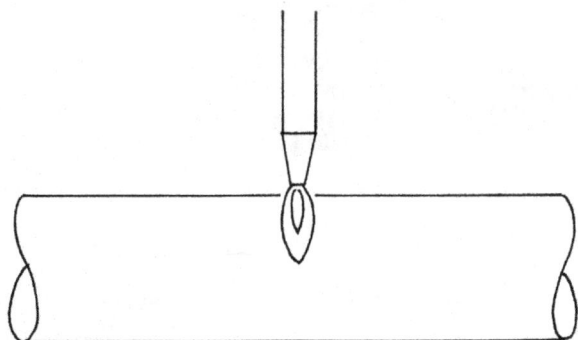

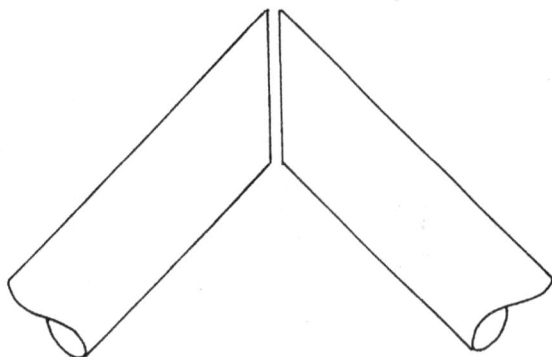

Bends can be achieved in pipes using two 45° cuts and welding them together

Even square bar up to 20 or 25 mm across can be bent in this way.

For heating the steel, use an oxy torch set on a neutral flame (that is, one that does not use excess oxygen, or gives off soot). Make sure you don't accidentally depress the oxygen cutting switch and cut the metal instead.

Bending thin pipes

Thin-walled steel tubing is often used in applications such as exhaust pipes on trucks, tractors or motor cars. While this material is easy to use in straight sections, bending it can be difficult. It can be joined easily by brazing, but, being thin-walled, it is difficult to arc weld.

This type of tubing (it often has a diameter of 25 mm to about 50 mm) will collapse if it is cold-bent such as in a pipe bender, a tool used to bend thick-walled pipes. Bending is best achieved by using localised heat from a blow torch, the flame again set to neutral. The tubing is heated to

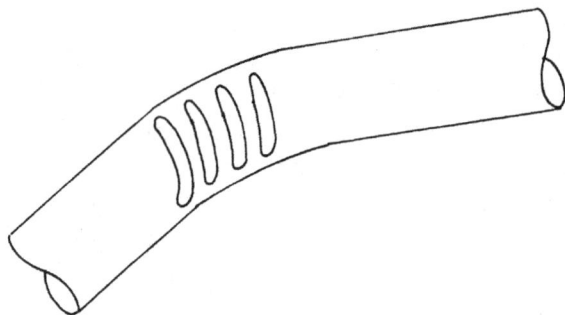

Sometimes a significant bend can be made in thin pipe with a series of smaller bends

redness, a little at a time, in narrow strips only on the side of the bend. Excess heating on exhaust pipes will quite likely see holes appearing where they are not wanted. Bend gently, a little at a time. A long 'bubble' will appear, and this is what you want to achieve. Move the flame along another 10 mm or so, and repeat the procedure, softening the wall and bending the tubing a little more, until the desired angle is attained.

Tubing which has a narrow diameter and thin walls, and particularly pipes made from soft material, such as copper water pipes, can be bent when they are cold by using a special non-compressing spring which is inserted into the tubing; the tubing is bent, perhaps in a pipe bender, and the spring removed. This will give a clean, neat bend — if you are able to buy those springs designed for this purpose.

Large-diameter pipes with thick walls cannot be bent using heat alone. They can, however, be shaped using a pipe bender. Such a tool has all sorts of possible applications on a farm, such as making your own farm gates. Pipes up to about 50 mm internal diameter can be bent with a pipe bender. The settings are variable, and can be adjusted for sharp and not-so-sharp bends. They are quick to use, and give an accurate bend each time. The walls of the pipe are kept in shape by a large cast iron former, around which the pipe bends.

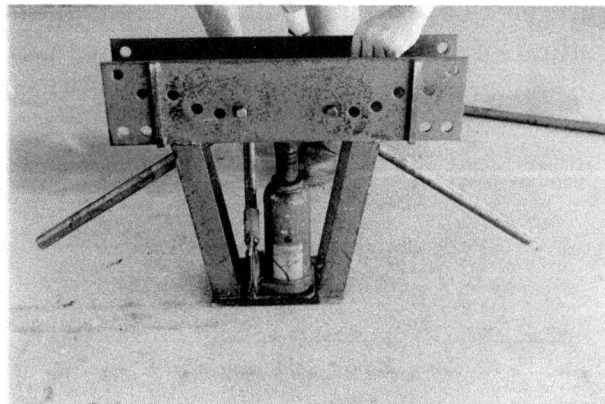

Mark the centre of the proposed bend, set the pipe in the pipe bender, and operate the lever of the hydraulic jack until all slack has been taken up between the pipe and the rollers on the bender. Check the flatness of the gate frame or whatever you are constructing, make any adjustments, then activate the lever of the jack again until the desired angle is attained. If the settings are correct, the bender will stop where it should, otherwise be careful that you don't push the angle beyond that intended. It's impossible to get bends out of pipes again.

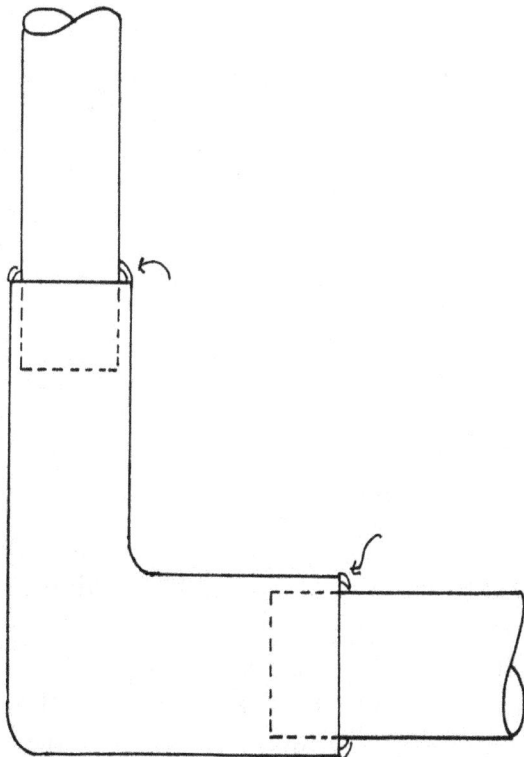

It is easy to achieve a 90° bend in pipes by using a sleeve of a larger internal diameter than the two pieces of pipe being bent

Making 90° bends in pipe

If a pipe bender is not obtainable by hiring, buying, borrowing or by other means, right angles can be formed in pipes by cutting the ends at 45° and welding two such angles together to form the right angle. It's simple, really. Just make sure the pipes are flat — that is, on one plane, because it is easy to weld an unsightly, immovable buckle into a gate frame. Clamp the two pieces together leaving the mandatory 3 mm gap for weld metal penetration, and weld the ends together. If you are welding galvanised steel (and most

pipe used on farms, particularly that used for gate frames, is galvanised) don't breathe in the unhealthy zinc fumes.

Often angles and elbows can be bought for various diameter pipes. If these are available, buy some if you think you will need them. They will save you a lot of work. Some are threaded, and the ends of the pipes screwed in. You may be able to modify a pipe of slightly larger diameter and use that as an elbow; one end of each pipe is inserted into the elbow and welded all round. This type of fitting could be used in particular irrigation systems.

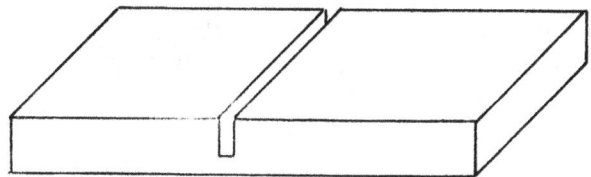

When bending flat bar, cut a groove, bend, and re-weld the joint

Bending flat bar

Flat bar is easy to bend if it is thin, regardless of its width, but very difficult to bend if it is 10 or 12 mm thick.

If full strength is required, bending can be achieved by either of two ways. The first is to heat the bar and bend it, using a vice and large adjustable spanner to provide leverage.

The other way to shape the bar is to cut it right through and re-weld it at the desired angle. Either of these two methods gives steel

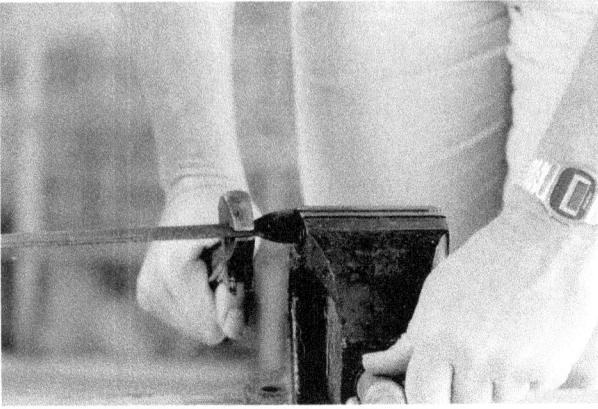

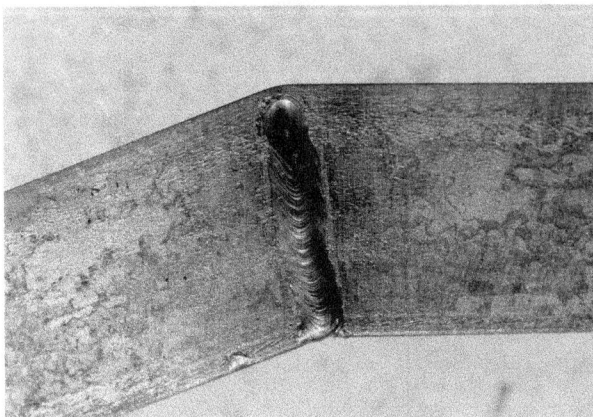

Make two cuts each at 45° and re-weld the joint

of more or less equal strength, provided of course the weld itself is up to scratch.

The lazy way of bending hefty flat bar is to cut partially through, perhaps six mm through a ten mm bar, bending the end to the required angle, then re-welding the cut to return at least some of the strength to the material.

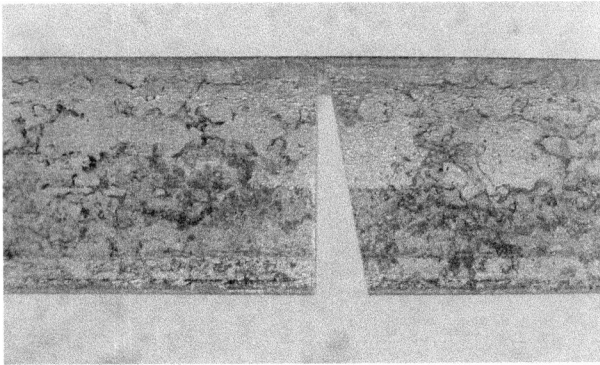

This lazy way is all very good if the flat bar won't be taking much of a load, such as if the steel is to be used in a fire grate where it will be needed to support only a couple of logs. Bending the steel in such a situation weakens it. A slight bend after making the cut won't affect the strength significantly, but beyond a certain point the steel will fracture

suddenly with minimal effort applied. But, for making fire grates or similar structures, this method is fine. But not, as mentioned already, for loads.

If you have a need for curved flat bar, steel six or even ten mm thick and 50 mm wide can be curved by using a hydraulic jack against the edge of the flat bar while the two ends are held securely by clamps or other suitable means.

Shaping angle iron

One of the attributes of angle iron is its great strength for a given weight. Bending angle iron to any shape is fairly easy.

If a right angle is required, then two cuts at 45° welded together will produce that 90° angle. With this method you can also use appropriate cuts for any other desired angle.

Another straight forward way is to cut a 90° vee, bend the angle iron to 90° and weld the joint. This is suitable for forming brackets for shelves in sheds to support timber, mesh or steel shelving, or even the supports on the frames of car ramps.

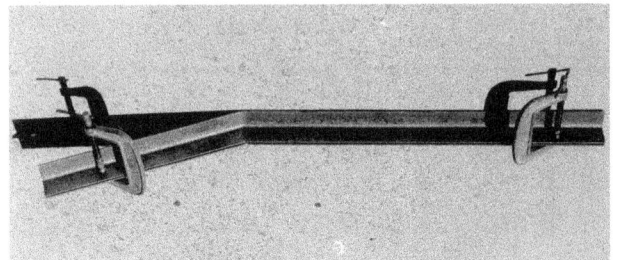

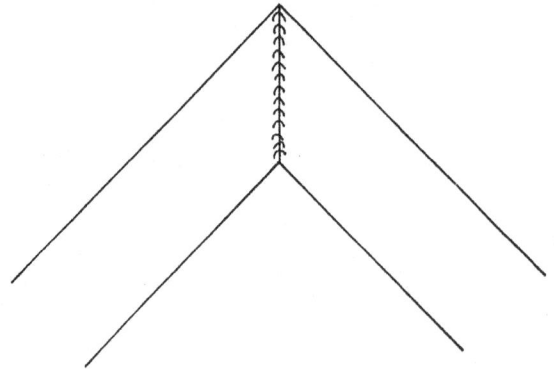

Shaping square hollow tubing

You will probably need to shape square hollow tubing. This is a versatile material to work with, but it will bend only slightly without a lot of special treatment, such as rolling it between large rollers several times.

But if you need to make distinct angles in the tubing, this is easily achieved by cutting through three sides and shaping it, and then re-welding over the cuts to form a strong joint.

This method is the easiest to shape this material. Determine the angle of the shape you want, and mark it on one side of the tubing. Make sure that the angle you mark is balanced — you don't want the angle to look awkward, as if the attempt was amateurish.

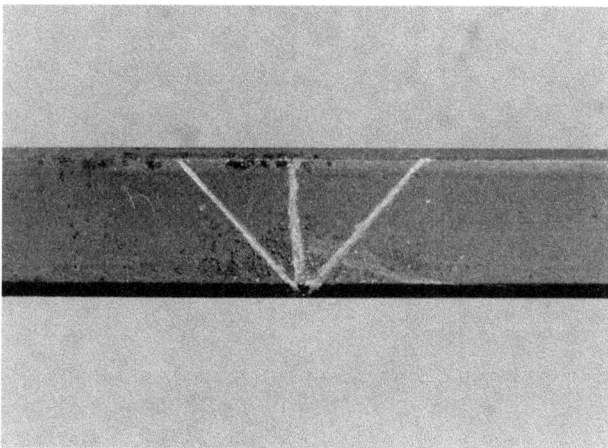

If you want a right angle, there are two ways of achieving this angle. You can cut the tubing right through at 45°, turn over one piece, and weld the two pieces together, checking with a square that the joint is exactly at a right angle. Make sure too that both pieces are on the same plane — that is, the structure you are making is flat.

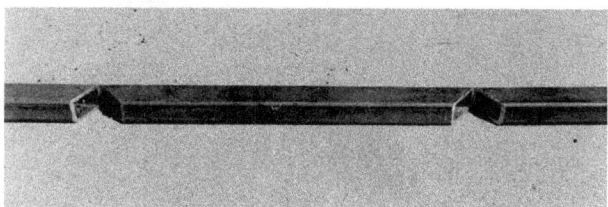

The other method of shaping square tubing is as shown in this series of photographs. Even for a right angle, you do not have to cut all the way through all four faces. You can cut the angle of 90°, but make sure the angle is balanced around the central mark.

Cut out the triangular pieces, and shape the tubing to the required angle.

This method is satisfactory for any angle, even one of more than 90°.

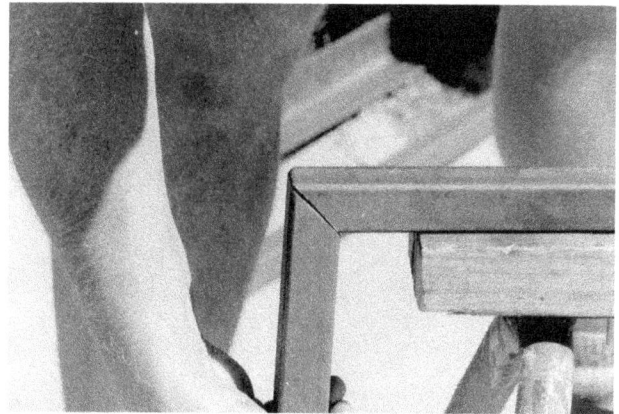

Always remember that when you weld the joint, it must be at least as strong as the original tubing. Anything less than this strength defeats the purpose of using thicker steel. If your aim is to achieve a joint of modest strength, consider using tubing that is thinner, although this might be more difficult to weld.

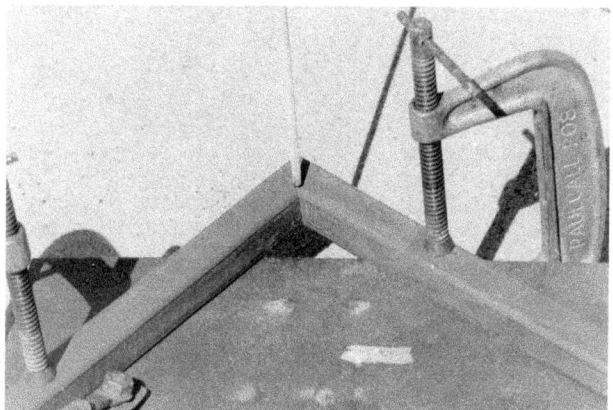

24 Painting and finishing off

All steel will rust if it is not treated properly to prevent corrosion or if it is not galvanised.

Rusting is nothing more than a chemical reaction between steel and oxygen in the presence of water or water vapour. Remove the water, and rusting won't occur. Remove the oxygen, especially from the water, and again rusting can't occur.

When you have untreated steel, rust will be inevitable. One of your jobs as a welder is to prevent that corrosion.

When you buy 'black' steel or shiny steel, this will mean anything that is not galvanised. It is likely that it will be either coated in a metal primer or some sort of protective coating, or it will have some rust on it. How much rust it will have depends on the conditions the metal has been stored in—whether in the open air, in a dry, hot shed, or anywhere in between.

You might think that galvanised steels—that is, those steels that have a protective zinc coating on them, will not rust. After all, that is the main purpose of the galvanising process.

But galvanised steels will rust where the coating has been removed either deliberately or inadvertently. When it is involved in the welding processes, such coatings will have been deliberately removed to facilitate welding or have been removed by the heat of the welding arc.

It is these areas of galvanised steel that will need to be re-coated. In Section 16 Welding galvanised steel, there is more information about restoring the protective coating. This can be done easily by means of a zinc-based paint applied with a brush to all areas, especially on welds.

Failure of paints and the rusting is often caused by paints that are manufactured for other purposes, such as for painting timber or masonry. Such paints will fail miserably when applied directly to bare steel if no primer has been applied.

The coatings produced by the various galvanising processes differ in surface characteristics. The correct primer and paint must be selected for each surface.

Certain environmental conditions can corrode steel, even galvanised steels. Rural, industrial and marine environments can affect the rate of corrosion of steels. In rural situations, the steels such as those used on farm gates will be outside for the life of the product without a cover over them. In industrial situations, fumes can be corrosive to zinc. Salt water can be disastrous on even the best galvanised steels if the zinc coating is not intended for marine applications.

Characteristics of galvanised steels

The coatings produced by the various galvanising processes all differ in surface characteristics, and must be considered individually in selection of painting pretreatments, primers and top coats.

Why paint galvanised steel?

In general, correctly chosen galvanised coatings used alone provide the most economic corrosion protection for steel. When coatings are painted, it is usually for aesthetic reasons, or for added corrosion resistance under severe exposure.

Duplex systems of galvanising-plus-paint are used. The galvanised coating provides a stable base which greatly increases paint life, while the paint film protects the galvanised coating to give an effect in which the combination lasts considerably longer than the total life of each coating alone.

Economics

Correctly chosen paints properly applied to galvanised steel provide outstanding durability and make good economic sense.

Much more complex and expensive paint systems are required on uncoated steel to achieve similar performance.

Galvanising-plus-paint systems

The longer life of correctly chosen and applied paint coatings on galvanised steel results from the zinc substrate that prevents initiation of corrosion at pores and scratches, and resulting creep corrosion beneath the paint film.

The economics of galvanising-plus-paint

The best protective coating for a particular project is usually the one which is considered to give effective protection at lowest overall cost, considering the planned service life of the structure.

In most circumstances dual systems of galvanising-plus-paint provide the longest available service life with minimum maintenance. The initial cost of dual systems is higher than for standard paint systems, but long term cost is considerably lower.

Painting galvanised steel

Two factors are critical to the satisfactory performance of paint coatings applied over galvanised coatings. The first is initial adhesion, and the second is the long-term adhesion.

Initial adhesion is achieved by use of a recommended pretreatment primer or self priming finish which provides a base for subsequent coatings.

Long-term adhesion depends on the compatibility of the pretreatment, primer or finish coats with the galvanised coating. Use of incompatible paint systems, or direct application of unsuitable finishes without the correct primer or pretreatment will result in early paint failure.

Preparation for painting

As in all painting operations, the surface to be painted should be thoroughly clean, free from grease and oil, and dry. Galvanised steel surfaces are clean and oil-free as manufactured but can become contaminated during transport, storage or fabrication. To be safe, non-oily soils and dirt should be removed by brushing or scrubbing followed by thorough clean water rinsing. Don't use soaps and detergents because of residues which may interfere with paint adhesion.

Grease and oil must be removed by mineral turpentine.

Thoroughly dry all areas that have been cleaned this way.

Pretreatment systems for galvanised steel

Many specialised paints require pretreatment of the zinc surface to extend the life of the parts.

Chemical etching of galvanised surfaces by the so-called 'mordant' solutions based on weak hydrochloric acid, acidified copper sulphate and others must not be used. Etching cannot be controlled and will often remove excessive thicknesses of the galvanised coating. While such treatments may achieve initial paint adhesion they do nothing to maintain long-term adhesion.

A simple, low-cost but lazy way of making the galvanised coating suitable for painting involves weathering of exposed surfaces until all bright zinc has changed to a dull surface layer. This may aid adhesion of some paints, provided any loose particles have been brushed from the surface. The deliberate use of weathering as a pretreatment for painting however is unnecessary and is not recommended as the minimum time needed for full weathering cannot easily be controlled

Primers for galvanised steel

Several primer types may be directly applied to galvanised steel without pretreatment other than cleaning and degreasing. These include specific formulations of waterborne self-priming finishes, etch primers, and zinc-dust-zinc-oxide primers.

Where painted galvanised structures will be subject to early handling in fabrication or erection with possible paint film damage, a cold phosphate pretreatment prior to priming is recommended to increase initial paint adhesion, even when an etch primer is used.

Use of a suitable primer is essential when galvanised steel is to be top coated with typical exterior house paints.

Water-based self-priming finishes

Many water-based self-priming finishes available from most hardware and paint shops give excellent performance on new galvanised steel if they are recommended by the manufacturer as being suitable. The economics of these water-based finishes on galvanised steel are superior to the oil based paints because of longer life and ease of application.

Suitable water-based paints are ideal for decorative and protective coatings on new galvanised steel used for exterior purposes. Gloss and matt finishes are available. Two-coat application direct to new clean galvanised steel surfaces will ensure many years of service without loss of adhesion.

Near the coast and under the more severe exposure conditions which may be encountered within a reasonable distance from the sea, conventional water-based self-priming finishes may not be suitable, since exposure results in formation of a white deposits on the paint surface which is particularly noticeable on darker paint colours. In such exposure conditions, water-based self-priming finishes containing chromate inhibitive pigments should be used.

Alternatively, the surface may be primed with an anti-corrosive water-based primer and top coated with a water-based finish.

Maintenance painting is normally carried out using the same type of water-based finish. Finishes designed specifically for galvanised surfaces may be top coated with oil or synthetic paints.

Etch primers

Two-pack etch primers or wash primers but not those based on hydrochloric acid are ideal for priming galvanised steel surfaces. Thin coatings should be applied. Suitable one-pack etch primers are also available, but care must be taken to ensure that they are formulated for use on galvanised steel.

General galvanised items require cold phosphate pretreatment prior to etch priming to achieve full initial adhesion.

The base product or first pack of a two-pack etch primer contains a resin in alcoholic solvents, and contains zinc chromate. The second pack or activator is an alcoholic solution of phosphoric acid which reacts with the galvanised coating, the pigment and the resin.

To apply, clean and degrease the steel, and dry the surface thoroughly. Stir the first pack of the etch primer thoroughly then add the specified quantity of activator. The pigment must be well stirred. Etch primer has a pot life of four to eight hours, depending on temperature, so that only sufficient for up to four hours use or less should be mixed. Don't add a freshly mixed batch to one that has been in use for some time. Apply a thin, even coat.

The etch-primed surface should be finish coated as soon as possible for best results. Etch primers are moisture sensitive and in humid conditions or if the surface is wet, the paint may gel or the dried film may reduce adhesion. Almost all paints will adhere to etch primer, which dries hard in 15 to 30 minutes, and is dry enough for re-coating in 30 to 60 minutes.

Finish coats for galvanised steel

Some of the primers for galvanised steel may also be used as finishing coats. In suitable applications water-based finishes are among the most economic paint coatings for galvanised steel because of their simplicity, ease of application and long life.

When galvanised steel is to be top coated with enamels such as those commonly used for exterior house painting, a suitable primer must be used in all circumstances. Where no primer is used, the slight acidity of most paints will react in time with the zinc coating to form brittle zinc products causing loss of adhesion. This undoes all the good work you put into fabricating and then finishing your project.

One-coat rust guard paints

There is good news for those painting non-galvanised steel — that is, 'black steel'.

We all know how easily black steel rusts. Until very recent times, few paints were readily available that did not need elaborate treatments of generous coats of primers, followed by at least two coats of a good paint for the top coat. This was the only way to stop that curse of all steel fabrications — rust. Very recently, some paint manufacturers have brought out a one-coat metal rust guard paint. It is generally based on an epoxy composite, and does not need any special primers.

They are slow drying paints. They usually need twenty-four hours to dry between coats. But that is a small time to invest when you compare the time taken to remove all rust after a few years, which may involve removing any rusted pieces, welding new pieces of steel into place, and starting the rust proofing all over again.

While one coat will generally provide adequate protection against rusting, two or more coats will give a good finish to the steel item you have fabricated.

Many such epoxy paints can be used to advantage to repair and revitalise rusted items, such as laundry cabinets that are made from steel. Although these are painted, they will not last more than a few years without rusting. If you have a need to revitalise old steel cabinets such as laundry cabinets under the troughs, sand back the rust using a fine emery paper or a power sander with a fine metal-sanding disk. Get the surface smooth to the touch, and paint with the epoxy paint. Two, sometimes three coast might be needed to bring the cabinet up to near-new appearance (but not necessarily to near-new condition because you could have a lot of rust behind the doors, the frame and in other inconspicuous places). At the time of publication, limited colours were available, but if you are painting a steel cabinet that was white for example, and white epoxy-based paint is available, then look no further.

A small tin of epoxy paint for $20 will be more attractive to the home owner than paying $600 for a new laundry cabinet. Plus the plumber's bill for installing it.

25 Welding steel plate

Many amateur welders produce a washboard from previously flat steel plate. Not only is the result impractical, but the result is not pleasing to look at. Yet the undesirable result is almost totally preventable once you realise the correct sequence for welding two pieces of flat plate together.

Whether you are building your dream boat, or welding a tank, a little thought can make the result pleasing.

Tack welds

A plate can be put in the correct place; once welding starts, distortion will pull it out of that position. It may have moved so much that its position now bears little resemblance to its original location. This can sometimes, indeed often, result in a steel plate that is so badly buckled that nothing can be done with it. For large areas such as plate, tack welding is the logical answer; these are small beads of weld metal placed short distances apart, about 30 centimetres or so, and only a centimetre or two long, just to keep the two components together until they are fully welded.

If distortion has become apparent at this stage, the tack welds can be broken or cut out and the job realigned.

Distortion can be minimised while welding plates together by staggering the welds and performing them in alternative directions, a process that involves welding small sections then reversing the direction on another part of the job; one small distortion in one part will tend to cancel that from another direction (well, at least in theory!).

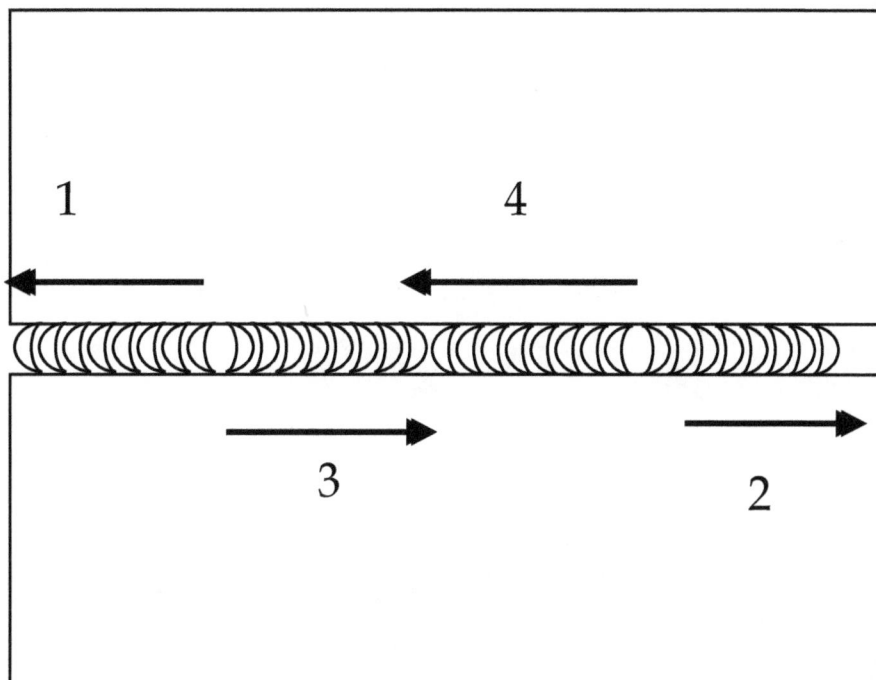

26 Bird dish stand

Bring life and colour to your garden with this stand that will support several dishes for bird seed or water.

A delightful way to enhance even the most colourful garden is to add more colour to it. Birds will do this splendidly. This bird table—or as some people refer to it, a bird tree—will be practical, strong and sturdy and will add much delight to your day as you watch the birds enjoy themselves. With the dishes filled with water particularly during summer, or with bird seed, you can attract a variety of colourful birds to your garden.

The bird table shown here is made from square steel tubing, which is reasonably lightweight, and very easy to build with the necessary metal working tools, including a welder.

There are four separate feeding dishes but the whole area occupies no more than a square metre. The arrangement shown in the photographs depicts the four arms at different levels, one on each of the four sides of the post. This tends to minimise squabbling among the birds so they can get on with their feeding. Well, usually!

One of the dishes is used only for water, and this one doubles not only as a source of drinking water, but also as a bird bath. In summer, you could use all four dishes for water, and this seems to make the site even more attractive for birds.

Materials

The materials you can use are a central post of square hollow tubing 50 mm by 50 mm with a wall thickness of 2.5 mm steel, two metres long; a piece of 50 mm by 50 mm flat bar, 50 mm long will cap the top of the post.

Four arms are also of 50 mm by 50 mm by 2.5 mm wall thickness square tubing, each 50 cm long. You may wish also to cap the ends of the arms under the dishes and for this you will need four extra pieces of 50 mm by 3 mm flat bar.

Sixteen lengths of 50 mm by 3 mm flat bar each 100 mm long will hold the dishes securely in place. Small off-cuts of steel welded to the end of the brackets will prevent the dishes from falling off their supports. And of course, you will need the four dishes themselves. Those shown in the photograph are terra cotta pot plant saucers and they are practical.

Construction

To make this bird feeder, cut the central post to the right length (two metres long).

Cap one end of the post with the small square piece of flat bar by welding all around. This will form the top of the post. Grind off the excess weld metal to leave a smooth finish. Make sure you wear adequate

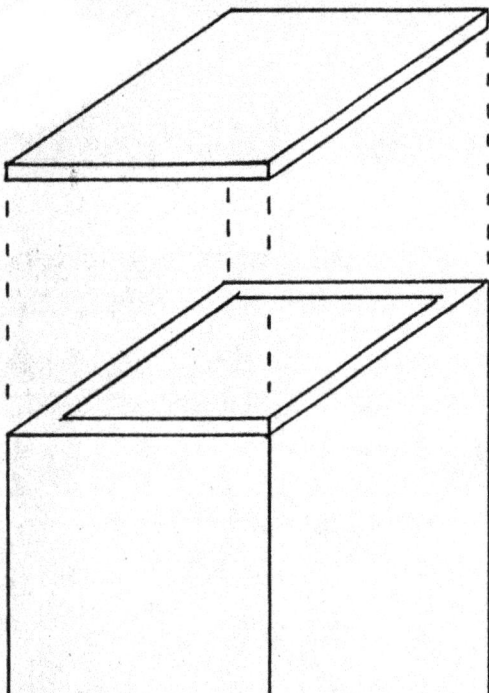

ear and eye protection when using any form of grinding wheel.

Next, cut the four arms. Each of the ends of the four arms are mitred in the opposite direction, but this doesn't mean there will be double cutting. Mark the steel the way shown in the illustration to minimise cutting and wastage.

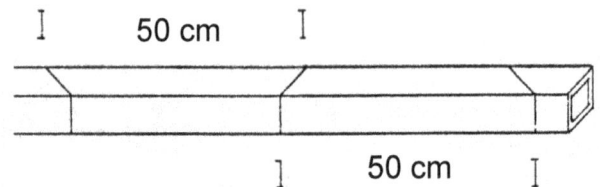

Mark the position where the first arm will be welded — about 100 mm from the top, and weld this in place. Weld each of the other three arms to the central post leaving 100 mm between arms on adjacent sides to give the appearance of the arms spiraling down when viewed from above the arrangement. Check that each one is at 45° with the central post and that the sides of each arm sit flush with that post before welding them.

Perhaps a tack weld (that is, a small amount of weld metal) on each corner only to begin with will keep each piece of steel in place until you have checked that the angles and the alignment are correct. Weld each joint fully and grind off excess weld metal from the joints.

Positioning the stand

You will want to watch the birds feeding from a convenient position in your house. Site the stand a little distance from the house but so that it can be viewed with ease from one of the windows or the deck around the house. Preferably, locate it near some trees or bushes — small birds in particular are vulnerable especially when they are busy feeding. If they are far from the protection of dense vegetation cover, they may feel vulnerable and may not come to the dishes.

This structure you have completed so far can now be installed in concrete in the ground — about 40 to 50 cm set in concrete will hold the frame rigidly in place.

The section that will be set in the ground should be coated with a metal primer before installing it; the rest of the structure can be primed and painted later. Check that the central post is perfectly vertical using a spirit level on two adjacent sides.

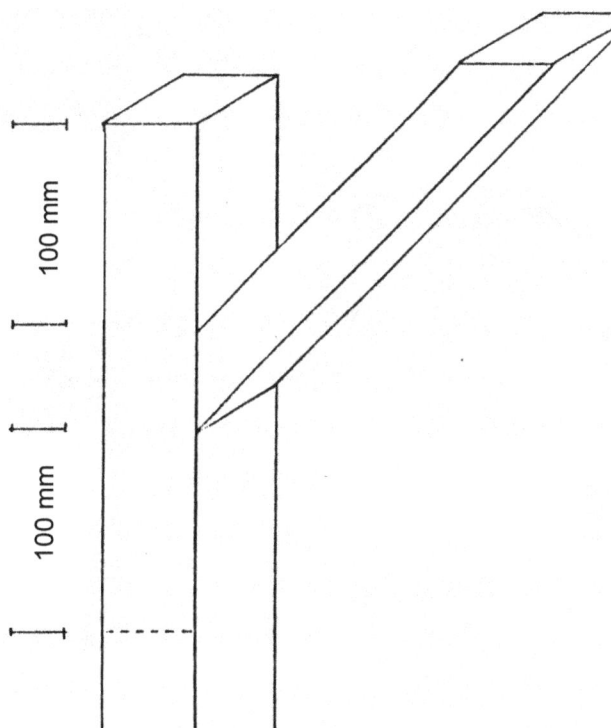

Leave the concrete to set for at least a couple of days before welding the brackets to hold the dishes in place. Disturbing the post before the concrete has set hard may render the whole table loose, and the birds will be frightened if the dishes move.

To make the brackets to hold each of the dishes, take four pieces of flat bar or angle iron, each 100 mm long, and weld them to the end of each arm in the shape of a cross. As there will be considerable moisture under the dishes, rust will be a major problem. If you can, use galvanised steel for the dish supports.

The flat bar will be sufficiently rigid to hold the dishes in place without any movement, and without their bending. Angle iron will ensure rigidity.

A small piece of steel welded to the free end of the dish supports protruding no more than 10 millimetres above it will prevent the dishes from slipping, or being knocked off the supports.

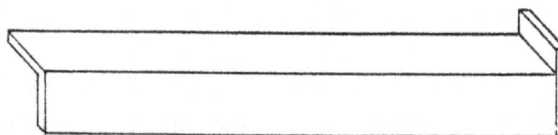

Tack weld each of the pieces of flat bar in place, check that it is perfectly level and square to the edge of the arm. Adjust it if necessary, then weld each one fully. Now, nothing will budge them!

You may, if you prefer, weld the brackets for the dishes to the ends of each of the arms before you install the post, but I have found that it is easier to get the levels correct if they are welded in place after the post has been set correctly.

Painting

Clean the whole of the steelwork thoroughly. Remove grime and scale with a wire brush and wipe it thoroughly with a cloth and turpentine. Prime with a good quality metal

primer and coat with two coats of a suitable paint, then wait for a while for the birds to arrive! They should do this as soon as they realise that there is a regular and ample supply of food and water left out for them.

Different birds prefer different foods; parrots like sunflower seeds (although there are special blends of parrot feed available in most supermarkets); others prefer fruit, but don't leave fruit out it you have fruit trees in your garden — this will attract the wrong type of birds.

Smaller seeds are popular with many of the small species of birds. And of course, some birds like the occasional meat scrap.

During dry seasons, most birds will prefer fresh water rather than seed. Water will be scarce in their environment, and you will be helping their survival.

If the birds depend too much on a ready supply of feed all year round, this could interrupt their migratory patterns, and will disrupt their normal life cycle and breeding cycle. Use your discretion here.

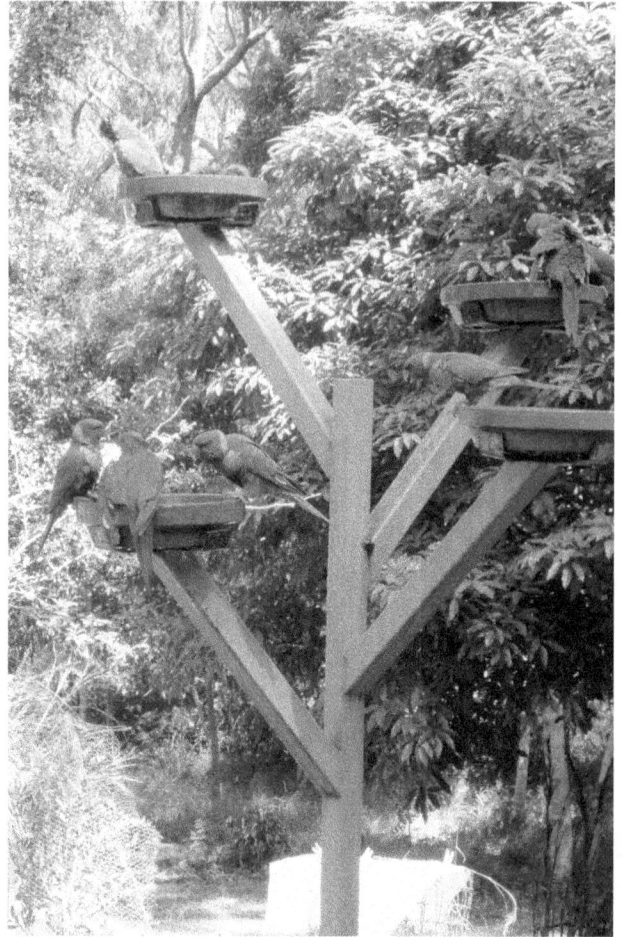

27 Hose support

Most hoses, if they are left over the lawn, deteriorate in the sun, or they can present a health hazard when someone trips over them.

This simple welding project will keep the garden hose tidy and out of the way of feet that are likely to become engaged with the tangle on the ground.

It is made from a length of galvanised 600 mm x 50 mm x 3 mm flat bar, curved as shown in the illustration, with three short lengths of 10 mm or 12 mm galvanised rod 100 mm long welded to the top of the flat bar. The hose support is attached to any convenient post or wall, but near where the hose can be attached to a tap. It is unlikely many people will want to connect the hose every time they use it. If you are attaching it to brickwork, use a masonry bolt but weld a lug with a hole in it to the centre of the flat bar. The masonry bolt is inserted through the hole in the lug and into a hole drilled into the mortar between the bricks. Do not drill directly into the bricks.

Begin by curving the flat bar. As it will not have any bracing or strengthening, it will form easily over a length of pipe, such as 100 mm diameter pipe, or even a large block of wood. Mark the centre of the flat bar where you want to make the bend. You will need only a little downward pressure on the two ends to achieve this. Push down on the ends until the desired curvature is achieved. By bending the flat bar beyond the point where it would normally spring back flat, you will be able to impart a permanent bend, or curve in it.

Now, 50 mm from each end, mark the place where two of the steel rods will be welded. And at the top of the curve, mark the spot where you will weld the third piece of rod.

All that is left now if to clean the steel, particularly around the welds, and apply a good quality metal primer particularly over the welds. You can paint the whole steelwork in a colour to match the house. Something like this does not have to be highlighted, so don't make it too brilliant when you choose a paint colour.

Attach the hose support to the wall, and that's this project completed.

28 Garden bench

A pair of these attractive benches will match the outdoor table described elsewhere in this book.

This timber and steel garden bench is comfortable and very sturdy, being much stronger than the average cast iron or cast aluminium types. It consists of 25 mm by 25 mm square hollow tubing with a wall thickness of 2.5 mm and a couple of lengths of 25 mm by 3 mm flat bar to which the timber slats are bolted.

Construction

Cut two lengths of square steel tubing, 1100 mm long, and cap one end of each by welding on a small piece of 25 mm by 25 mm by 3 mm flat bar.

Using a steel scribe or a felt-tipped pen to mark the steel, set out two V-cuts in each length, the first 400 mm from the capped end and the second, 750 mm, but on the opposite side to the first.

Cut the vee using a metal-cutting disk mounted in a disk grinder. You can, if you wish, use a hacksaw with an 18 teeth/inch blade, but a disk or angle grinder is much easier and faster and also very handy for grinding welds and cleaning up rust and rough edges.

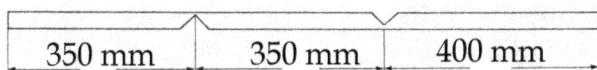

| 350 mm | 350 mm | 400 mm |

Make the vee cuts but leave enough metal at the bottom of the cut so that the tubing can be bent at that point without separating in two. Bend the tube to the required shape. Remember that you are not trying to form a right angle, but a bend of about 105° so that the back has a slight tilt and the front leg

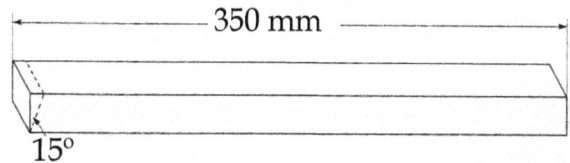

350 mm
15°

splays slightly forward. Weld the tubing at these joints, ensuring full weld metal penetration in the joint you are forming. Clamp the tubing to a piece of backing plate to minimise distortion. For all the welding in this project, an electric manual arc welder, with a 2.5 mm general purpose welding electrode set on about 80 amps is ideal.

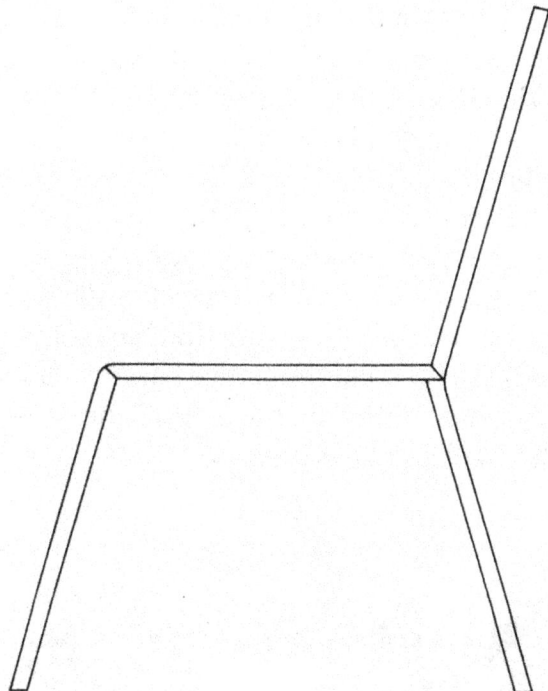

Now cut two pieces of square hollow tubing 350 mm long for the rear legs. Cut one end at an angle of 75° and weld the leg to the rest of the frame. You will need two identical ends, so it is preferable to make the frames together and check one against the other to make sure they are identical. By placing the second and subsequent frames over the first one, you can ensure that the angles are all identical.

Mark the bottom angle of the feet by placing any straight edge (for example, a length of steel) along the bottom of each frame. Cut along the marks you have made and weld a piece of 25 mm by 25 mm by 3 mm flat bar over the ends to ensure that the feet don't dig into the pavement or concrete.

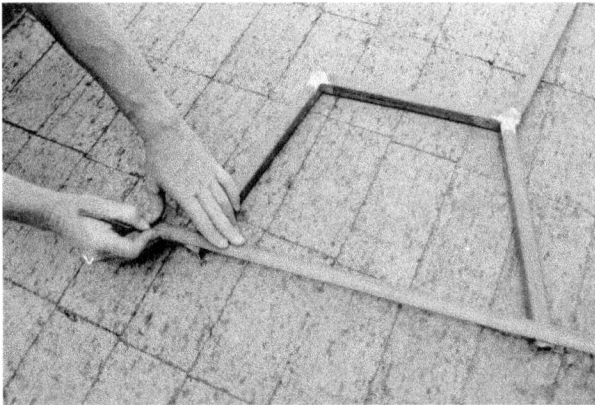

Take two 800 mm long pieces of 25 mm x 3 mm flat bar and round off the ends with an angle grinder. Attach the flat bar to the outside edge of the frame so that for every pair of frames there is a left and right overhang.

Start welding the bar to the tubing with an overhang of 50 mm above the capped end of the seat back, using 25 mm welds 100 mm apart. Rather than following the shape of the tubing, you can curve the flat bar around a piece of pipe with a diameter of 75 mm. The flat bar will bend easily.

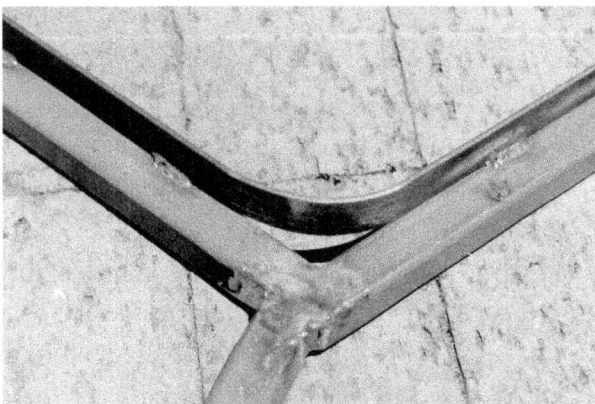

Making the scrolls

Now add the scrolls. These will not only make the seat more decorative, but will strengthen the legs. The scrolls are made from 25 mm by 3 mm flat bar 800 mm long, rounded off at each end, and formed around a scroll-making tool, a technique illustrated elsewhere in this book. Curve the flat bar around the pipe until a perfect circle has been formed. Now weld the scrolls into position between the front and back leg of each frame.

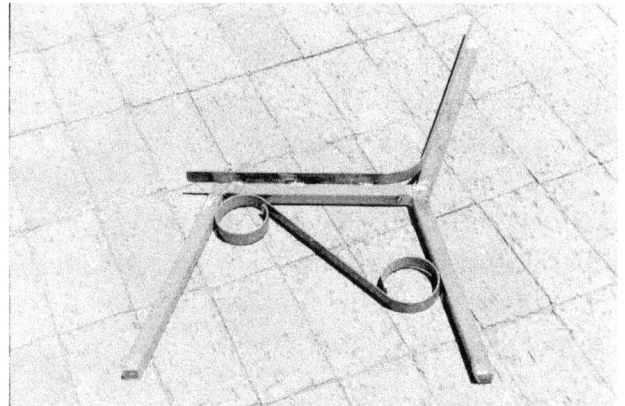

Assembly

The two end frames are held in position by welding a length of square tubing 1125 mm long between them. Use a square to make sure that everything is at right angles to each other. As a tip, before welding the second side into position, look along it to make sure that the seat, legs and back are in line. This will eliminate any unsightly twist that you could otherwise weld into the frame.

Grind off excess weld metal to leave smooth, shiny joints.

Remember to always wear adequate ear and eye protection whenever using a grinder as well as full protection whenever you are using an electric welder.

Cut nine 1250 mm long slats from 70 mm x 20 mm hardwood, selecting a durable exterior grade timber. Mark the position of the bolt holes and drill both the flat bar and the wooden slats to accept either galvanised or zinc-coated bolts. Ensure that one of the slats covers the tubing joining the two side frames.

paint, stain or other wood preserving treatment to resist the effects of the weather. To achieve complete coverage it is better to coat the slats before they are installed.

Materials list

(for one double seat)
All dimensions in mm
RHS (2.5 thickness walls)
2/1100 x 25 x 25 (end frames)
2/350 x 25 x 25 (rear legs)
FB bar 6/25 x 25 x 3 for cappings) 2/800 x 25 x 3 to frames)
2/800 x 25 x 3 (scrolls)

Scroll formers

1/75 diam x 150 mm long steel pipe
Timber 9/1250 x 75 x 25 exterior grade hardwood
18/38 long galvanised bolts, primer, paint and timber finish
square pieces for capping the open ends of the tubing
18 galvanised bolts 25 mm x 6 mm for attaching slats

Rust can be a problem with steelwork, so make sure you use a good quality metal primer, followed by at least two coats of an exterior paint, allowing adequate drying time for each coat.

The timber slats can be bolted in place. The slats should be treated with an outdoor

Making a single seat

The only difference between this double seat and a single — one of the same design — is the spacing of the sides and the length of the slats. For a single chair, use tubing 500 mm long to join the sides and timber slats 625 mm long.

135

29 Mail box stand

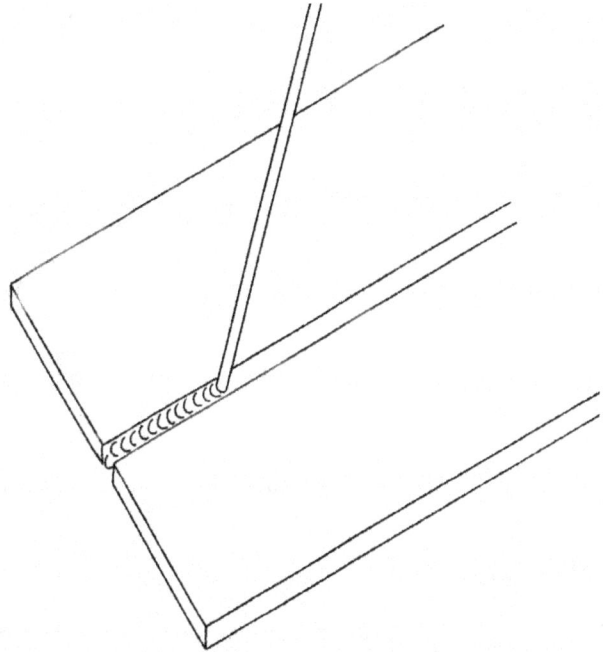

Weld the steel pieces together to form a strong joint

This project uses 25-millimetre by 25-millimetre by 2.5-millimetre rolled hollow square steel tubing for the stand. You will need one piece 1300 millimetres long for this, of which 300 millimetres will be set in the ground in concrete.

To attach the letterbox, which will be available from most hardware stores, weld a small plate, about 50 millimetres by 100 millimetres to one end of the square tubing.

Bevel the edges before welding them to ensure maximum weld metal penetration

Drill two holes in the plate to bolt on the letterbox.

A feature of this project is the small wooden insert that supports the house numbers. This is held in place by two pieces of 25-millimetre by 3-millimetre flat bar, 230 millimetres long. Round off one end using a grinder (protect your ears and eyes as you do so). Weld the other end 300 millimetres from the plate you welded to the top of the stand, tack welding this temporarily in position (that is, use a small weld to hold the flat bar in position). Check that the flat bar is at right angles to the stand. Weld it fully to the square tubing.

The last part of the steelwork is the addition of a scroll. This not only enhances the appearance of the letterbox stand, but strengthens the support for the timber. The scroll is made from a piece of 13-millimetre by 3-millimetre flat bar, 600 millimetres long. Round off both ends of the flat bar. Instructions for making the scrolls are given elsewhere in this book.

Weld the scroll in position using only light welding. Welding is incredibly strong, and there is no point in over-welding.

Grind off any excess weld metal to give a smooth finish. Use a good metal primer to prevent rusting, and paint the letterbox and stand in your favourite colour.

Cut the timber and stain it. The wood shown in the photograph is a cedar offcut. It is held in place with four screws, two at the top and two at the back. The numbers are screwed to the timber.

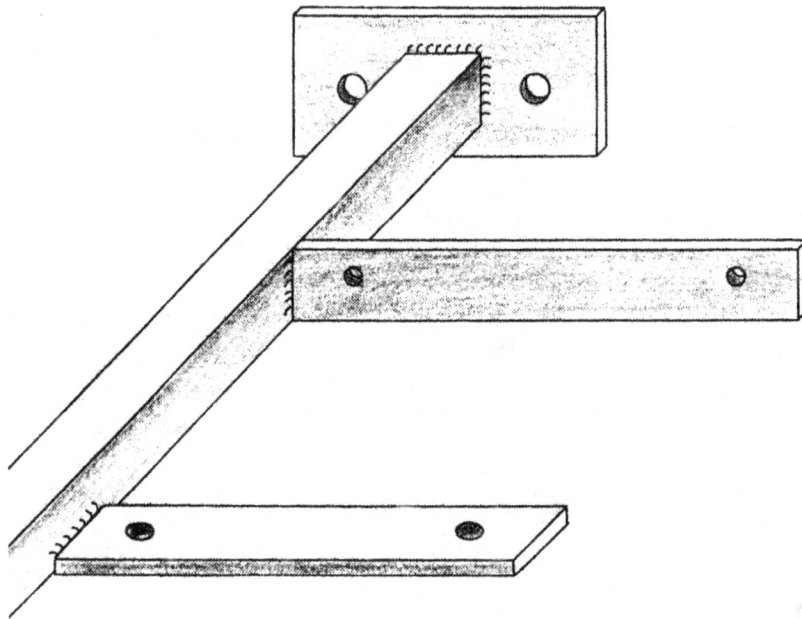

30 Steel trestle

Whenever you try working with lengths of steel, the first thing that becomes apparent is that they are always long and awkward. However, with this sturdy trestle that you can make yourself, you will be able to support long lengths of steel (and yes, some of them are eight or ten metres long).

You will make this project more easily if you first read the section on working with pipes. The whole project is made from 25 mm OD pipe with 2.5 mm wall thickness.

The steel requirements given here are for one stand, but you will need three such stands for convenience. You will need one to support each end of the long lengths of steel, and the third one will be placed in the middle to give it sufficient support. This will make cutting so much easier, as you can be sure that all cuts will actually be vertical — but of course that depends on your competency with your cutting.

You will need two small sections of a slightly larger pipe (32 mm OD) pipe each 75 mm long for the hinges. The simplicity of this stand is that the top section of one half fits into the short lengths of pipe welded to the opposite side and it is this junction that forms the hinges.

Cut four pieces of 25 mm OD x 2.5 mm pipe 1200 mm long. These will form the outermost part of the frame of each half.

Now cut the cross pieces. You will need three of these, two at 900 mm long and one of 800 mm in length, but you can make them wider if you can see a need for larger trestles.

If you make them of different dimensions, one length will still need to be 100 mm shorter than the other two.

Place the short pieces of 32 mm OD pipe over one of the cross pieces of pipe (that is, one length that is 900 mm long). This will form the top section of one half of the stand.

Weld two longer lengths of pipe (that is, those of 1200 mm in length) to the shorter length (800 mm long) for form an 'H'.

Now for the opposite side, place the two short 75 mm lengths of 32 mm OD pipe over one of the 900 mm long sections of pipe. This will form the hinge at the top as shown in the illustration.

Weld the second length of pipe half way along the frame.

The second trestle must have the same configuration as the first one, otherwise you could be working with steel that is not level.. This would make your work much more difficult. If you get all three trestles the same height, and they are level, the steel you will be cutting will also be level, so at least in theory, the cuts you make should also be vertical, but that of course depends on the care you give to your cutting.

If you want to add a length of chain so the support does not open out under the weight of heavy lengths of steel, make sure you weld it to the underneath of the pipe as shown in the illustration.

So the support does not slide easily, you can attach rubber feet of the open ends of the bottom. This will also prevent the sharp ends of pipe digging into a valuable floor.

To complete the project, clean the welds thoroughly and apply a good quality metal primer to prevent rusting. You can, if you want to, paint the whole stand to give a more professional appearance.

You will find this type of support can take a considerable weight of steel — perhaps several lengths of heavy angle iron or heavy pipe or tubing.

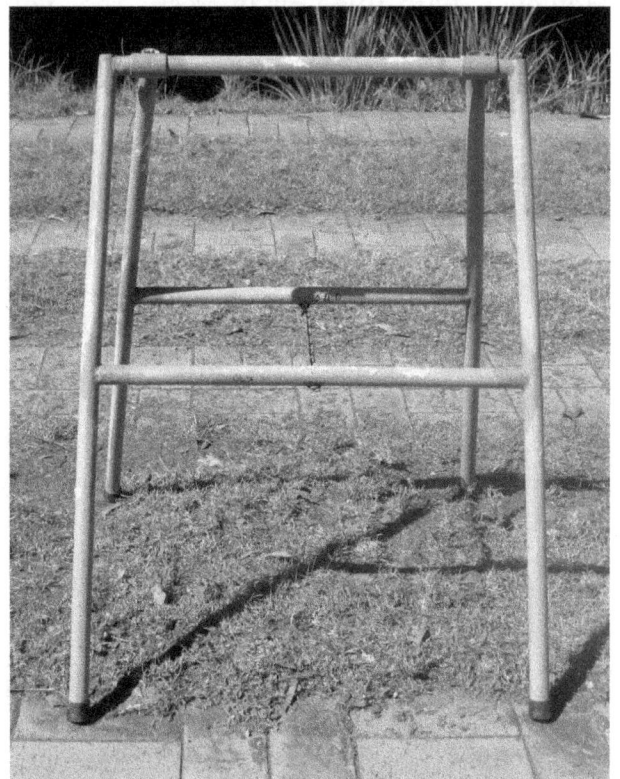

31 Security grille

By the time you've accumulated tools for your workshop, you will have spent perhaps many hundreds of dollars on them and other equipment. You'll want to protect them, rather than have someone enter your work room via the window without your approval.

You can keep intruders out of your work room and your tools safe with a security grille over the window. This style will cost you only a few dollars but will protect hundreds of dollars worth of equipment.

It consists of a frame made from 25 mm by 25 mm by 3 mm angle iron, and vertical and horizontal bars made from 10 mm by 10 mm square steel. Secured over the window, it should deter any would-be thief.

Very few windows are exactly the same size, so if you are making security grilles for more than one window, measure each window individually. And if your windows are all of a slightly different size, do not mix the framing, because nothing will fit the window.

Measure the inside of the window frame, as the grille will be placed within the window frame. Allow no more than one or two millimetres clearance all around, so the grille is a comfortable fit within the window frame.

Cut the angle iron with 45° mitred cuts, so that two adjacent sides will fit together neatly at right angles.

Clamp two adjacent sides together to a steel backing plate, and check that the angle formed by the sides forms a right angle. You should check this with a square for accuracy.

Weld the first joint together.

Turn the pieces over, still clamped to the steel plate, and weld on the opposite side of

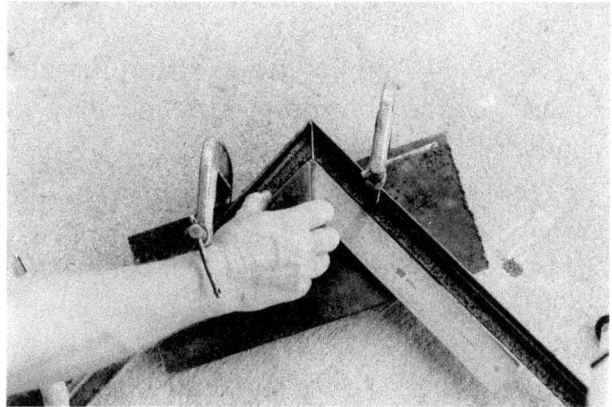

the frame so you get maximum strength at each corner.

Weld the rest of the frame together.

At this stage, you should check that the frame fits comfortably within the window. You have allowed only a very small margin for error, so any adjustments should be made at this stage in the construction, rather than later, which would involve a lot of extra work to put it right.

The vertical bars will be sufficient if they are placed at intervals of about 150 mm. They should be evenly spaced.

Mark off along the top and bottom of the frame, intervals of about 150 millimetres, but you should determine the correct spacing for each window grille, but get them even!

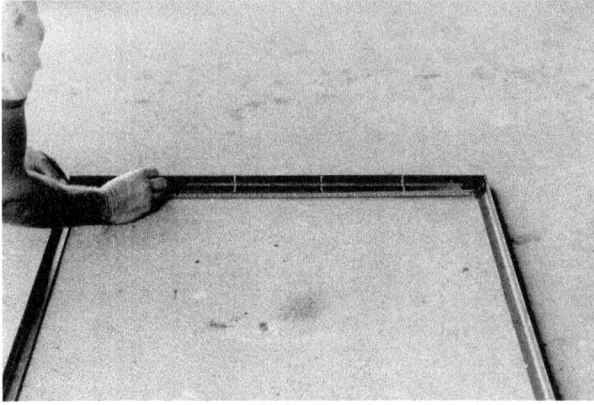

Cut the 10 millimetre by 10 millimetre square bars to the right length so they fit neatly into the angle iron frame.

Weld each bar on both sides to the flat surface of the frame.

Bars like this can still be bent by a determined thief. They will need lateral support.

Along the sides of the frame, mark off three intervals by dividing the distance from top to bottom into three equal sections. You will have two marks along each side of the frame.

Measure and cut the horizontal bars. These should come close to the sides and almost touch the angle iron, allowing only for a small gap for weld metal penetration. Remember also that these two bars won't be welded to the flat side of the angle iron, because they will rest over the vertical bars. They will be welded 10 mm higher than the vertical bars, or near the outer edge of the angle iron.

The points where the horizontal bars cross over the vertical bars should be welded to provide rigidity to all the bars so they can't be forced apart.

To mount the grille to the inside of the window frame, buy security screws. These are specially made screws that can be screwed into the window frame, but they are nearly impossible to extract.

Drill a couple of holes each side of the frame to take the mounting screws.

Alternatively, you can use bolts and flatten the end of the bolt slightly with a hammer.

A security grille like this in place will allow you to relax and not worry about thieves. At least, not in you workshop!

32 Outdoor table

This simple wrought-iron style timber table is a very useful addition to your garden furniture as well as being a conversation piece amongst your friends at your next barbecue.

The frame is welded from square hollow tubing, 25 mm by 25 mm with a wall thickness of 2.0 mm or 2.5 mm, except for one length of 50 mm by 25 mm tubing. These sizes are quite sufficient to give a sturdy and rigid table. The scrolls are made from thin flat bar that can be easily rolled into the design shown.

Tubing with a 2.0 mm wall thickness was used for the original table, but if you are a novice at welding, I suggest material with 2.5 mm thick walls — it is much easier to weld. All welds are either butt joints or tee joints, so only basic welding techniques and metal working tools are required.

The top is made from any durable timber suitable for exterior use.

Welding the frame

Most small electric manual arc welders are suitable for this project. Use a 2.5 mm general purpose electrode set on about 80 amps.

Start with two lengths of hollow tubing 720 mm long to support the timber top and two lengths 600 mm long for the feet. Cap the

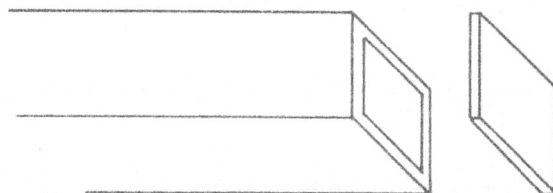

Cap the open ends of RHS tubing with a small length of flat bar

open ends of each piece with a square of 25 mm by 3 mm flat bar. Grind off any excess weld metal to give a smooth, neat finish.

Always make sure you use adequate eye and ear protection when using a grinder.

Take one of the 600 mm lengths of tubing and mark the centre. Butt a 630 mm piece of tubing at this mark to form a tee. Clamp both pieces of tubing to a backing plate (any offcut of thick steel plate will do), use a square to check that the joint forms a right angle and then weld the sections together.

The other end of the 630 mm length is then welded to the centre of one of the capped 720 mm long pieces. Again, before welding the two together, clamp them to the backing plate and check the right angle.

Complete the second side of the frame in the same way and grind off excess weld metal from all joints.

Two further sections of hollow tubing, each 1200 mm long, act as spacers to complete the frame. The top bar is 25 mm by 25 mm hollow tubing; the lower piece, welded to the centre height of the two end uprights, is 50 mm by 25 mm tubing. Before welding these two pieces in position, ensure that everything is square and true.

To secure the timber slats in place, two lengths of 25 mm by 3 mm flat mild steel bar, each 720 mm long, are welded on edge to the

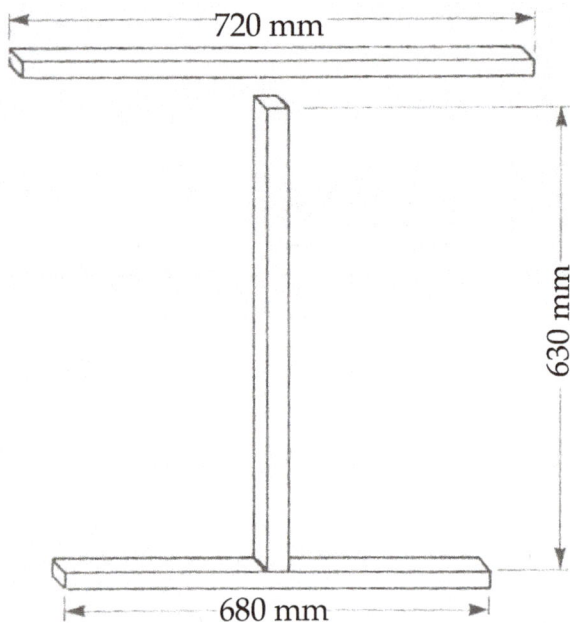

720 mm

630 mm

680 mm

Cut the three pieces of RHS for the frame and weld them together

furniture you can be proud of, but they will also make the frame even more rigid. Incidentally, scrolls such as these are much easier to make than is generally thought. The tool to make them is simple, too—all you need is any offcut of pipe with a slot cut in one end. Instructions for making scrolls are given elsewhere in this book.

Weld a length of 25 x 3 mm flat bar to the outer edge of the top member of the frame to take the timber slats

outside of the top section of the end frames. Three or four small welds about 25 mm long on each bar will be adequate. Grind off excess weld metal to leave the top of the frame flush. Position the timber slats temporarily in place, adjust them until you are happy with the spacing and then mark the location of screw holes in the flat bar. Drilling one hole for each end of each slat is sufficient to hold the timber in place. When the slats are later installed, the flat bar is hidden from view.

The table is quite strong without further work to the frame. However, the scrolls shown in the photographs will not only turn an ordinary table into a piece of crafted

The scrolls themselves are formed from 13 mm by 3 mm flat bar, although 20 mm by 3 mm flat bar will bend quite easily too. Cut the lengths required (600 mm for the large scrolls and 300 mm long for the small scrolls), grind one end of each piece to a rounded profile and insert the rounded end into the slot in the pipe to a depth of about 3 to 4 mm. Wrap the bar around the pipe, pulling it in tight to the pipe at all times.

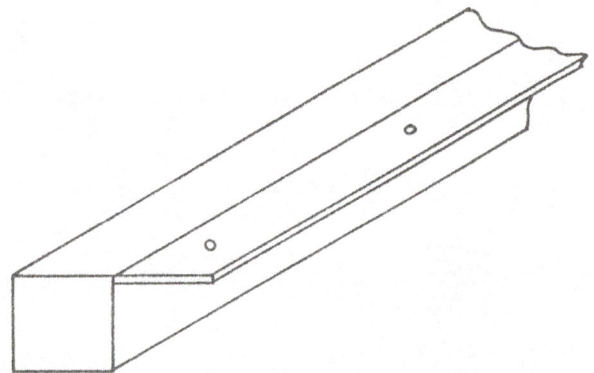

For the large scrolls, wrap the steel around the pipe one complete turn. Turn the flat bar over and curve the opposite end, but

144

no more than one quarter of a turn. For the smaller scrolls, one complete turn around the pipe for one end of the bar is all that is needed.

The scrolls are welded in position, using a 5 mm weld at each point of contact.

Clean the steel with a wire brush and turpentine and apply a good coating of a metal primer and two coats of compatible exterior paint.

After the paintwork has dried, the timber can be attached. Ten straight pieces, 1350 mm long by 70 mm wide, are fixed in position by galvanised screws, fitted from underneath through the flat bar into the wood.

Paint the timber using a good quality, durable exterior paint, and the table is ready to put into position.

Materials list

All dimensions are in millimetres
Rolled Hollow Square Section (tubing)
2 pieces 720 x 25 x 25 (top)
2 pieces 600 x 25 x 25 (bottom)
2 pieces 630 x 25 x 25 (legs)
1 piece 1200 x 25 x 25 (spacer)

1 piece 1200 x 50 x 25 (spacer)
Mild steel flat bar
2 pieces 720 x 25 x 3 (top)
8 pieces 25 x 25 x 3 (caps)
8 each of 600 x 13 x 3 (large scrolls)
8 each of 300 x 13 x 3 (small scrolls)

Scroll formers
1 of 75 mm outside diameter x 150 mm long steel pipe
1 of 40 mm outside diameter x 150 mm long steel pipe

The length of steel for the scrolls are based on scroll formers of 75 millimetres and 40 millimetre outside diameters. If you wish to use scroll formers of different diameters to those suggested here, adjust the length of flat bar you use for the scrolls.

Mild steel flat bar offcuts for capping open ends
Paints: Metal primer for the steel and paint for the wooden top
Timber: 10 x 1350 x 19 mm
Screws. 20 galvanised or stainless steel wood

33 Steel door

The underneath area of a house is a splendid place to store pieces of timber, cardboard cartons, steel tubing and pipes, and a thousand other household things that are not needed on a daily basis, but which you don't want to throw away.

If you have such an area, and you want to stop intruders from seeing what your house is made of, you might like to construct this simple steel door.

It is made from a frame of galvanised angle iron or square hollow tubing, with a thin coated sheet of steel pop-riveted to the outside of the frame.

You might prefer to add a piece of timber if you have a brick wall so the door can be hung easily using wood screws. If you add the timber, make sure you take the thickness of that into consideration before measuring

and cutting the steel. Attach the timber first, and work your measurements around that.

Measure the height and the width of the doorway. Allow for a small clearance between the edge of the door and the door frame. Three millimetres all around should provide adequate clearance to ensure that the door won't get caught. The angle iron is cut at 45°. With proper planning, you can minimise the number of angled cuts you will need to make. Remember that a cut one way through the angle iron will provide the correct angle for the piece on the opposite side of the frame.

So cut the four pieces to the right length, and check each one and make sure that the door will fit comfortably into the space allowed.

Lay out the pieces in the correct position on a flat surface to give you a clear idea of where each piece will go.

Now tack weld the four pieces together. A couple of short welds at each joint will be sufficient at this stage. But make sure the whole frame is flat and that there are no buckles or twists in it. A good fit is what you will require, and that is not possible if the frame has a large buckle in it. Get it flat at this stage, and you will minimise the work ahead of you.

You should also check carefully using a square that the corners are at 90°. This is of course assuming that the door frame was built correctly with right angles at each corner. Some builders didn't care too much about the neatness of their work in out-of-the-way places such as under the house, so check the accuracy of each corner before you start cutting and welding. You might have to be a bit creative to accommodate second-rate work.

Check that the frame fits the space allocated, with enough clearance for it to swing without catching anywhere.

If any part of the frame catches on the wall at this stage, it is easy to break or cut the weld, remove a small piece of the angle iron that is causing the problem, and tack weld the joint again. Check that it fits better this time. You might have to repeat this procedure a couple more times before you get it right, especially if you are new to welding.

Once you are satisfied that the frame fits into the entrance comfortably, fully weld all the joints.

Now add bracing. Even the lightest weight door will be too flexible. A diagonal length of angle iron from the top outer to the bottom inner corners will provide sufficient rigidity to your project. As shown in the picture, angle iron bracing in at least two of the corners will ensure rigidity to the door.

Attach the hinges. These can be welded to the inner frame and attached to the wall or to the timber you have placed in position to take the door.

You will need a catch to keep the door closed. Determine the level of security you will need. If the door is going within an area that is already locked, then you won't need a secure look, just one strong enough to keep the door closed.

If more security is required, consider a slide bolt that can be secured with a padlock. But the lock or securing bolt is attached after the steel sheet is put in position.

Cut the sheet steel by laying the door frame over the sheet of steel. Move the frame around until you have the best fit so the ridges of the sheet steel end where it is easiest to drill and attach the sheet.

For a light-weight door such as this, it should be sufficient to use pop rivets to attach the sheet of steel. Clamp the sheet of

steel to the frame on diagonal corners, but make sure you do not compress any of the ridges on the sheet of steel. It is usually a very soft material, and one that can be easily deformed.

Starting on one corner near where you have the clamp, drill a hole to take the rivet. Drill subsequent holes and fix the rivets at around 300 mm spacings all around.

But before you attach the sheet steel, clean all the steel frame, paying particular attention to the welds. Give the frame a coat of good quality metal primer to prevent rust, paying particular attention to the welds. This is most likely the spot where rust will begin. Then give the frame two coats of paint to complete the preservation process and lock out all moisture and thus prevent rusting as much as possible. The underneath areas of most houses are damp, so expect significant rusting to occur if you fail to prime the metal sufficiently.

Hang the door, check that it fits comfortably, and the job is finished.

34 Lattice and steel door

This is a variation of the steel door described elsewhere in this book.

The frame is constructed from angle iron, but instead of using sheet steel, wooden lattice makes an ideal substitute. This type of door is particularly suitable for closing off an area, such as under a deck or balcony where a high degree of security is not required. It acts more as a screening rather than for a security benefit.

As in the metal door, the frame is constructed from angle iron. Because the lattice made from timber will be heavier than the sheet steel covering, you would be advised to use angle iron 50 mm x 50 mm x 2.5 mm. If you can buy it in your area, use galvanised steel for this project. It will give you many years of trouble free life.

Measure the area where the door will be fitted. If it is too wide (more than 2.4 metres wide) make two doors identical and make them smaller. This will make it easier to open and close the door, and will minimise the weight of each individual door.

Choose hinges that are suitable for attachment to the frame. If you are attaching the doors to a timber frame, you can use smaller hinges and wood screws. If you are attaching the doors to brickwork, then you will need to use hinges that have a wider reach so the securing bolts are not drilled into the brickwork too close to the edge and cause cracking of the brick.

If you are using masonry screws or bolts to hold the doors to the brickwork, make sure the protruding head or nut does not interfere with the edge of the door frame. You can use countersunk heads so the tops of the screws are level with the edge of the hinge. This way,

there will be no protrusion that will interfere with the closing of the door. If the screws are not flush with the surface of the steel framing, you will be putting too much strain on the door frame, and possibly on the brickwork as well. You might be able to position the hinges so they don't interfere with the closing of the door, depending on the type of hinges you use. Buy hinges that are suitable to this project. You might be able to secure the hinges to the outside of the brickwork that would prevent any protrusion interfering with the closing of the door, or doors.

Measure the lengths of angle iron you will need to cut, but allow the thickness of the hinges, and a clearance between the two doors if you are making more than one to ensure ease of closure. A gap of 3 mm should be sufficient to enable the two doors to close easily.

Tack weld the steel together in case you need to make any adjustments to the height or the width of the doors. Check the angle with a square to ensure that the angle you are about to weld is 90°.

If you are satisfied that the door, or doors will close easily, fully weld the joints so they are strong and permanent.

Weld on the hinges to the outside of the frame 300 mm from the top and the bottom.

Now add bracing. Diagonal bracing formed from 25 x 2.5 mm galvanised angle iron will be ideal. Weld in place from the top of the free end diagonally to the bottom to provide the most rigidity. It will help prevent vertical movement within the door or doors. Extra bracing using a 300 mm length of angle iron welded in the two innermost corners, at 45° will ensure the door won't collapse for many years.

Clean the steel thoroughly, paying particular attention to the welds.

Prime the steel with a good quality metal primer, or if you have used galvanised steel, pay particular attention to the welds. This is the area that will tend to rust.

Now give the frame or frames two coats of paint. You won't be able to paint the frame once you have attached the lattice to it.

The lattice you use should be treated pine, especially if it will be subjected to rain and inclement weather. Soft, untreated pine and even many of the hardwoods will not last more than a few years.

Cut the lattice by placing the frame over a section of the lattice, marking it and cutting carefully each piece of wood.

If you want to paint the lattice, now is your chance, because you won't be able to do so easily once the lattice is attached to the metal frame. Two coats of paint will be required.

Attach the lattice by drilling holes through the ends of the wood and into the steel to take stainless steel metal screws. One screw each 300 mm though the end of the lattice and into the steel should suffice. Attach the hinges to the timber or to the wall as you had planned.

Attach the catch or the lock to hold the door closed, or to close it in a more secure way.

35 Patio bench

This simple patio bench will be easy to make for one of your first welding projects. It bolts on to verandah posts, or to a solid wall.

The frame is constructed from 50 mm x 50 mm x 3 mm angle iron, galvanised of course to prevent rusting, and it will have bracing of another piece of angle iron at an angle of approximately 30°. Although there will be only two such frames, the bench will comfortably support the weight of two people, depending on the strength of the supports to which the bench is attached.

Don't make the seat too long. It should comfortably seat two people of average weight, perhaps three people at the most. Any more weight than that, and the boards will sag and eventually develop a permanent bend.

The length of steel to which the supports are attached to the deck frame post or wall should be sufficient to accommodate most weights. A minimum length of 40 cm should be adequate, giving a reasonable height for the bench seat itself. Any longer than 40 cm,

the seat will be too high for most people to sit comfortably with their feet on the ground. Think of the user!

The top section to which the boards are attached should be wide enough to take the width of the boards used. You should leave a gap, perhaps 3 mm between the boards to allow water to drain freely away rather than pooling on the seat. No two boards are ever the same width, so buy the boards first, determine roughly how wide you want the bench to protrude from the support, and cut the steel for the top of the bracket so that the end board overhangs the frame by about 10 mm. Using a disk grinder, round off the edge that will protrude from the wall or post.

Once you have tack welded the first frame together, check that everything looks about right—the length of the top support (check this again against the width of the two or three boards you are using for the seat), and make sure the height will be comfortable for the users. It is easier to make adjustments at this stage rather than when the bench is painted and is in place.

Measure and cut the angle iron you will weld in place for the bracing. You will need two lengths—one for each bracket.

Now drill the two holes for the attachment bolts. Use 12 mm or half-inch bolts for safety—galvanised of course as the bench will be subjected to a lot of rain. If you are using treated pine timber for the seat, you will not be able to use coated bolts. They must be fully galvanised. An adverse reaction is set up between the coated bolts and the treated timber. Remember that treated pine timber is much softer than most hardwoods, so if you are using this timber for the seat, you might consider using thicker boards.

When marking the position of the bolt holes, make sure that you will be able to drill fully through the post. Make sure there are no steel pipes, drain pipes or other objects behind the post that will make drilling and attaching the bench more difficult for you.

Now make the second end frame a mirror image of the first. A little planning before you cut the pieces of steel will help ensure that you get this right.

Paint the supporting brackets. If you used black steel (that is, steel that was not galvanised), you will need to use a good quality metal primer to prevent rusting over the years. When the primer has dried to manufacturer's specifications, use two coats of good quality exterior paint.

Bolt the first support in place, checking that it is vertical (use a spirit level to ensure it is upright), otherwise the appearance will detract from your efforts.

Using a board and the spirit level again, mark the position for the second frame bracket. Don't assume the deck will be flat. Usually it will be, but sometimes they aren't. It depends on the builder and his methods of construction.

Mark the position of the second frame, and bolt that in position.

Now you can attach the boards for the seat. Use two bolts for each board on each end otherwise expect the boards to buckle and warp and render the seat uncomfortable.

For the seat attachment, use round headed bolts so the head protrudes only slightly above the timber. Don't countersink the bolts because water will pool in the holes around each bolt and damage the timber.

Paint the boards, leave the paint to dry, and the patio bench will be ready to use for your next barbecue.

36 Roof trusses

Roof trusses made from galvanised pipe are a simple yet effective method of constructing the roof framing for sheds or garages.

Please read the section of this book about Pipes. It contains enough information so you will feel comfortable using this material.

The main thing to remember with using pipes for roof trusses is that the whole frame should be strong enough to take the weight of the roof, and strong enough to endure the force of the winds in your local area (and then add about 50 percent of average sustained wind speeds for your area just in case). They should be at a sufficient angle to prevent bowing under the weight of the snow and timber and the metal roofing that will be attached. They should not be so steep that they encourage tremendous forces to be exerted on them from the wind.

A general rule would be to have a slope of between 15° and 45°, but try to aim for a slope or pitch of about 30°. Less than 15° and the roof will sag under its own weight and you should use much heavier steel pipe. More than 45° and the wind sheer will present a problem.

For the roofs of garages and sheds, it should be sufficient to work with pipe with an outside diameter of 25 mm and a wall thickness of 2.5 to 3.0 mm.

You will naturally need more than one roof truss. But to begin with, make one, and make sure that everything fits together

perfectly before cutting the pipe for subsequent trusses.

Start with the longest piece—that is, the bottom length, or the length that spans the distance between the outer walls of the garage.

Make sure you allow sufficient length at the ends for attachment to the outer walls so they can be attached to the brickwork, steel framing or any other material you will be attaching them to.

If you are attaching them say to brickwork, you might consider using a length of flat bar (galvanised of course) welded to the pipe so that with one masonry bolt at each end, you have secured the truss adequately.

The next stage is to calculate the length of the top pieces. As they will be at an angle, their lengths will not be exactly half that of the cross piece.

Determine the centre of the cross piece and mark that clearly. Using a square of sufficient length, place a length of steel between one end of the cross piece, and measure the distance to the appropriate place on the square. You should have determined the pitch of the roof, hence the angle of the top pieces. This will give you the length of each top piece. But please note that this method of determining the length of the top pieces of pipe only applies if the roof line is to be symmetrical. Some roofs are not, and each section of the top could be at different angles on purpose.

Remove this section of pipe from the walls. Weld on a concrete floor or on the ground as long as these surfaces are flat. If the pipe spans a considerable length between the walls, you can expect appreciable bowing that will throw out all other welds and give a grotesque appearance to your beloved garage.

Now tack weld the three lengths of pipe together, but make sure the tack welds are sufficiently strong so the frame can be moved without it falling apart as soon as you lift it off the ground.

Put the truss on the wall and again make sure that everything fits together perfectly. The more care you take at this stage, the easier it will be for you to attach the roof later on, and to be proud of your building efforts, or at least your welding efforts. If you are satisfied that everything is okay, you can weld all the joints fully.

If that fits perfectly, cut the pieces for subsequent trusses. Make sure they are all the same length and that the angles of each are identical to those on the first truss you made, otherwise your roof line will be wavy, and that is certainly not something you will want people to comment on.

Make up the rest of the trusses using the first one as a template, building each one on that first truss. That way, they should all be at the same angle, the same length and so on.

Weld the attachment plates to the ends, at the same distance from each end.

If the trusses thus far constructed are not braced, they will not support the weight of the roof. But you won't need many braces to achieve a strong roof. One at one and a half metres to two metres apart should be sufficient.

Use the same diameter pipe for the bracing.

Cut each piece, squeeze the ends together slightly to facilitate welding (this being done in a strong vice), and tack weld each end in place. Note that one piece of bracing will be attached to the top section of pipe at an angle of 90°, but where it meets the bottom, or level section, it will not be at 90°. Cut this at the correct angle, squeeze the ends together to

154

facilitate welding, and tack weld this into place.

After you cut the pipe for the bracing, you will have an odd angle at one end of the remaining length of steel. This is good, because it will save you the need to make the next cut at the same angle. Simply turn the pipe around and make the next cut at 90°. With good planning, you will be able to minimise cutting and wastage.

You will need plates, or some other point of attachment to which you will bolt timber to which the metal sheets will be attached.

Cut the pieces from a length of 50 mm x 5 mm flat bar about 70 mm long, galvanised of course. Drill a bolt hole in each, and weld it to the top (sloping) truss members. Make sure this weld is strong, as it will take the force of the wind that can, in some areas, blow incessantly.

With the trusses all welded together, you will need to clean the weld areas with a wire brush and turpentine, and treat the welded area and that around the welds with a good rust inhibitor paint.

When they are in place, check that they are all evenly spread across the distance, ensure they are all vertical, and bolt them to the side walls, or to the other frame members that will comprise the walls.

You can then attach the timber beams and the roofing material to complete this job.

37 Saw-horses

Those long lengths of steel you will be handling from now on will be awkward. Often pieces as long as six to eight metres come from the steel merchant. You'll need something to rest them on while you cut them into usable lengths. While there are instructions in this book for the construction of steel trestles, saw-horses are an ideal addition to any metal working workshop as well as the trestles.

This is where you'll appreciate at least one saw-horse. But don't limit your stock of saw-horses to one. I have found that for some of the long pieces of steel, three saw-horses are the minimum. That's the number I would recommend you making.

The method of construction described here assumes you have access to a pipe bender. This method is very fast, with a minimum of cutting and welding, and the results are professional.

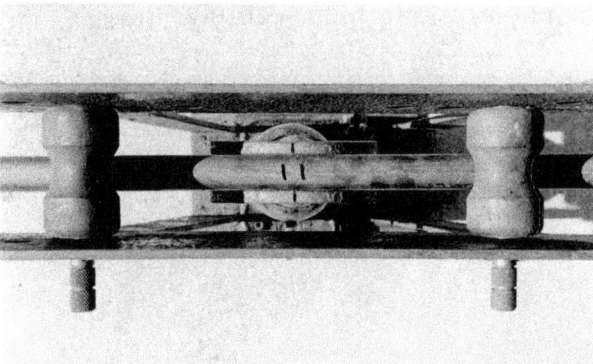

However, it's not essential, because you can cut and re-weld steel pipe at the required angle. Since you may want to make three or more saw-horses, the hire of a pipe bender for a couple of hours may be worthwhile.

To construct each sawhorse, cut two lengths of 20 mm inside diameter (ID) (or 25 mm OD pipe) pipe, 1100 mm long. Mark the centre of each of these pieces of pipe. Each of these will be bent over to form one air of legs.

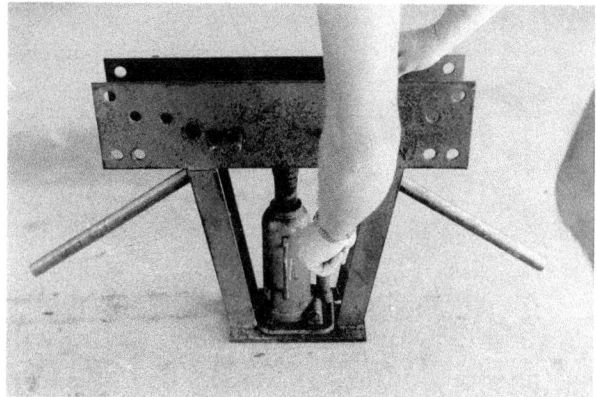

Place the centre of each piece of pipe in turn into the correct sized former, and activate the hydraulic lever of the pipe bender until the pipe has bent sufficiently. The two ends of the pipe will bend towards each other, and they should be 500 mm apart.

The former will come to rest as the hydraulic jack reaches its maximum height. Bring the pipe bender to this position.

Remove the first set of legs and bend the second piece of pipe the same way. When the

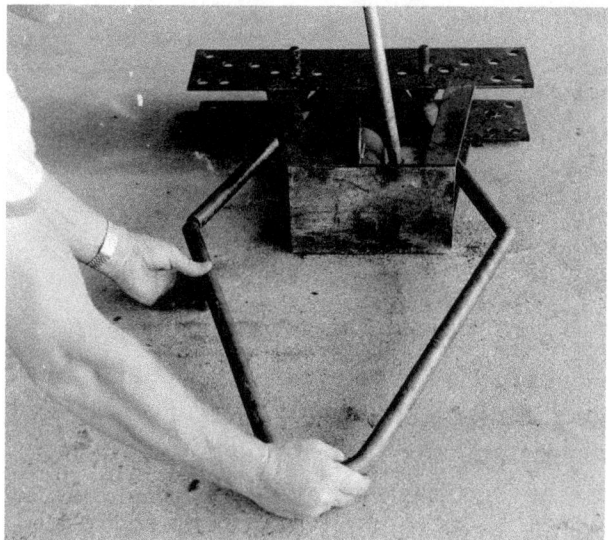

157

pipe bender reaches its maximum height, release the pressure on the pipe, but before removing the pipe from the former, check that both pieces are now bent to the same extent. Hold the ends of one pipe against the ends of the other one to check that they are at the same angle and thus are the same distance apart.

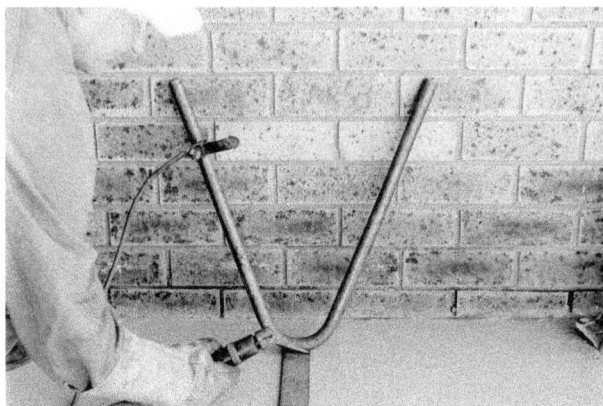

You will be making most of the saw-horse upside down. By doing it this way, you will be able to weld the legs to a flat bar, and also set the angle of the legs so they are identical. Here, a brick wall of your workshop or house will provide you with the means to make sure everything is level.

The legs are welded to a flat bar 50 mm by 5 mm and 700 mm long.

Lay the flat bar perpendicular to a wall, so the end of the flat bar is 100 mm away from the wall.

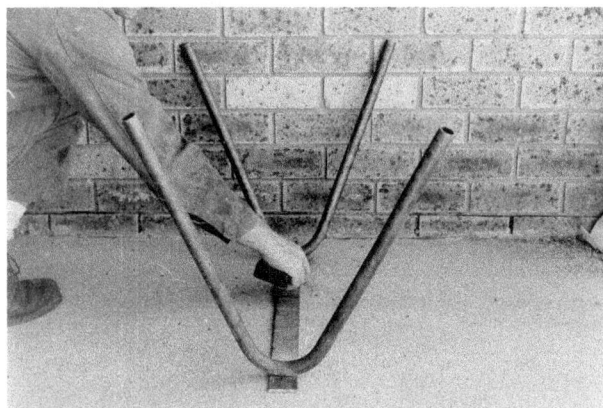

Now lay the centre of one set of legs over the flat bar 50 mm from the end of the steel, that is, 150 mm from the wall, with the ends of the legs in contact with the wall. If you're using a brick wall, you can make sure

immediately that the legs are level by lining up the two ends with a row of bricks.

Weld the legs to the flat bar, making sure that you weld on both sides of the pipe to gain maximum strength. Remember, these sawhorses will have to support heavy weights at times, so strength is essential.

Turn the frame around and weld the second set of legs to the flat bar. The same method applies.

Drill a hole 6 mm in diameter 100 mm from each end of the flat bar. These will be used to attach wood to the steel plate.

It's often a good idea to clean, prime and paint the steel work at this stage of construction, as you won't be able to cover all the steel once you have attached the wood.

Cut a piece of '4 by 2' timber (100 mm by 50 mm) 800 mm long.

Place the timber on the floor, and rest the saw-horse frame upside down on the timber.

Drill holes through the timber to coincide with those in the steel. Make sure you place an off-cut of timber under the wood you are drilling through so the drill tip doesn't come into contact with the concrete floor. This is the quickest way to ruin an expensive drill bit.

You can now turn the frame, and the timber, the right way up. Attach the timber to the steel frame with a 6 mm bolt through each hole, and tighten securely.

All you will need to do now is to press on four rubber feet. These are often sold as chair tips, and they fit over the ends of the pipe. These will prevent the steel pipe from digging into the floor of your work area, and they will lessen the noise as you cut the steel.

38 Driveway gates

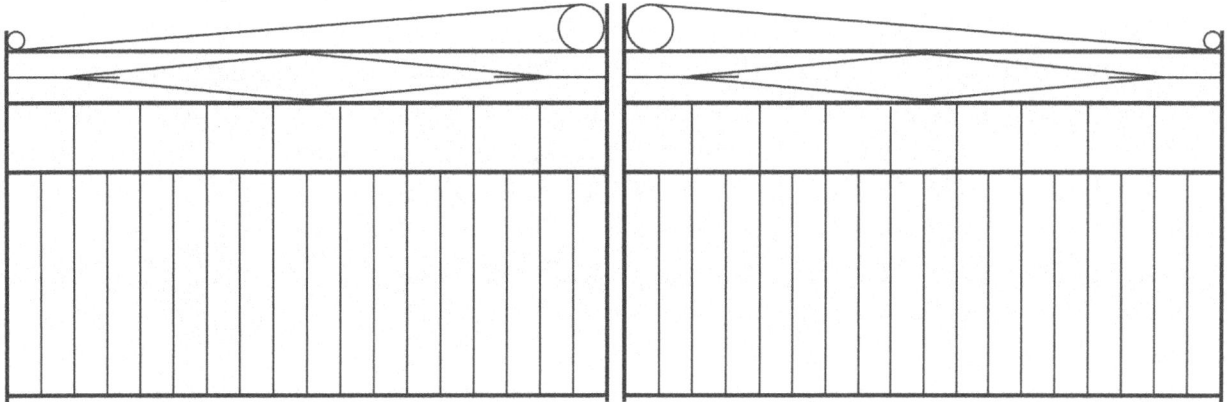

Often home owners tend to keep away from installing wrought-iron gates because of their belief they are too expensive. If you construct them yourself, then the cost is comparable with gates made from timber.

Wrought-iron gates are permanent too, as long as they are treated to prevent rust. Timber gates will certainly have a finite life if they are not maintained.

You can save around seventy percent of the cost of manufactured steel gates by welding them yourself. This represents a considerable saving for even a modest job, but one from which you will derive considerable pride in a job well done. Wrought-iron gates do not have the same inherent problems that many timber gates have. They do not fall apart. The nails don't rust, causing the boards to fall off. They do not buckle. They don't warp in the weather. They are made as one, strong, complete unit.

Everything you do around your home will add value. So the set of decorative wrought-iron gates will be a feature that will be considered favourably if you need to sell your house at a later date.

So choose your design and begin the construction of this worthwhile project. The design shown here is only one of many to guide you. You can incorporate any features you can think of to enhance the beauty of the gates — you can include the name of your house, if it has a name. You can install cast aluminium panels, or arches, and more scrolls. The design here will be a starting place. But make sure that any design you select is pleasing to you, and is within your level of competence as a welder.

The style of gates you make should complement the type of house near which they are being installed. Sometimes flashy gates can clash with a more conventional house.

If you are putting gates into an archway, make sure the gates too have an arch. Don't try putting flat-topped gates into an archway.

If you were to get a manufacturer to build your gates to your design, you would probably be governed by price. However, by doing all the work yourself, price will not be a real consideration, as any extra work, such as extra scrolls or including the name of your house into the design, will be a matter of your labour only, not someone else's time that you would be paying for.

Keep in mind there will be very little

difference in price for gates you are building yourself between basic, plain design and a highly decorative style with lots of extras.

Drive around your neighbourhood and select features from gates you like, and design your own, based on components of several you have seen and that you like.

Because no driveway width is standard, the exact measurements of gates are not given for this project.

If you are building the gates as shown here, the main thing to remember is to make sure the vertical rods are appropriate. For those that appear to extend above the first horizontal bar at the top, the number will be an even number. For those that stop at the first top bar you will need an odd number.

To calculate how many vertical rods you will need, there are a few measurements you will need to consider. First, the total distance between the gate posts. Don't make the mistake of making the gates first and then installing the posts later. You will have to be incredibly accurate in your work for this way to be entirely successful.

The vertical rods can be solid 10-mm square rod, or a better option is to use a 13-mm rolled hollow section, or square hollow tubing. These gates will be much lighter to work with, to install and to open and close.

The frame could be 25 mm rolled hollow section, or RHS, square hollow tubing. Wall thickness of 3.2 mm will be easy to weld, but you could go to thinner walled thickness if you are a competent welder.

The scrolls at the top are made from 20 mm x 3 mm flat bar. You will be able to form the scrolls easily with steel this thick without the need for heating it. See the sections of this book about making a scroll former and making scrolls.

And the diamond shape in the top section is made from 20 mm x 3 mm flat bar.

Often people will ask the same question — how strong will my gates be? The answer is that they will be as strong as you wish them to be. But don't use steel that is too thick and too heavy. Beyond a certain point, which is around the dimensions given above, you will be gaining almost no extra security by using steel tubing twice the thickness, or rode twice the size. Steel is incredibly strong, so take advantage of that inherent property and scale down the dimensions, rather than going for extra weight, extra cost, and extra work.

If security is a real issue in your neighbourhood, go for extra height, not extra thickness of materials used. Make it harder for any would-be thief to scale the gates.

But be reasonable. If you make a gate too high, the gate posts will need to be taller, and the taller they are, the more movement you will end up with. Gates up to 1.2 metres high will need posts made from 50 x 50 x 3.2 mm thick rolled hollow tubing. Taller than that, the posts will need to be much thicker, otherwise they will sag under the weight of the gates.

Don't make gates that are higher than you need with lots of footholds for a would-be thief to climb. That is, keep the horizontal sections far apart so people can't use the gates as they would use a ladder.

A gate needs be no higher than that of the fence. Gates higher than the height of the fence will look ridiculous, and they would serve no further deterrent. Instead of climbing over the gate, the thief would merely climb over the fence.

There is a well-used saying in the housing industry that locks only keep honest people out. That is true too for gates. You can make gates harder to open by using a short length of chain around the gates and secured with a padlock. Or you could use a couple of small padlocks — one on the bottom drop bolt that keeps the two gates closed, and another one of the small D catch that keeps the gates closed. But remember that every time you want to go through the gates yourself, you have to unbolt every lock you have. After a time, you will probably tire of this practice and leave the padlocks off. So much for the extra security you installed, and the very reason you installed heavier, higher gates.

You will need hinges that are strong enough to support the gates for many years. Small hinges used on lightweight wooden doors will not be adequate. Use only heavy duty, galvanised or plated hinges.

So you have now measured the distance between the gate posts. Calculate the spaces needed for hinges on both sides. There will be a space of around 5 mm between the gates when they are closed.

To calculate the length of horizontal frame members, delete: the space needed for two hinges; the space between the gates (5 mm); the thickness of the end frame members (four lengths of 25 mm width, or 100 mm). Cut the eight lengths according to the result of this calculation.

For the two outermost vertical frame members, calculate the height of the gate to get the length of steel you will need to cut. Allow 10 mm at the bottom of the gate; allow 50 mm above the top frame member for the small scroll.

For the two inner frame members, you will cut these longer because as shown in this illustration, the larger scrolls come together in the middle when the gates are closed. Allow 100 mm above the top horizontal frame member.

You can now assemble the frame. Lay out all the pieces for the frame so you will get a clear idea of where the pieces fit together. This simple procedure will take the worry and guesswork out of the puzzle as you weld the joints together.

Making the frame

Start with one of the bottom corners of the gate frame. Clamp the vertical member against the bottom horizontal piece. Check with a square that the two pieces form a right angle. Now weld this joint together on one side only.

Clamp the pieces for the next bottom corner of the gate frame to the steel backing plate, and check with a square that they form a right angle.

Before you weld this joint, look along the side of the frame and line that up with the opposite side. You may have to support the frame in one or more corners to ensure that each section is on the same plane. This is the only way you can be sure that your gate won't develop an unsightly buckle.

When you weld the top piece in position, weld it to the outer frame member first. Allow for the scrolls. Again, clamp the pieces to a steel backing plate and check that they are at right angles.

Again, ensure that all pieces are on the same plane—that is, they are all level with one another. Look along one edge of the gate frame and line it up with the opposite side.

You might need to adjust any of the corners up or down until they are all on the same plane. That is the only way you can ensure that your gate frame will be flat. If it isn't, you will have to cut the weld later, prepare the joint all over again, and then re-weld. Get it right the first time, and you save yourself a lot of work.

Clamp the first horizontal frame member to a steel backing plate and weld it in position.

Turn the frame over and weld on the opposite side—all joints must be welded all around, otherwise water will get into the frame causing rusting.

As you weld each joint, make sure you clamp the joints to be welded to a backing plate to avoid bucking and distortion.

Assemble the second frame the same way as the first frame.

Once you have finished the frames for both gates, check once again that each frame is flat and that no distortion or buckling has crept into the work. Look along each side and line it up with the frame member on the opposite side.

If there is an appreciable buckle, relax. It can be fixed.

Cut almost through the welds in each corner of the frame where the buckle seems to be. Do not cut right through the welds—you will need to leave a small amount of weld metal in place to secure the members.

Straighten the frame and line up all the sides so they are on the same plane.

Clamp each corner in turn and re-weld it, checking again that the frame is straight, and that another buckle has not come into your work.

The need for good workmanship and accuracy will now be apparent.

The next stage in constructing your gate is to weld the vertical bars on the inside of the gate frame.

How far apart are you going to place them? This really depends to some extent on the purpose for which the gates are intended. It also depends on the configuration of the vertical bars. If you are building one such as that shown in the main diagram, make sure you do not end the run of vertical bars with a number that makes the gate look rather strange. Add an extra bar, or eliminate one to suit and space out the intermediate bars.

As a general guide, bars with spaces of 100 mm will keep most small children in, and most small dogs out—and of course your own small pooch in your yard where it rightfully belongs. Decide on the number of bars you will want.

To get the centres of the vertical bars an even distance apart, measure the distance between the outer frames.

You might end up with a fractional number.

Round off this number either up or down, depending on the design of the gates, and the number of vertical bars in your design so that it looks appealing without an odd bar looking conspicuous.

These marks will represent the centres of vertical bars. The actual distance between the bars will, of course, be less than this because of the thickness of the bars themselves.

Cut the bars according to the size you need.

Make sure each bar fits within the frame. If it is too long and you have to force it into position, this will bend the bar and it will spoil the appearance of the gate. If the bar is a little loose, you will need to use more welding rod to fill the gap.

You will probably be using bars of 13 mm rolled hollow section (square tubing) or 10 mm solid steel. These can be welded at 45° to give the gate more personality.

Scrolls

You can now weld into position any other pieces you want to incorporate into your gate, such as scrolls or the name of your house. Here are some examples of designs that have been included in wrought-iron gates. Instructions for making the scrolls are given elsewhere in this book. If you like the idea of including scrolls into your own gates, you will find they are just so easy to make, yet the difference they make to a gate will be amazing. You are making wrought-iron gates. You are investing in only your time. This is the chance to create those amazing gates you have always wanted, have always talked about, and have always wanted to show off to your friends and neighbours.

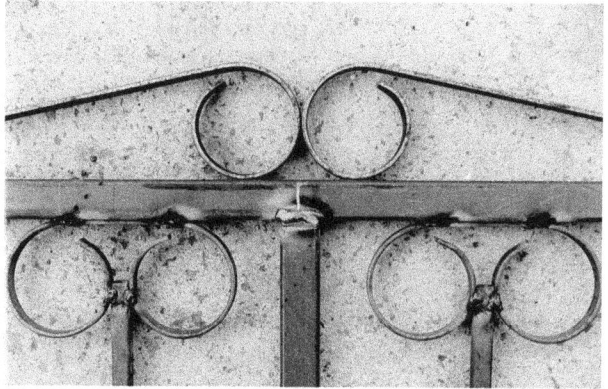

A little imagination will enable you to configure any arrangement of scrolls on your new gates

Half scrolls arranged in a diamond pattern will add interest to any gate

Half scrolls combined with full scrolls will enhance any gate design

Half scrolls and diamond-shaped configurations can enhance any gate

Catches and locks

Gates will have to open inwards or outwards depending on sloping ground, or obstacles such as drain pipes against walls or garden edging.

Here, it is assumed your gates will be opening inwards, the most common arrangements for driveway gates. If, however, you need a different configuration because of slope of the driveway or obstacle that prevents your opening gates inwards, make sure you apply the correct configuration to suit your own needs rather than following the instructions here.

To keep the gates closed, you will need a catch. The most commonly used catch for securing gates is the D catch. This simple yet effective self-locking catch has a plate that lifts up as the striker bar or tongue on the opposite gate closes against it, then drops

A D catch is the easiest way of closing double gates

again, holding the gate in a closed position. Both components are welded to the inside of the gates, one on each gate. Make sure the parts align correctly.

One of the gates is kept closed with a drop bolt. This is secured to the inside of one of the gates by welding it to the frame. The bolt drops into a hole drilled into the concrete, or into a steel pipe set in concrete in the ground.

A drop bolt attached to one gate will keep that gate closed allowing the other gate to be opened easily

Make sure the D catch and the drop bolt are both secured to the same gate. You and everyone else using the gates will gave difficulty of access if they are on the wrong gate.

Since one gate is kept closed by the drop bolt, juggling the drop bolt, the striker bar and the D catch will ensure the gates will open with the minimum of inconvenience.

Once you have finished the gates, clean them, remove slag from the welds, excess weld metal, and clean the steel thoroughly. Then use a good quality metal primer and at least two coats of exterior paint to prevent rusting.

39 Personalise your gates

Does your home have a name? Why not incorporate that name in your wrought-iron gates? This can be an attractive way of showing people that you care for your home and are proud of the name.

If the name is only one word long, repeat it in each gate. If it consists of two names of similar length, put one name on each gate.

The name can be painted in a colour different from the rest of the gate, so that it will stand out more.

You can make the letters from 13 mm by 3 mm flat bar. Make the letters individually, ensuring that they are all the same height and of similar width. Most letters will occupy a similar width. However, letters such as I will take less space, while and M and a W will require a wider space. Allowance must be made for narrow or wider letters in the layout.

When making letters such as N or A, cut the outer pieces first and secure them in place and then add the other components such as sloping or cross pieces.

When you make curved letters such as J, S or D, form the curve over a piece of pipe in the same way as if you were making scrolls.

It is easier to form the curve first, and then cut the stroke to size. Letters such as D are of course comprised of a straight bar with a curved component.

Space the letters evenly within the gate frame, and tack weld each part of the letter

in place. Check that the letters and spacing are even and then weld them fully and securely.

A small scroll on both sides of the name will highlight the name even more.

40 Outboard motor stand

If you or your friends have a small boat with an outboard motor, you will need one of these stands to support the motor while you carry out maintenance or are simply flushing the motor with fresh water.

It is constructed from 25 mm OD galvanised pipe, a short length of durable timber, and four galvanised bolts to attach the board to the supports.

A convenient height to work on is around 1.2 metres (four feet). Cut two lengths of pipe one metre long, and two pieces 600 mm long for the feet.

About in the middle of the uprights, or the one-metre lengths of pipe, bend each one at an angle of around 10°. By doing this, you can make the legs further apart to give stability to the motor, but you can minimise the length of board required.

Mark the centres of the two shorter pieces you have cut. If you have a pipe bender, use it to bend these two sections of pipe at 30°.

If you do not have a pipe bender, you can get around this by making the longer pieces not one metre long, but 1.2 metres long, and welding the feet straight to the end of each pipe at right angles. You would not have to bend the sections used for the feet.

Once you have welded the feet to the uprights, clean down the pipes, paying particular attention to the welds.

Paint them, particularly the welds, with a metal primer to prevent rusting. Although you will be using galvanised pipe, the welding will burn off the zinc coating, rendering the welds liable to rusting.

Cut a board 800 mm long, 300 mm wide and 25 mm thick. If planed down smooth, the board's finished thickness will be about 19 mm. This will still be sufficient to support the weight of most smaller outboard motors. Smooth the edges where you have cut them.

If you are using rough-sawn timber, you might prefer to sand the surfaces to remove the roughness. If you use a power sander, make sure you use a dust mask and ear muffs for safety to protect your hearing and your health.

Treat the timber with a good quality wood preservative or a quality exterior timber treatment to preserve it. It will get wet when you flush the engine out after it has been immersed in salt water.

Drill two holes in each vertical pipe, the first 50 mm from the end, and the second 200 mm below that. Make sure that the position on each pipe is identical, otherwise the board will be tilted and the result will look less than professional. Make sure that the holes are in line with the feet. If they are at an angle to the feet, you will find that the board and the feet do not align correctly. Don't be surprised by the comments you get from friends about your workmanship.

Make sure the feet are parallel with each other, and clamp the board to the two supports.

Tighten the nuts on all the bolts, and check that everything looks straight and even.

Most outboard motors will be stable on this stand.

41 Bull-bar

Despite what conservationists say, there are still lots of wild animals in this country! And stray animals, like sheep and cattle on the roads. In fact, animals on the roads, particularly at night, are rather common on country roads. These animals may pose a hazard to drivers travelling to their farms, or on country roads anywhere after dark.

Any extra protection you can give your vehicle will be worthwhile. A bull-bar (or 'roo' bar as they are sometimes called in Australia) will give the vehicle a lot of extra protection.

Vehicle owners sometimes prefer to buy ready-made bull-bars. This is alright if one is available for a particular model. Often it is not. They are generally available for more

popular vehicles for around $1000, but many vehicles have been overlooked, and waiting for perhaps weeks while one is made for your particular vehicle can be frustrating.

Here are the instructions for making a bull-bar. The construction is straightforward and will give a satisfactory bull-bar in a matter of hours.

A bull-bar should be rigid enough to withstand a mild collision, such as with a stray animal, if the vehicle is travelling at a reasonable speed. The remains of the animal are another story. Bull-bars also offer added protection in collisions (at moderate speeds) with other vehicles and with trees.

Nothing, of course, can protect a vehicle if it is travelling too fast.

The bull-bar should give a little in any collision. If it doesn't, the alignment of the vehicle can be thrown out, costing even more in repairs.

Anchorage points are a problem on some vehicles—there just don't seem to be any. Ideal attachment points would be on the chassis if there is one but any reasonable and strong part of the frame (perhaps the bumper bar attachment points) will usually do.

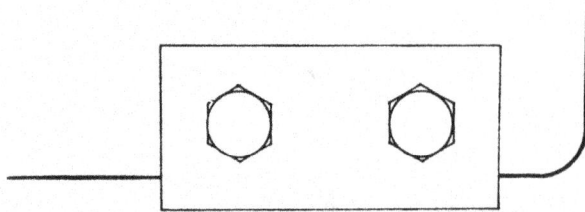

The supports for the points of attachments will need to be strong, so make them out of steel 6 mm thick

A steel plate 100 mm wide and 6 mm thick by about at least 150 mm long will be ideal on which to build the rest of the bull-bar. The steel plates should protrude slightly below the bottom of the chassis or point of attachment. At least two holes should be drilled in each of the plates to take bolts. The holes will line up with the attachment points you have identified on the vehicle.

Secure the mounting plates in position with the bolts. You will have to remove these to weld the bull-bar fully, so don't bother at this stage to tighten them securely. Only tighten them enough to let you get the right positions for the rest of the bull-bar.

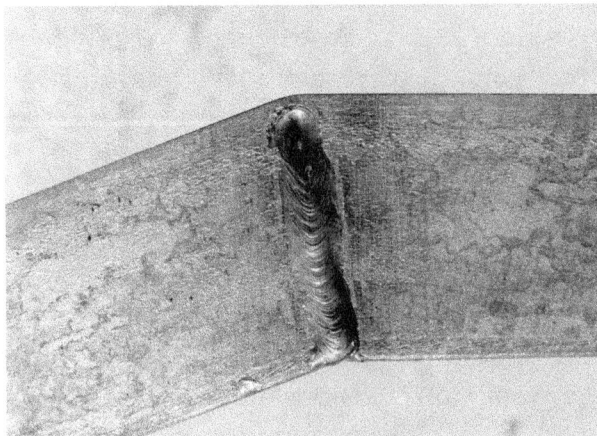

Cut the supports, shape them and then weld them together strongly

You will possibly find the job easier if you build at least some of the bull-bar on the vehicle. If you do so, disconnect the battery otherwise the current from an electric welder can damage it. Disconnect the wires to the alternator or generator. This is essential for electric welding.

Weld the supports at the correct angle so they are straight

You will need to take a rough profile of the front of the vehicle where the bull-bar leaves the points of attachment, turns under and forward and finally in front of the vehicle.

Make an H-frame. This is made from several pieces of steel, cut and welded together, to allow for clearance of the vehicle.

You will need to make a loop of pipe using pipe with an internal diameter of at least 25 mm (OD of 32 mm). The outer edges of the loop must clear the headlights and the

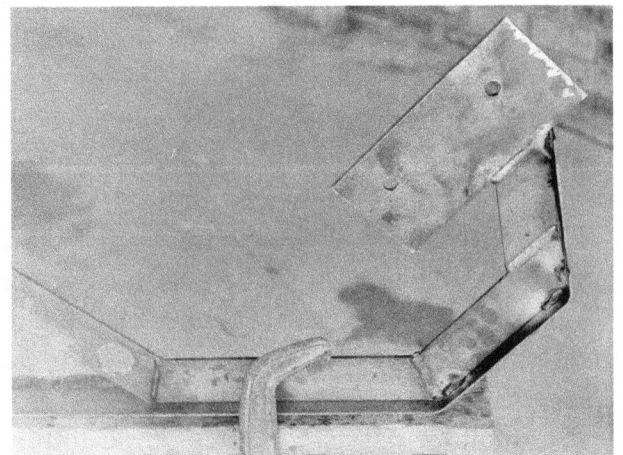

Every joint on the frame needs to be strongly welded. One weak weld may cause failure on impact

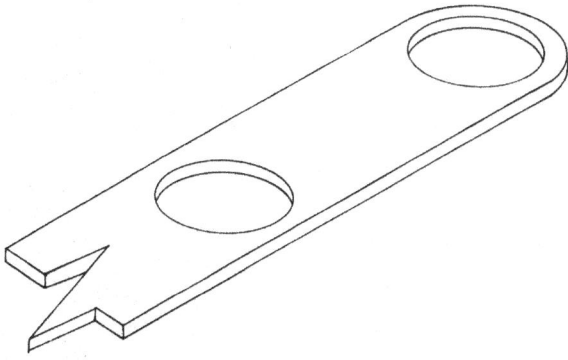

Drill two holes in each support for the pipe

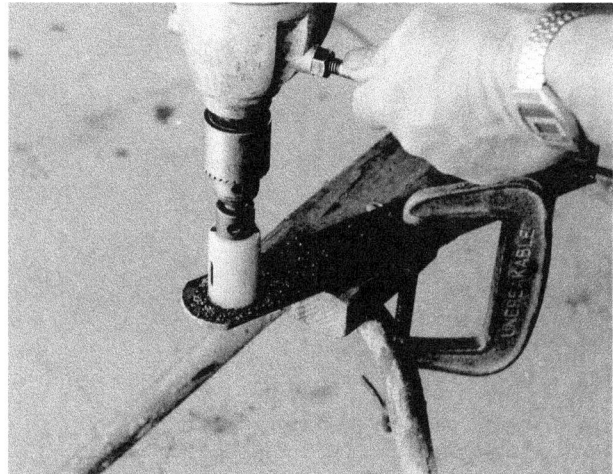

Cut the holes for the pipes with a circular saw

indicators, but preferably be as wide as, but certainly not much wider than, the vehicle.

If a pipe bender is available to bend the pipe to shape, use it. It will give excellent results. Another method that is rather easy is to cut the four sections of pipe at 45° and weld the sections together. The bull-bar will have sharp corners, but it will nevertheless be functional.

around this support a length of flat bar 40 mm wide by 3 mm thick. The flat bar you use here will bend easily at this stage. Weld at intervals of about 100 mm, running a weld about 25 mm long each side of the support.

Make sure that both pieces of pipe are identical so they are easy to weld

Use a pipe bender to bend the pipe to the right shape

Make sure the welds are strong. A weak weld anywhere will render your bull-bar totally useless if it snaps under impact.

In making H-frame supports, cut flat bar 50 mm wide and 6 mm thick to the profile of the front of your vehicle. Round off the ends.

Cut two holes, top and bottom, for the steel pipe to pass through. The pipe should, for appearance if for no other practical reason, line up with prominent horizontal parts of the front of the vehicle, such as the top of the bonnet and the bumper bar. Wrap

Weld both pieces of pipe together and grind off the excess weld metal

171

Paint the completed bull-bar before attaching it to your vehicle

You'll be surprised at the strength of this structure!

Weld all the joints fully and strongly. Finish off your bull-bar by cleaning the steel with a wire brush to remove mill scale from the surface of the steel, and turpentine to clean off any grease.

A good quality metal primer will help to prevent rusting. Pay particular attention to the welds, the bends, and the hidden corners.

Apply two coats of enamel paint. Most people choose black for their bull-bars.

42 Box trailer

No matter what size the farm ute or truck is, the time will come when, for some reason or other, it will be too small. A trailer will be useful for effectively expanding the carrying capacity of the vehicle for carting hay, chemicals, hoses, irrigation bits and pieces, and even the odd farm animal or two. While excellent commercially-made trailers are available, it is nevertheless often convenient, practical and less expensive to build your own. You can make the one that you need, and, to the basic design, you can add an animal cage or high sides for carting hay.

These instructions will take the welder through every step in the construction of the very popular 6′ x 4′ (1.8 m x 1.2 m) box trailer. They assume no previous experience in building a trailer, only some competence in welding techniques.

Even if you do not have the facilities to bend the sheet steel that will be used to form the sides and the mudguards, sheet metal workshops will guillotine and bend steel to individual specifications.

Trailers with a steel frame, floor and sides are the most popular construction for home-built trailers. However, construction using a steel frame and floor, and timber sides, may be preferred by those with woodworking experience.

Parts such as axles, hubs, springs and wheels can be purchased from trailer and caravan accessory dealers who specialise in trailer components. These dealers can also provide the necessary lights, draw bar couplings and plugs. Wheels, stub axles and springs could be bought from a motor wrecker at a considerable saving in cost.

Springs should be adequate for the job: a generous scoop of soil can weigh more than half a tonne.

All trailers to be used on public roads must be registered. Third party insurance may be optional, or it may be covered by the towing vehicle's third party insurance policy. Nevertheless, this type of insurance is strongly recommended. Trailers can break away from the towing vehicles and cause serious injuries to other road users.

All metal parts should be treated with a good quality metal primer to prevent their rusting. Some parts can be treated before the trailer is fully assembled. However, all primer in the vicinity of the welds should be removed before welding to prevent the inhalation of toxic fumes. Impurities can weaken the weld, but, more importantly, fumes from the burning primers (and paints too) are a health hazard. The use of galvanised steel is preferred.

Apply two coats of an enamel paint to the finished trailer.

Accuracy in both marking and cutting will ensure that assembly and welding is easy. A cut that wanders from the true by several millimetres is more difficult to set up and weld.

Set the pieces out prior to cutting them to get an idea of the angles of cuts and lay out the frame pieces so you know which pieces go where in the finished frame.

Lay out the frame components

Lay out the pieces of angle iron for the base. The front piece will have one face out (to the front), and one face down; the two sides will each have one face out and one face down.

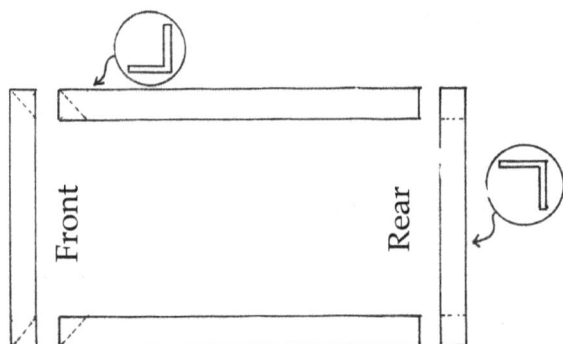

The rear piece will have one face out (to the rear) and one face up.

Mitre the corners

When cutting the angle iron for the frame, both ends of the front section must be cut to an angle of 45°.

Bevel the edges

If you are using angle iron thicker than 3 mm, bevel the edges at each joint to ensure full weld metal penetration.

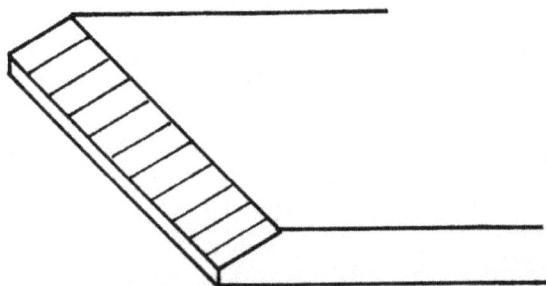

End section of the frame

The end section will be upside down in relation to the other parts of the frame. Cut one piece from each end as shown in the diagram.

Welding the frame

Clamp the pieces to be welded onto a backing plate of scrap steel, and check for accuracy using a square of good quality (some cheap squares are not really square—if you use one of these, your trailer might be a bit irregular in shape, and hard to fit together). Leave a space of 3 mm between each piece for full weld metal penetration to give the weld proper strength. Welds must be the strongest

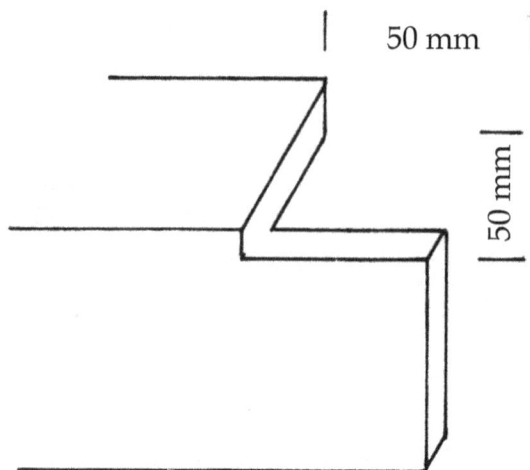

attainable, because with vibration caused by the trailer being towed on the often bumpy roads can develop fractures if the welding is not done properly. Weld each joint from both sides to ensure maximum weld strength.

On the second and subsequent welds, check the alignment of each piece of steel by line of sight. All pieces should be on a flat plane—that is, the whole frame should be 'flat'. Adjust one or more corners up or down to ensure the correct alignment.

Floor supports

25 mm x 25 mm x 3 mm angle iron floor supports are welded to the frame 600 mm apart, so you will need two of these. The floor (sheet steel) will later be tack welded to these supports.

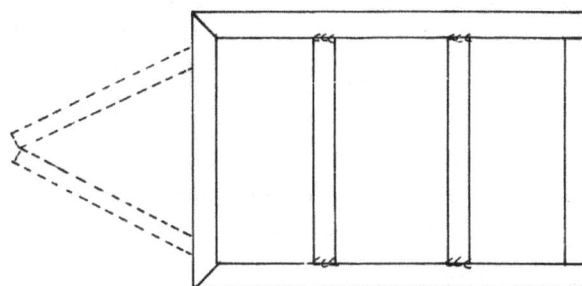

Once welded, the base may seem rather flexible, but don't worry—the springs and the axle will increase rigidity.

Side supports

Weld supports for the sides at 90° to the base. Check the accuracy with a square.

The front supports fit over the corners of the frame. Leave a 3 mm gap between each support and the base for weld metal penetration.

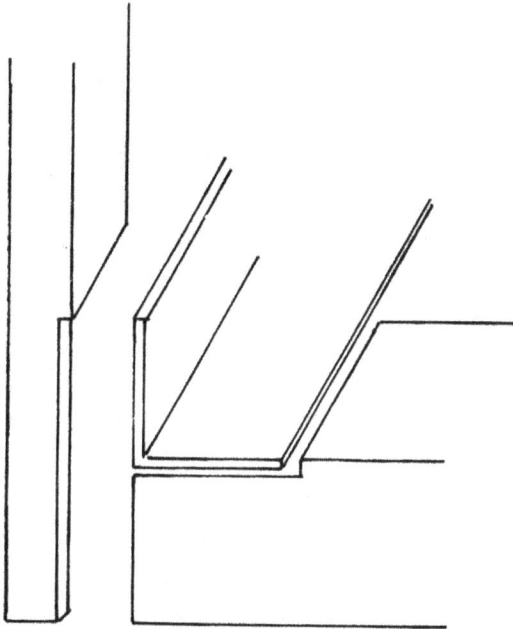

Rear side supports

Cut and weld the rear supports as shown in the diagram.

Attaching the draw bar

The draw bar is welded to the bottom of the frame. Its attachment is simplified if the frame is turned upside down. The illustration shows the frame as inverted, ready for the attachment of the draw bar. The two lengths of RHS are placed in a vee as shown here.

300 mm

Ensure that both pieces of RHS are on the same plane. Check by line of sight. Clamp the RHS to the frame, and weld both pieces in place.

Weld the edges of the RHS together where they touch.

Attaching the coupling plate

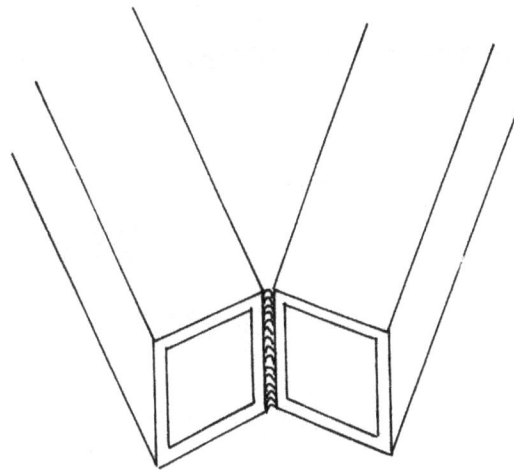

Mount the 200 mm x 100 mm x 5 mm coupling plate neatly over the end of the RHS and weld top and bottom. More than one run of weld metal may be required for strength in this important component of your trailer.

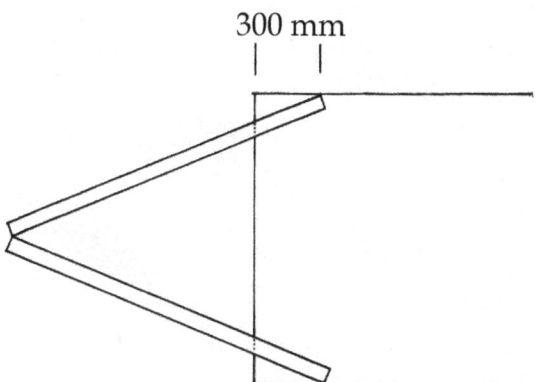

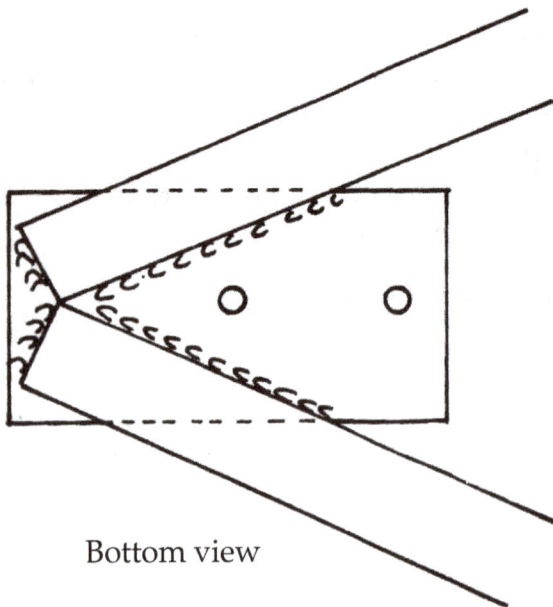

Bottom view

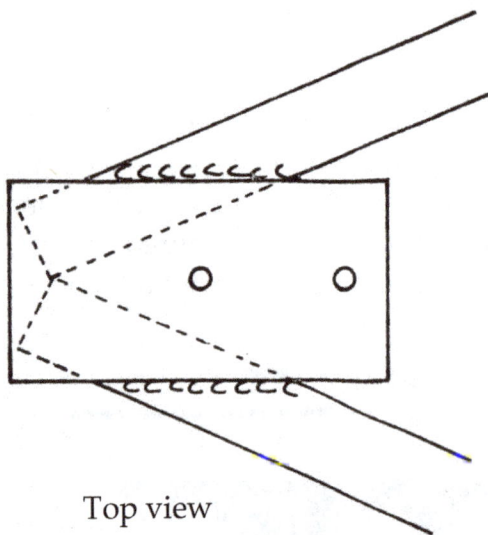

Top view

Attaching the coupling

Couplings are usually made from cast iron and they should never be welded to the coupling plate. Mark and drill the bolt holes. Small holes can be enlarged to the required size with a round file if an adequate drill and drill bit (usually ½ inch or 12 mm) are not available. Always use the correct size bolts so there is no lateral movement of the coupling. Small bolts in large holes will cause movement and will weaken and eventually fracture the bolts with disastrous results.

Shaping the sides

Steel sides and the front should be cut and shaped as shown. Sheet metal workshops can shape the steel to the required size and shape.

Alternatively, timber sides may be used. Mitre the ends where the side pieces of timber meet those comprising the front

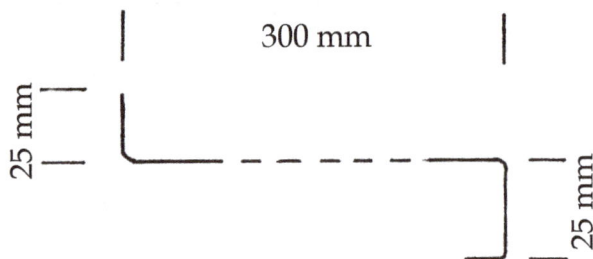

300 mm

25 mm

25 mm

pieces. Holes are drilled into the vertical supports and the sides are bolted to these.

Fitting the sides into position

Fit the sides and the front sheet into position and align the top. Use clamps to pull the steel sheet to the angle iron to ensure a good fit. Weld the sides and the front to the angle, with 25 mm welds each 300 mm, using a small electrode on a low amperage. Weld in short bursts to minimise burning through the thin sheet steel.

Weld the edges together. Use a small electrode on a low amperage.

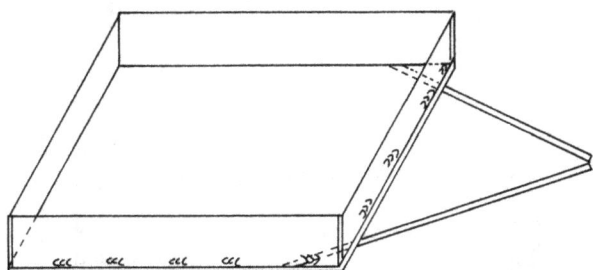

iron before the sides and the front are fitted into place.

Weld the floor to the angle iron and the two floor supports, using 25 mm welds spaced at 300 mm intervals.

Positioning of the springs

The centre of the axle should be 25 mm **back** from the centre point of the trailer frame, excluding the length of the draw bar. With an evenly distributed load, the draw bar should rest gently on the ground.

Attaching the springs

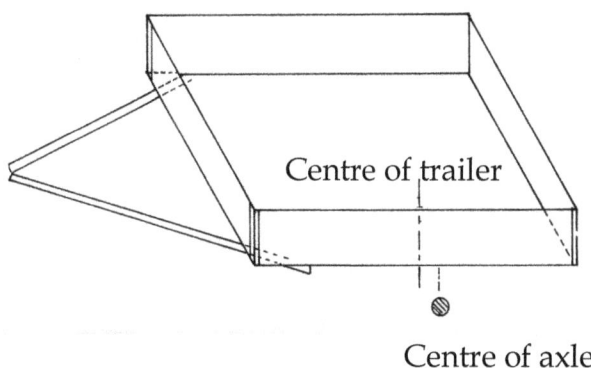

Centre of trailer

Centre of axle

Filling the corners

There will be a gap in the two front corners between the rolled edges of the sides and the front. This can be filled by welding in place a small off-cut of sheet steel shaped as shown.

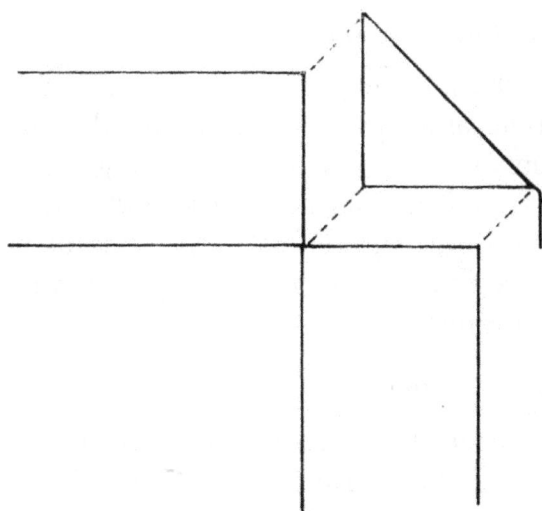

One end of each spring is fixed in place with a high tensile steel bolt mounted through a U-shaped anchor point.

The rear of each spring is free floating to take up the flattening out of the spring when it is under load. A bolt is inserted through rubber bushes.

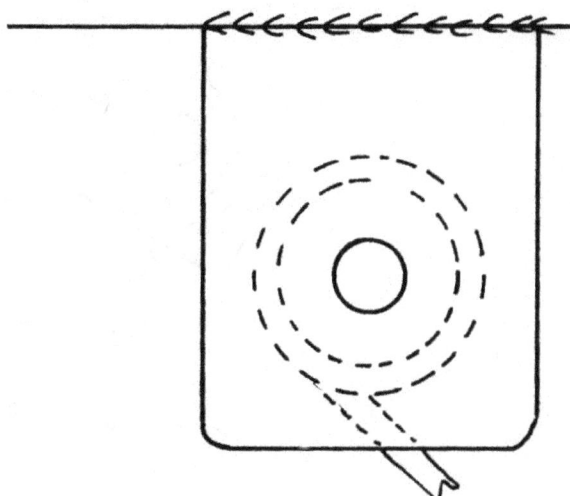

The floor

The floor can now be placed in position. If you are using timber sides and front, the steel floor should be fitted directly onto the angle

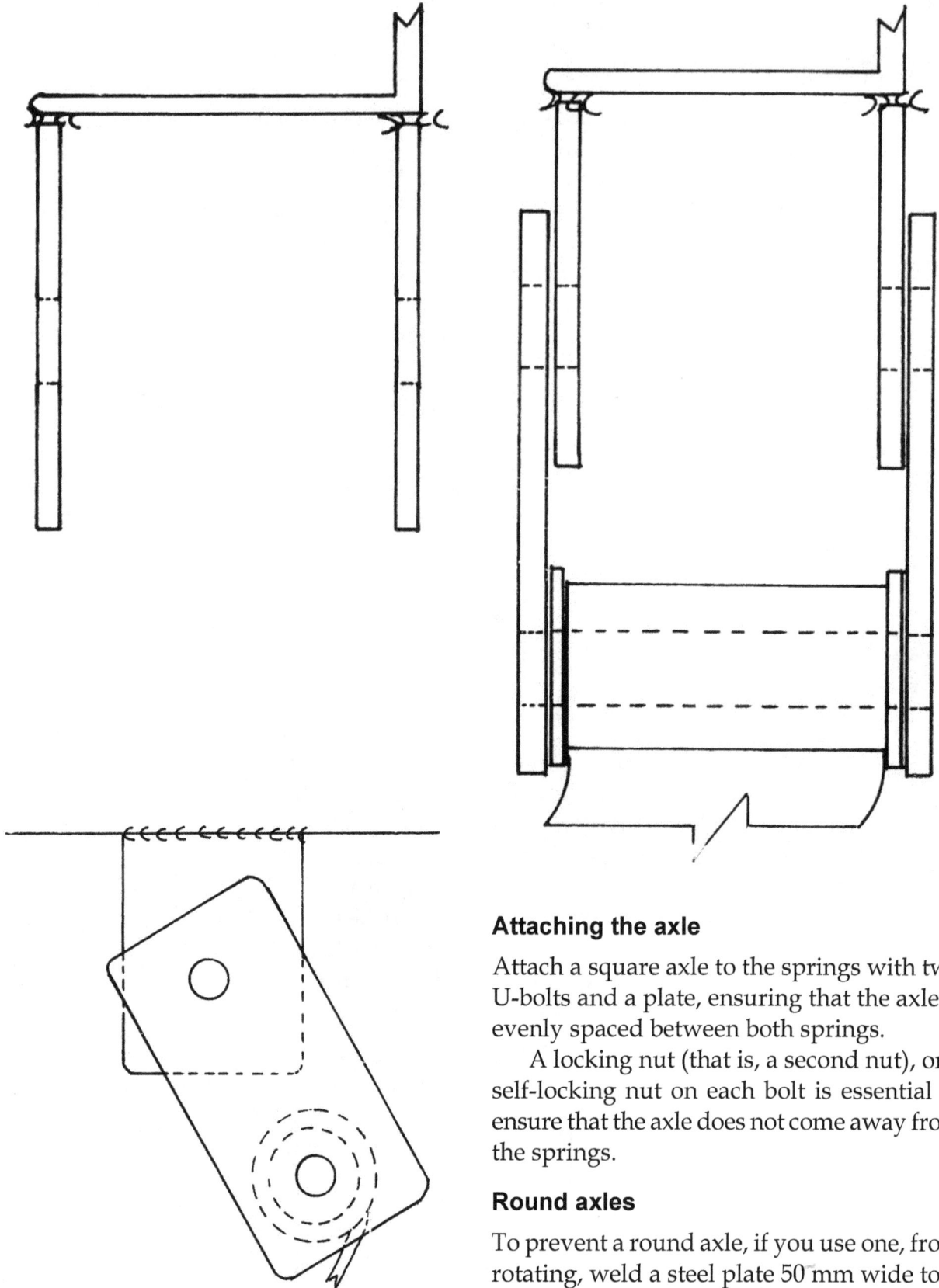

Attaching the axle

Attach a square axle to the springs with two U-bolts and a plate, ensuring that the axle is evenly spaced between both springs.

A locking nut (that is, a second nut), or a self-locking nut on each bolt is essential to ensure that the axle does not come away from the springs.

Round axles

To prevent a round axle, if you use one, from rotating, weld a steel plate 50 mm wide to it where the axle will meet the springs.

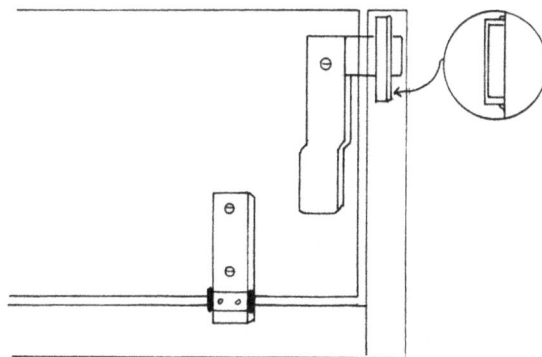

Adjusting the bearings

Bearings should be packed with grease and adjusted to take up any free play.

Shaping the tailgate

The tailgate can be shaped by any sheet metal workshop to the dimensions shown.

Or timber can be used. This may be a preferred alternative, especially if you are using timber for the sides and the front.

Weld the corners

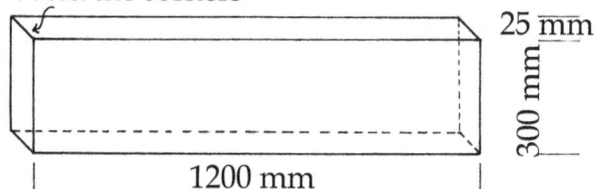

25 mm

300 mm

1200 mm

Attaching the tailgate

Attach the tailgate to the frame with two hinges.

Tailgate locks

Sturdy catches such as those shown which you can make yourself will keep the tailgate closed, while ensuring a quick release. Alternatively, there are many other methods of keeping the tailgate closed which will suffice, such as sturdy slide bolts that can be bought from most hardware stores.

Mudguards

These are formed from sheet steel in accordance with the dimensions shown. They can be guillotined and formed by a sheet metal workshop. Alternatively, the sheet steel is cut, and the edges rolled, a small section at a time, over a sharp edge. The edges are essential for strength.

If you need to engage a sheet metal workshop to guillotine and roll the front, sides and the tailgate steel, then get the mudguards formed at the same time.

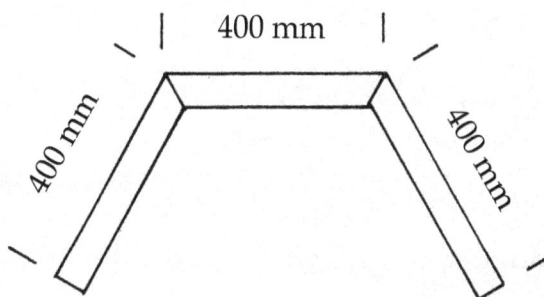

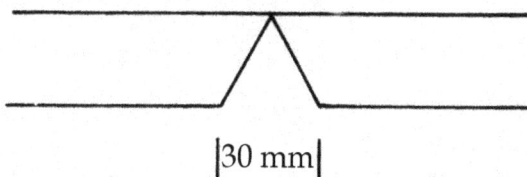

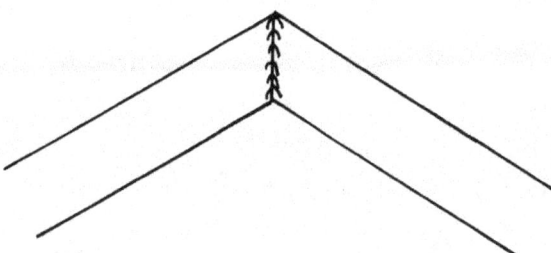

400 mm

400 mm

400 mm

|30 mm|

Cut through the edges with tin snips or with a hacksaw and form the mudguard as shown.

Weld over the cuts where the sections overlap to strengthen them.

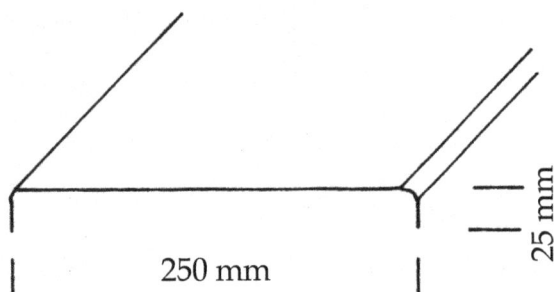

250 mm — 25 mm

Attaching the mudguards

These should be welded directly over, but high enough above the wheel, so that when the trailer is fully laden, the wheels will not rub on the mudguard. A distance equal to that of axle-to-base above the wheel is recommended. Weld the mudguards directly to the side of the trailer and to the frame, using 25 mm welds spaced at 300 mm apart.

The rear of the mudguard should be not less than the level of the axle. However, the length of the mudguard can be extended if necessary by the attachment of mud flaps or flexible rubber pieces the width of the mudguards, bolted to the rear of each of the mudguards.

Tie-down rods

Use pipe or rod of 12 mm diameter for tie-down rods on both sides and the front of the trailer. Supports for the rods can be made from small scraps of angle iron welded to the corner supports.

The side tie-down rods will rest directly on the top of each mudguard.

Safety chain

You must include a safety chain on any trailer being towed on a public road in case the trailer disengages from the towing vehicle. The chain should be short enough to prevent the draw bar from touching the road,

but should not impede turning. Therefore, the attachment of the chain to the trailer should be just behind the draw bar coupling. Make sure that when the trailer is attached to the draw bar by only the chain, that the front of the draw bar does not touch the ground. Keep the length of chain short. Weld an end link securely to the coupling plate or front of the draw bar.

Lights

Regulations require that indicator, stop, and number plate lights be fitted to a trailer being towed on a public road. There are various combinations of lights for trailers available.

The indicator/stop lights are best placed on an additional thin plate welded to the side of the trailer at the rear. A special multi-pin plug should be available from trailer accessory dealers, and it should be wired in accordance with the wiring on the towing vehicle. These are generally 7-pin plugs designed specifically for trailers.

The number plate light is placed above the number plate, usually in the middle of the tailgate.

43 Farm gates

Making your own farm gates will mean the convenience of having your gates when you want them—not after they've been ordered, manufactured and eventually delivered.

Judging by the number of orders I have received for non-standard farm gates, such as 7'5", 9'3" it appears that many entrances are not a standard size.

The cost of having a non-standard farm gate made up is exorbitant. There is a surcharge added to the price of the gate to offset the cost to the manufacturer of resetting the equipment (the jig) to make a one-off gate. That's time consuming, and you, the consumer, must pay for the labour, lost production etc. Not to mention the delay, of course, as it may take several weeks before a specially ordered gate can be made up.

So there's the cost and the convenience to consider when you make your own farm gates—the size you want them and when you want them.

The methods described here assume that readily available gate infill mesh and 25 mm ID galvanised pipe are used. You may have special requirements such as very sturdy cattle gates, which will require different mesh. The method will be the same but you may have to alter some of the measurements given here.

Gate infills are available ready cut for ten, twelve and fourteen-foot (3.0, 3.6 and 4.2 metre) gates. These are convenient to work with for a standard size gate.

If you are likely to make gates of different sizes, consider buying a 30-metre roll of mesh. From it, you cut off the length you want when you want it, and there is very little wastage apart from the pieces left over at the end of the roll.

The frames are usually made from galvanised steel pipe 25 mm internal diameter (ID) which gives an OD of 32 mm. This material is strong enough for most purposes.

There are two popular methods of making the frame. The first is to use a pipe bender. If you are making lots of gates it will be convenient to buy, borrow or at least hire one.

Alternatively, you can make satisfactory gates by cutting the sides, top and bottom sections of the frame separately and welding the sections together at right angles.

But before you cut anything measure the entrance. As I said, not all entrances are a standard size.

Cutting the mesh

Calculate the length of mesh you will need. Allow 25 mm for free movement between the gate and each post, and for the fittings. You must also allow for the width of the pipe at each end of the frame. So deduct 25 + 25 + 32 + 32, or 114 mm from the width of the entrance. Cut the infill mesh this length after you have made the frame.

If you are using a roll of mesh, unwind it sufficiently so you can measure it and cut it. Put weights at the end of it as you unwind the mesh, otherwise it may rewind rapidly and the ends will spike you and they are sharp! Put weights each side of the cut you make for the same reason.

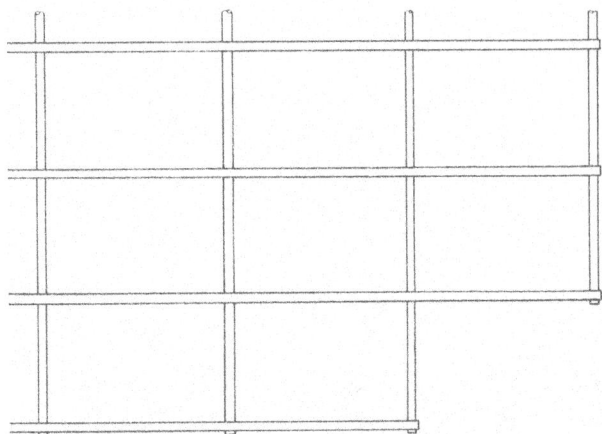

To make the frame for a farm gate, use a pipe bender, or cut the corners of the pipe at 45°

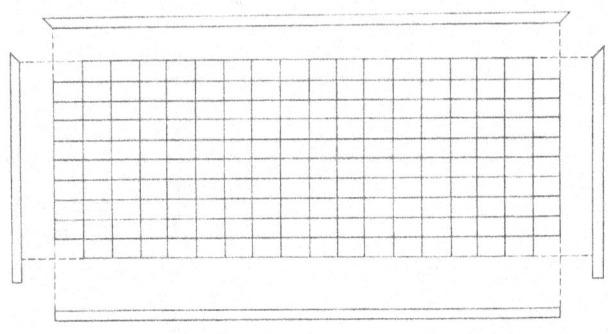

Cutting the corner section out of the mesh will ensure a much better fit

You may have to flatten the mesh slightly once you have rolled it out. Straighten it by hitting some of the joins with a hammer, if the curvature is pronounced

A felt pen will mark the mesh, and a pair of small bolt cutters will cut it, although other conventional methods, such as using a hacksaw, are satisfactory.

The corners of the frame will prevent the mesh from fitting correctly, so remove one section from each corner of the mesh.

Making the frame

Calculate how long the end sections of the frame will be. Allow about 10 mm below the bottom of the gate, 32 mm for the bottom of the frame, and of course the width of the mesh itself. If you are using a pipe bender, mark the pipe this distance from one end of the pipe. So if the mesh is 900 mm wide, add 900 + 32 + 10 or 942 mm from the end.

Put the pipe in the pipe bender at this mark and activate the pipe bender until the pipe is bent at right angles.

Pipe benders differ in accuracy, and that accuracy sometimes depends on the setting used. Most pipe benders will have several settings.

This is the time to check that the mark on the pipe lines up with the inner edge of the frame. If it doesn't, adjust the measurement for the second mark accordingly. Check for flatness. Allow for any discrepancy before making the next bend in the pipe.

Before you begin to activate the pipe bender for the next bend in the frame, ensure that the end of the frame—that is, the shorter end you have bent—is exactly parallel with

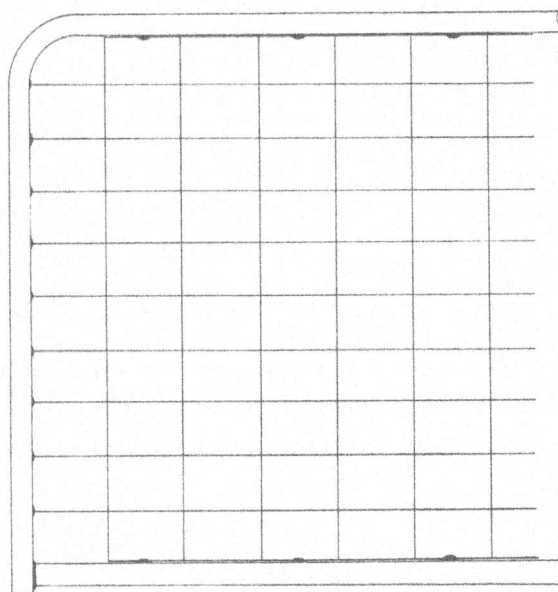

A pipe bender will ensure a more professional-looking gate. Weld the mesh into the frame

the side of the pipe bender. This will ensure that there are no buckles in the gate—a most inconvenient, but permanent reminder of your carelessness.

Welding the mesh

Weld the mesh in place. The infill should be welded to the centre of the inside of the frame to give a very neat, professionally built gate.

Begin at one corner, and work your way along the mesh, making welds about 25 mm long each 300 mm or so apart.

Set the welder about 30 amps higher than recommended for the particular electrode you are using. This will ensure better removal of the zinc coating, better deposit of the weld metal, and a stronger weld. The first run of weld metal will melt the zinc from the galvanised steel—both the mesh and the pipe. Remove the white coating of zinc oxide using a wire brush, and re-weld over the same area.

A smooth, even weld is required. Take your time and allow the weld metal to be deposited at a slightly slower rate than normal.

The preferred electrode will be a 3.25 mm electrode, set on about 110-120 amps. Use an E6012 or E6013 electrode.

Perhaps one word of warning is necessary. You are welding galvanised steel (the pipe and the mesh). Zinc fumes are not going to improve your health, and they should not be breathed. Work in a well ventilated area to avoid inhaling any welding fumes and in particular the zinc fumes.

If you are not able (because of the length of the gate) to cut the mesh with a vertical rod at both ends, you will be left with straight pointed ends of the mesh. Each of these must be welded to the frame separately.

Bottom of the frame

Measure the distance between the two ends of the gate after the mesh has been pulled tight. A tightly fitting bottom bar is preferable to one where the mesh will be very loose, but don't force the ends apart too much.

Cut the pipe to the required length.

Flatten both ends of the pipe to about half the original diameter so the pipe can be welded easily in place. A few blows with a heavy hammer, with the pipe resting on a solid surface will soon modify the pipe to the required dimensions.

Weld the bottom bar in position, ensuring that it is in contact with the mesh infill.

Turn the gate over and, with a wire brush, remove the white powder near each of the welds. The powder is an oxide of zinc and will brush off easily.

Weld over these points (that is, directly opposite the welds on the other side of the gate).

That's the first gate finished, but it is assumed that you had access to a pipe bender. Often farmers who make only the occasional gate, or have little need of a pipe bender will not invest in one. So here's an alternative to the previous method of making the frame.

It involves cutting the pipe for the frame at 45° and welding adjacent pieces together to form a right angle.

The measurements for this method are easy to calculate.

The two ends are cut the same size. Allow 10 mm at the bottom of the gate, plus 32 mm for the bottom pipe, plus the width of the mesh (900 mm). Cut the pipe at 45° a distance of 1145 mm from one end.

The length of the pipe at the top of the gate can be calculated from the length of the mesh.

Cut the pipe for economy. One 45° cut will provide the angle for the next piece and will eliminate making unnecessary cuts.

Clamp two adjacent pieces of the frame together against a steel plate offcut keeping the ends of the pipe about 3 mm apart for weld metal penetration. Make sure they are at right angles. Check this with a square and weld them together.

When you weld the next corner, check that the two ends are on the same plane — that is, that the frame is flat—to eliminate any buckle. Look along one end and make sure it lines up exactly with the opposite end. You may have to adjust one end up or down to achieve the accuracy necessary.

Weld the mesh infill and the bottom bar in place as described earlier.

Bracing

Gates up to 3.6 m (12′) long usually don't need bracing. Over that length, some form of bracing may be required. Often this is in the form of a pipe set diagonally within the frame, set from the top of the unhinged end across to the bottom hinged corner.

Finishing off the gate

That's all the welding done but the gate will rust in places where the welds have been made if left untreated. The mesh and the pipe are galvanised to prevent rusting. However, the weld metal that was deposited, and the area around each weld where the zinc was burnt off, will now be unprotected.

After chipping off and removing the slag, clean the areas with a wire brush.

Apply a generous coating of a fast drying cold galvanising paint. This is applied over the bare metal and allowed to dry for a few minutes. The gates are now complete, ready to hang.

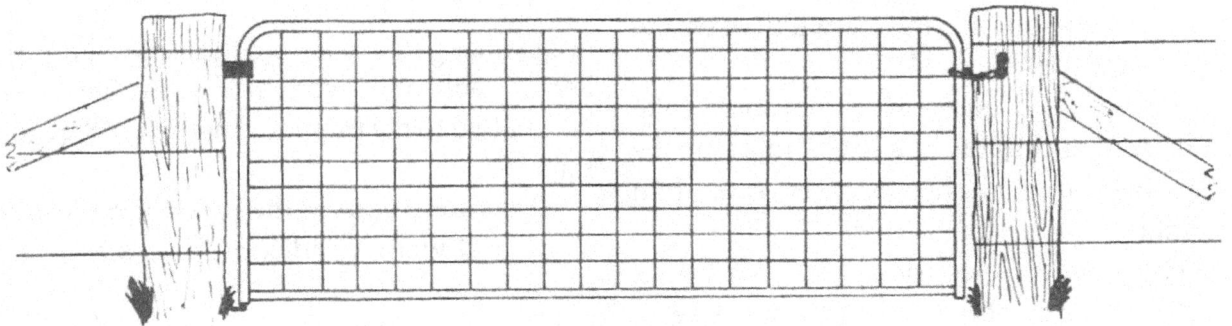

44 Fencing roller

Recently I noticed two would-be farmers laying out the fencing materials across a paddock by pushing the roll of wire netting up a slight incline. Surely, they would have told themselves, there's gotta be a better way of laying out the fence!

That's doing things the hard way. One wonders how they would have handled the barbed wire. With a few bits of steel pipe, a welder, some simple tools, these fellows could have laid out all the fencing materials, including the barbed wire, the quick and easy way.

There are three things you'll need for easy fencing (if there is such a thing): the netting dispenser, the barbed wire dispenser, and the steel post driver.

Wire netting dispenser

You will have two options here. The first is a simple type—the dispenser is towed behind a utility or tractor, or simply pushed or pulled like a roller by hand if the total distances are short. The second is a trailer- or utility-mounted dispenser.

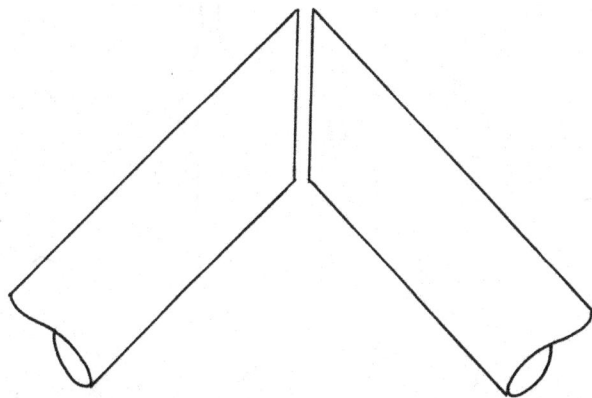

Form a vee either by using a pipe bender or cutting the ends at 45° and welding them together

Netting comes in different widths but the measurements given here assume rolls of 900 mm width. Adjust the lengths of the pieces of steel accordingly if you are using netting of a different width.

The dispenser made from pipe 25 mm ID pipe or 32 mm OD (the same as that used on most farm gates) will be fine; pipe with 20 mm ID should suffice, but might be inclined to be a bit too flexible for heavy rolls. Use galvanised pipe for the dispenser—it will save you the time of priming, painting and removing rust almost every year. However, with welding galvanised steel come the precautions. Don't breathe in the vapours from the welding process as they're a bit nasty. And work with a slightly higher amperage than you would normally use, to remove much of the zinc coating from the pipe; clean the white zinc oxide from the welded area after the first run using a wire brush, then weld the pipe together in the usual way. And don't forget to add some rust proofing to the welded area—that will have no rust protection after the weld metal has been deposited. Cold galvanising paint applied locally will be as good as anything.

Cut a piece of pipe 160 cm long. If you have a pipe bender, bend this piece in the centre to form a right angle. Pipe benders are extremely useful for making items such as farm gates on the farm. If you don't have a pipe bender, or if you don't have access to one, cut through the centre of the pipe at an angle of 45° so the two pieces put together will form a right angle. Weld these together.

To each of the free ends, weld a piece of pipe 600 mm long. Again, make sure the whole structure is flat before you begin any welding. Prop up the ends where necessary. Look along each length to again check for flatness.

Once welded properly, this frame should be quite rigid without the need for further strengthening or bracing.

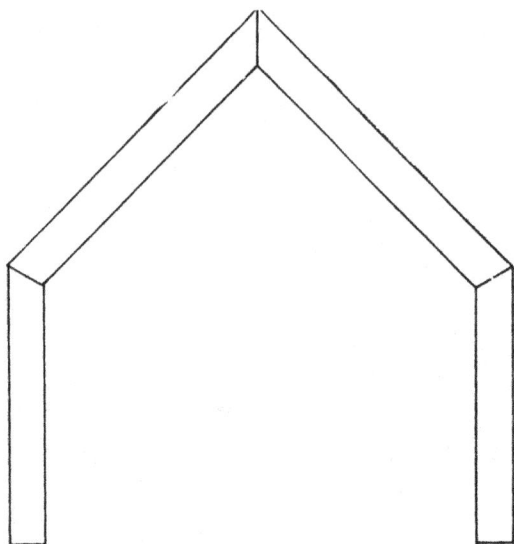

Look along the length to check for flatness of the whole frame before welding to avoid welding in a distortion

The roll of netting is held in place by means of an axle that passes through the roll of wire, and is in turn attached to the ends of the dispenser frame. The method described here of attaching the axle to the frame is only one possible way. Depending on the resources in your area, and the hardware available, there could well be easier and better ways of attaching the roll. Remember though, if you are planning on laying out rolls and rolls of netting, the easier it is to hitch up the netting each time, the better.

One method of securing the axle to the assembly is to weld about 50 mm of a slightly larger pipe, such as pipe with an internal diameter of 32 mm to each end of the frame. You may have to cut along the length of the sleeve, open it out slightly and re-weld it if you can't get pipe that gives a comfortable fit. The axle, comprising 25 mm ID pipe, slides comfortably through these sleeves, and is kept in place with a pin, a cotter pin of substantial size, or simply a bolt of about 6 mm (1/4 inch) diameter passing through

each sleeve. Put the axle in place to attain correct alignment before welding the sleeves in place. Cut the end of the pipes before welding on the sleeves as shown in the diagram. Drill the hole in each sleeve and through each end of the axle. The axle is easily removed for the next roll of fencing material.

This type of dispenser as constructed so far can be pushed or pulled along by hand. Certainly it will be an improvement on the method the two fellows were using. However, depending on the terrain being fenced, and the length of fencing to be laid

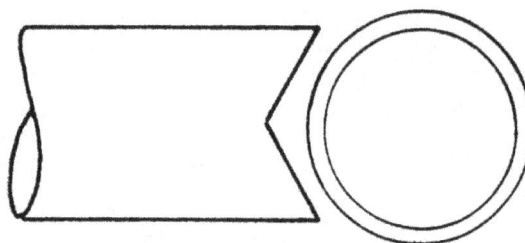

Cut out a shallow vee to ensure a better fit when welding to an adjoining piece of pipe

out, it can also be towed behind a vehicle if one further modification is made: weld a short draw bar (about one metre long) to the apex. To the other end, weld a steel plate 200 x 100 x 5 mm thick. Weld the plate securely to the pipe after squashing both ends of the pipe in a vice to facilitate a better fit for

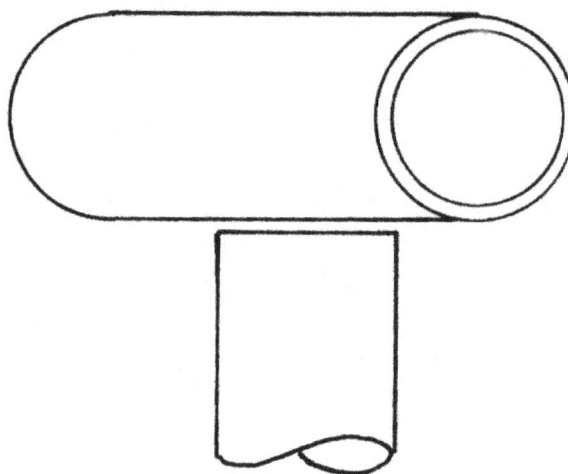

Weld the sections together

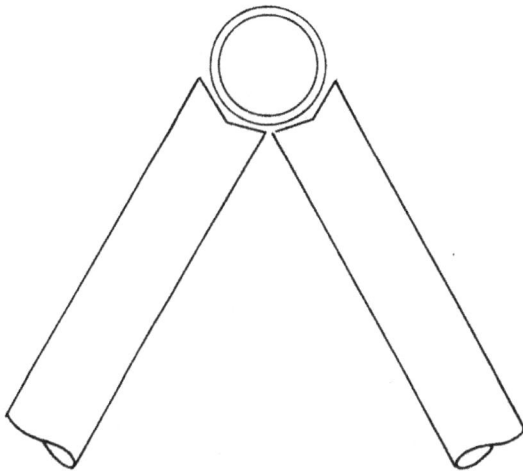

Any type of coupling will suffice, but this arrangement will be inexpensive. You could use a proper tow bar attachment and bolt it to the draw bar of the frame

welding. Buy a trailer coupling (they're not very expensive) and bolt the coupling to the plate. Couplings are made from cast iron and should never be welded (it says so on the coupling). This device can be hitched to any tow bar using a conventional tow ball. Fencing becomes easier, doesn't it? Solve the problem of crossing the creek beds as you come to them.

Doing it in style (although with the weight of materials involved, I have my doubts about this claim) involves a dispenser that can be trailer or utility mounted. What you will end up with is a stand. The netting is placed on an axle and run out behind the vehicle. Make sure your off-sider is prepared to do much of the heavy lifting for you. Wire netting is not really light to lift. Even the 200-metre rolls weigh about 75 kg, closer netting much, much more. Each roll would have to be lifted onto the vehicle. That's the advantage of the netting running on the ground.

So start by making the stand—simply a triangle mounted to two parallel pieces of pipe to form a rigid structure. In this type of apparatus, the height of the axle must be higher than the radius of the largest roll of netting you will be using.

The same type of axle attachment will work just as well on this device as on the previous one. Weld sleeves of a slightly larger diameter to the tops of the stand, after temporarily inserting the axle through the sleeves to attain correct alignment.

With both these methods, attach the free end of the netting to some attachment point such as a couple of pegs in the ground to prevent the roll from coiling up again once you are out of sight.

Barbed wire

Keep barbed wire separate from netting while unravelling it. And keep the strands of barbed wire separate too. Trying to unravel them is like harvesting prickly pears by hand.

The dispenser is again made from galvanised pipe, but as the wire is far less weighty than the netting, lighter gauge pipe can be used — 20 mm ID should suffice. The construction is straight-forward, and indeed is similar to that for the dispenser. A simple handle will facilitate pushing or pulling.

Steel post driver

And the third implement to make fencing easier is the steel post driver. You can of course buy these, but why not save your money for other farm improvements?

For this, you will need a length of pipe one metre long with an internal diameter of 60 mm. Black pipe (that is, pipe that has not been galvanised) might be a better proposition for this gadget because of the ease with which plain steel can be welded compared with galvanised pipe. You will need a piece of rather solid steel plate 12 mm or more thick for the top, cut to the shape and size of the pipe. It's the top of the driver that does the thumping, so it must be solid, and it must be welded properly to the end of the pipe. But before you weld this in place, weld three guides inside the pipe. These are, of course, optional, but they do keep the driver straight and square to each star post.

Three lengths of 20 x 6 mm flat bar, each piece one metre long (about the length of the pipe itself) are arranged evenly around the inside of the pipe Weld the flat bar to the inside walls of the pipe. You will be able to

187

reach only the last 25 to 30 mm of each end of the flat bar with the welding electrode, but that should be sufficient to hold each one permanently in place. Make sure that the pieces of flat bar are quite straight, otherwise you could experience some jamming on the post.

Weld the ends of the flat bar to the inside of the pipe

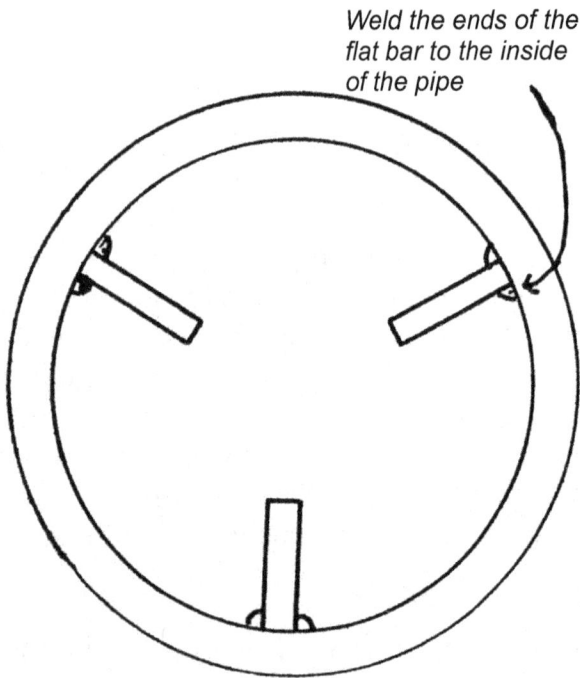

Make sure the internal flat bar is welded securely in place before welding on the capping. Once the capping is in place, you will not be able to re-weld the flat bar

Now you can cap the pipe with the hefty piece of plate. Bevel the outer edge of the pipe all around to ensure maximum weld metal penetration. If the construction gives way at any of the welds, it will be at this join. Lay down the weld metal in small sections of about 25 mm at a time on opposite sides until the joint has been completely welded all around.

Handles welded to the sides of the driver will complete this project. If you have a pipe bender, bend a piece of pipe (about 20 mm ID will suffice) into a wide but shallow 'U' and weld one securely to each side of the driver.

Alternatively, cut the pieces at 45° and weld the pieces of pipe into suitable handles. If the cap stays on okay, then it will be the handles that will fall off if your welding is not up to standard.

Bend the pipe to make a handle, or mitre the ends and weld them

45 Hay feeder

This hay feeder can be built easily in your spare time, and will provide an ideal means of feeding livestock when green feed is scarce. Such a feeder can be made from 25 mm ID galvanised pipe and welded mesh similar to that used for the construction of farm gates. The dimensions given here assume that gate infill mesh will be used for its construction. Distributors who sell farm gates and other rural products should be able to supply the mesh you require.

A couple of lengths of pipe of 25 mm internal diameter will provide the frame. And as the hay feeder is not subjected to any stresses other than cattle eating greedily from it, a length of three metres or perhaps a little more would not be unreasonable for such a structure.

Preventing rust

Use galvanised pipe for the frame of the feeder as this will prevent rusting. Some mesh (such as black mesh) has not been treated and can be expected to rust. Galvanised materials won't rust at all except on welds, or where the removal of the zinc coating has been caused by the welding process, but even here, cold galvanising paint applied when the job is finished can replace that lost. When welding galvanised steel, use an amperage 30 amps higher than you would for most applications. That extra heat will burn away the zinc coating, facilitating a strong, or at least a better, weld. Remember not to breathe in any of the zinc fumes that will be given off in the process.

Cutting the mesh

To ensure that the frame is made to suit the mesh used, it is often more satisfactory to start with the mesh. Cutting the mesh to three metres long will give a feeder of good proportions. Cut it so there is a vertical rod at each end. You will need two pieces the same length for the sides. Cut the mesh for the ends later.

Making the base

The base consists simply of two pieces of pipe, about 1200 mm long, bent slightly in the centre to raise the feeder off the ground by about 150 mm. A pipe bender can be used for this to great advantage, as it is quick and easy to use. Alternatively, if a pipe bender is not available, the same configuration can be achieved by first cutting most of the way through the pipe, bending the pipe to the required shape, and re-welding the now-enlarged cut you made.

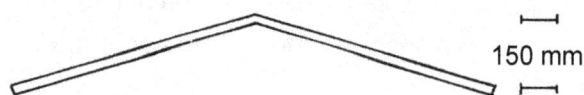
150 mm

Measure again the length of the mesh you have cut so that the lengths of the pieces for the frame can be calculated accurately. A pipe welded between the two sections of the base will add stability and strength to the structure. Cramp both ends of the pipe to make them fit into place more easily. A few heavy blows with a heavy hammer will compress the ends sufficiently for the purpose. Make sure that both feet are parallel and straight so that the completed feeder has a firm base when it is in use.

Constructing the frame

The next stage is to weld the frame onto the base. Check the width of the mesh you are using. Let's assume that mesh 900 mm wide will be used. Two pieces of pipe, each 900 mm long but this of course depends on the width of the mesh, are welded at an angle of about 60° to form a vee. The top of the feeder will then be a little over one metre high. It is preferable to compress the ends of each of these pieces to ensure an easier fit when welding them to the base, and when securing the top. Make sure that the pieces forming the end section are perfectly straight (that is, vertical when the base is resting on a horizontal surface).

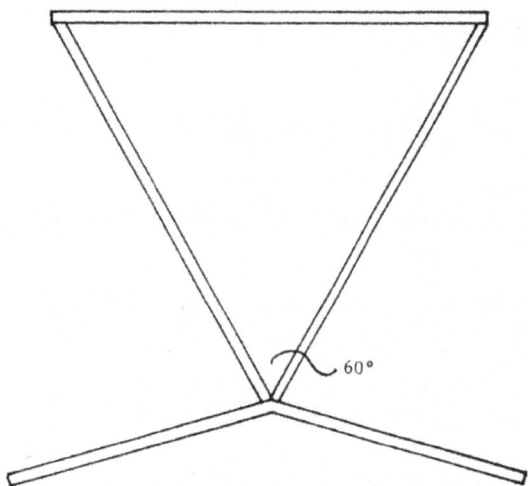

Now you will need to attach a pipe at the top of each end (the vee). Measure the lengths required, cut them, and weld them into place.

Complete the frame. Measure and cut the pipes to complete the top. Accuracy of measurement as well good workmanship are important, as an error of only a few millimetres in the length of pipe can cause a lot of floppiness in the mesh.

Welding the mesh in place

The last part of the construction of the feeder is to weld the mesh in place. This should be located within the pipe frame if possible, the same way as it is welded in a field gate. Start by welding in one corner of the mesh, pulling it tight into the frame as you proceed. Go across the top for a part of the way, then down the side before finishing the top. Welding of the opposite side and the bottom can then be completed, but at all times pull the mesh tight.

The bottom edges of the mesh used to form the sides will touch. For added strength, these two edges should be welded tightly together with intermittent welds. It's simply a matter of pulling the edges together and welding them. Throughout the construction of this project when welding the mesh, use 25 mm welds each 200 mm apart.

Now you can cut he mesh for the ends of the feeder. Obviously you won't be able to cut it as easily as you did for the sides. Align a small piece of mesh that adequately covers the end of the frame, clamp it in position, and mark the outline of the pipe on this; a felt-tipped pen will mark the mesh clearly. The mesh can be cut along the marks using a small pair of bolt cutters.

Weld the mesh to the frame so that there are no rough, jagged ends to catch the unsuspecting cow on the jaw. You should also check the rest of the feeder to ensure that there are no irregularities or sharp, jagged ends anywhere that will destroy a beast's good looks.

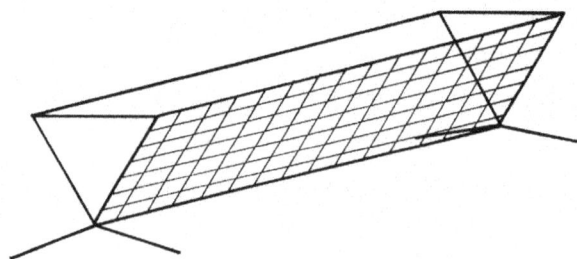

Finishing off

Welding galvanised steel will leave a white coating of zinc oxide on the surfaces. This is powdery and is easily removed from the metal by using a wire brush. However, the coating of oxide also means that the galvanised coating has been burned from the metal. This can be replaced by applying a cold galvanising paint on each side of the welded joints. Cold galvanising paints impart a zinc coating to any bare steel treated and they are fast drying. Their application should prevent the steel from rusting for many years.

Bales of hay can be teased out to make it easier for the livestock to remove the feed. The animals will be easily able to reach over the top of the feeder, as well as put their tongues through the open mesh to obtain the feed.

Anchoring the feeder in place

The dimensions of the base given in this article should be wide enough to ensure stability in most situations. However, with over-ambitious or hungry livestock, there may be a chance that the animals may topple the feeder. Extra stability can be added by putting pins like a tent peg, and formed from thin round rod about 300 mm long over each foot and hammering them into firm ground.

46 Loading ramp

A loading ramp is an essential piece of equipment for loading livestock safely onto a truck or trailer. The ramp described here is lightweight and is suitable for sheep, pigs and goats.

Its construction is simple. The sides are similar to a farm gate, using the same type of galvanised pipe and similar mesh, while the base consists of an angle-iron frame with a hardwood timber floor bolted to it. Crosspieces will ensure an adequate foothold for the livestock using the ramp.

Some farmers may prefer to construct the ramp as a permanent fixture and in a fixed position. The method for constructing this type is probably easier than that for a more mobile, adjustable ramp.

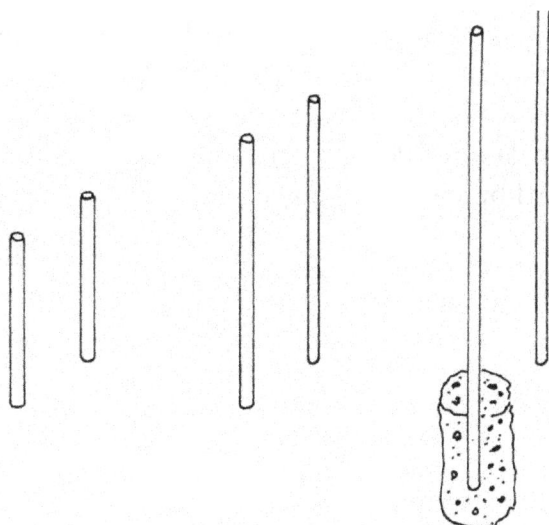

The fixed loading ramp

With the fixed type, pipes of 76 mm diameter are set 1200 mm apart into the ground with 500 mm in concrete – one with 900 mm above the ground, the second with 1500 mm above the ground, while the third has 2100 mm above ground level.

Pipe is welded to the tops of these posts, while the frame for the floor will be welded in position 900 mm below this, allowing mesh to be welded between the top railing and the floor.

While this type of ramp will possibly be more rigid and secure, it should be appreciated that not all vehicles are exactly the same height, and the fixed ramp will have limitations with different vehicles.

Constructing the sides

Making the sides of the adjustable ramp is a bit like constructing two farm gates, only these 'gates' are skewed at 30 degrees. The sides are 2.8 metres long, but their height could vary slightly depending on the type and width of the mesh used. The mesh used for the field gate infills will suffice, but any variation in width is insignificant, as long as this is taken into consideration. Details described here will assume a mesh width of 900 mm.

You will need two lengths of 25 mm internal diameter galvanised pipe. That's the

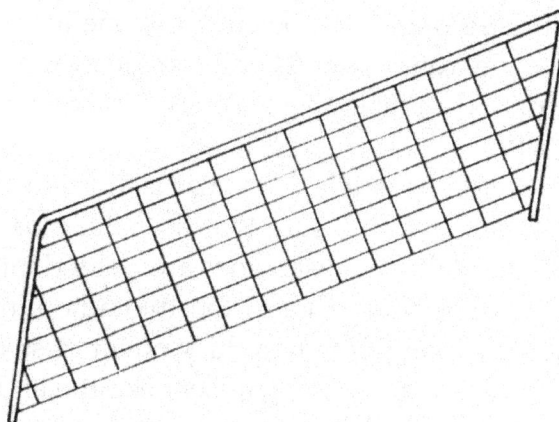

diameter of pipe used for a field gate. Each length will be 4800 mm. Using a pipe bender, form an angle of 60° one metre from an end. At the same distance from the other end, form an angle of 120°. Ensure that the frames for both the sides are as similar in angle, length and height as it is practicable to get them.

Cut the mesh to shape. A small pair of bolt cutters will be ideal for this, but of course most farm workshops will have a range of other tools that will do an admirable job in reducing mesh easily and painlessly to the desired size and shape. The mesh should be located on the inside of the pipe—in that position there will be no rough edges or sharp spikes that are likely to catch animals and injure them. Lay the sheet of mesh over the frame and mark the place of each cut with a felt-tipped pen.

Weld the mesh into the pipe frame using 25 mm welds each 300 mm apart, but as you make each of the welds, pull the mesh tightly into the frame (and later, to the base) to take up all play in this material and keep it tight.

Use a wire brush and clean the white zinc oxide coating from the metal after the first run of weld metal. A 2.5 mm general purpose electrode should be used for this, but, because of the zinc coating, increase the amperage by 30 amps and a reduced rate of travel.

Constructing the base

The base will be constructed from angle iron, 50 mm by 50 mm by 5 mm. Use four pieces for this, two at 2800 mm, and two at 450 mm. All these pieces can be cut from one length of angle iron. The ends of the angle iron will be mitred—that is, they will be cut at an angle of 45°.

Weld the angle iron in the form of a rectangle, making sure that the whole base is flat and that no distortions are welded into the construction. Clamp the two adjoining pieces of angle iron to a thick offcut of steel plate, leaving a 3 mm gap between the ends to ensure adequate weld metal penetration.

Ensure too that all the corners form right angles. Check these angles with a square before you begin welding.

Assembling the sides and base

Next, the sides are welded to the outside of the base before the timber floor is bolted into place. Begin by tack-welding the sides to the base to ensure the best fit. If any adjustments are to be made it is easier to break a tack weld than to cut and re-weld a more substantial joint.

Now weld the pipe forming the sides securely to the angle-iron frame. You are welding galvanised steel, so the usual warnings about breathing in the zinc fumes naturally apply.

The bottom of the mesh can now be welded to the outside of the angle iron frame that forms the base. Weld at the same intervals as for the sides, but of course it is possible to weld only on one side of the mesh here.

The sides may seem a bit floppy at this stage, mainly because the angle iron will tend to flex slightly. Rigidity to the whole ramp can be provided by adding three braces under the base. These are formed from short lengths of the pipe from which the sides were constructed. Bend these in the pipe bender and weld them under the base at intervals, one about 300 mm from each end, with a third brace in the centre.

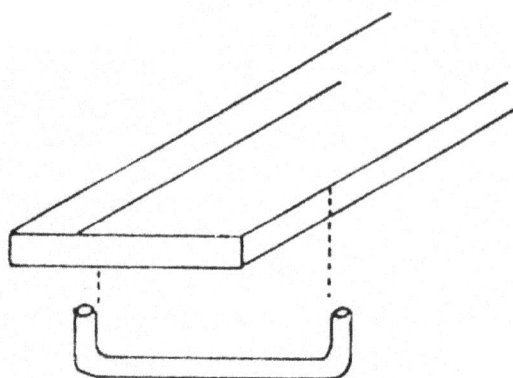

Attaching the floor

The timber floor is bolted to the ends of the angle iron frame with two galvanised bolts through each end of the boards. Any hardwood 40 mm thick will suffice for the floor, the width of each board being about 150 mm. To prevent springiness or flexing of the timber, you may feel that it is desirable to weld two or three pieces of flat bar under the timber and bolt the wood to the steel. The flat bar of course will be welded between the two inner edges of the angle iron.

Boards on their own will provide insufficient grip for livestock when animals are ascending or descending the ramp. You will need to attach crosspieces of timber. Pieces 25 mm by 25 mm of suitable hardwood each 150 mm to 200 mm apart attached to the hardwood floor will prevent the animals from slipping.

Supports for the ramp

The ramp can be pushed against and supported by any vehicle for the convenient loading of animals. Two steel supports welded to the end of the frame may be sufficient to enable easy loading of the vehicle, as long as there is no chance of the ramp slipping off the tray. A hook over the tray will provide a better means of locking the whole ramp securely to the vehicle.

A better method, however, is to install two steel posts 75 mm square and 500 mm apart at the loading area. These will provide the means of adjusting the height of the ramp to accommodate any vehicle used to transport the animals. These supporting posts should be three metres long — 2400 mm above the ground, with 600 mm set into the ground. Single chain links can be welded to the flat sides to provide the adjustable support. A steel rod 12 mm diameter is inserted through any two links, providing an easy adjustment on which the ramp will rest. Enough links can be cut from about one metre of chain bought from most hardware stores. While round pipe with a suitable cap is alright, I prefer to use square posts for this purpose; these will be 75 mm square, with a plate welded to the top to keep out the rain. The choice is one of convenience.

47 Cattle grids

It's easy to tell the likely candidates for cattle grids. They're the farmers who have to open and close a dozen gates between their houses and the main road.

Cattle grids are a practical and sensible solution to all those gates. They keep the cattle in while giving free access to vehicles.

Consider a few points when building and installing grids. The first is the weight of vehicles that will be driven over them. Think ahead to the heaviest truck that will be likely to go your way. One truck weighing thirty tonnes, or with an (illegal) axle weight of, say 20 tonnes, will cause more damage to the steelwork than will a thousand lightweight vehicles passing that way.

Secondly, if a grid is installed between paddocks, a gate will be needed somewhere, installed either next to the grid, or further along the fence to allow cattle to pass from one paddock to the next whenever required.

The construction of grids and their bases varies from farm to farm, depending on the person making them. Sometimes, for example in wet areas, the grids are best set in a concrete base which is free draining— that is, open ended with a gentle slope in the direction of flow to allow water to pass under the grid without accumulating.

The frogs won't be happy being denied their pond, but this will prevent a build-up of water that might otherwise overflow on to the access track or become a breeding ground for mosquitoes. And if installed on a sloping roadway, a drain above the grid will take any runoff from the road away from the grid.

Some grids on farms are constructed from disused railway lines. True, these are strong, and probably little or nothing will bend

them, but they'll break the farmer's back as he tries to lift one to clean accumulated debris from underneath. Lightweight grids will prove adequate for vehicles within the legal axle weight limits.

Because of their weight and size, cattle grids are perhaps best constructed *in situ*. A portable electric welder, or one run off farm machinery will be required.

Since whole lengths of the steel are heavy and awkward (the square hollow tubing is available in 8-metre lengths) and less than easy to cut, it would be preferable to have all the steel cut to the right size by the steel merchant. Your job then would be to weld the steel together. So for a base (or trench) 4000 mm long and 2000 mm across, you will need: 6 bearers 100 mm by 50 mm RHS tubing with a wall thickness of 4 mm and 2.5 metres long; 12 cross pieces 75 mm by 50 mm with a wall thickness of 4 mm.

For the sides, you will need: 4 pieces of 50 mm by 25 mm by 3.2 mm square hollow tubing 1200 mm long for the verticals; 4 pieces of 50 mm by 25 mm by 3.2 mm square hollow tubing 2500 mm long for the horizontals; and gate infill mesh to fill the gap.

Alternatively, round pipe 72 mm OD with a 4.5 mm wall thickness can be used for the joists on square tubing bearers, although most times the tubing serves the purpose admirably, and is much easier to work with on structures like these. But with pipe of this diameter, the spaces between them will be slightly different.

Of course, there's the disused railway line you can use to get fit with at the same time. You'll possibly have to cut that yourself to the required lengths, so have your oxy cutting equipment nearby.

Whether you choose to use square tubing or round pipe, you might like to cap the ends. This won't add anything to the strength or appearance, but it will reduce the possibility of rusting from the inside. For capping, you will need 2500 mm of 50 mm by 50 mm flat bar. Cap each of the open ends and grind off the excess weld metal.

First though, build the base.

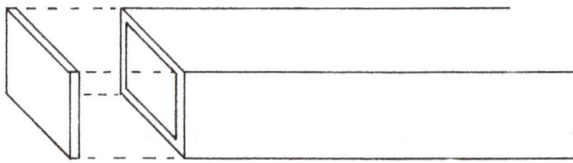

Cap the ends of the tubing to help prevent rust

Concreting around the trench will be necessary. The section of the trench where the bearers will rest is probably more practicable and longer lasting if it is of reinforced concrete.

Ideally cattle grids should have a full concrete base. This should be constructed on a solid surface, with any packing material such as sand or gravel firmly bedded down. This type of base is preferable in wet areas or where there is a likelihood of water flowing under the structure.

The bedding material should be prevented from washing out from beneath the concrete. The ends of the concrete base can be dipped several centimetres into the soil to prevent water from running under the

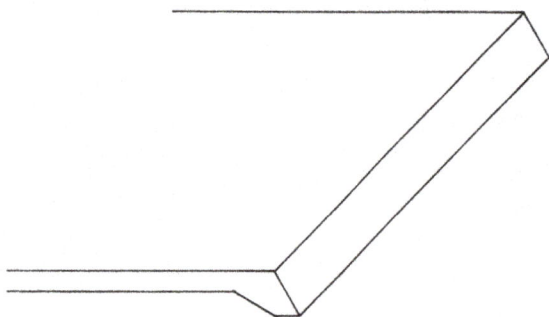

By extending the concrete below the base at the ends helps reinforce the ends as well as reduce washout from under the concrete base

base and removing finer material like the packing sand. The soil is then backfilled to the edge of the concrete.

Boxing or some sort of form-work will keep the concrete straight and neat. A sloppy concrete mix without form-work will give a really bad result. The concrete base should be at least 100 mm and preferably even 150 mm thick over its entire area. Heavy trucks will be driven over it.

The sides, also 100 mm or 150 mm thick, and which must be parallel to each other, will be built on to the slab. The top of the concrete should only come to 150 mm below road level.

The concrete base should be smoothed out and the form work for the sides put into place. The form work should be straight and smooth and should not buckle or bend under the weight of the wet concrete as it is poured. It should be easy to remove when the concrete has set. Make do with any suitable materials that are handy, such as smooth sawn timber. Make sure the base is free draining or it will become a frog pond.

Now to the steelwork. Here's a way to construct just one of possibly dozens of designs of grids.

The six bearers are placed narrow side up across the trench as shown in the diagram. They should all sit flat on the concrete and must all be level. The bearers are evenly spaced along the length of the concrete. Ensure that each of them is at 90° to the edge. Anything other than a right angle will detract from the whole appearance of your work.

To the tops of the concrete are bolted 100 mm by 75 mm by 5 mm angle iron primed on the underside to prevent rusting. Channel or flat bar will do, but make sure it is primed on the underside to prevent rusting.

The bearers are welded to the angle iron. These lengths of angle iron are bolted to the concrete by three or four 12 mm diameter anchor bolts. Unless cowboys arrive from the city to visit you on weekends and do wheelies in their high-powered mounts on the grid, the bolts will suffice in holding the structure firmly in place.

Allow a gap of a few millimetres between the inner face of the angle iron and the concrete wall for expansion of the steel in summer. Bolt the angle iron firmly in place.

Space the twelve joists, narrow side up, beginning at the ends of the bearers. Check

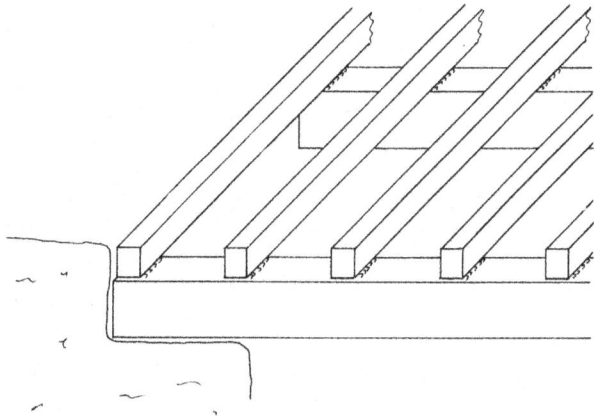

The bearers are placed narrow side up

that they are at right angles, and weld them to the bearers. When the road material is backfilled, the end joists will prevent the gravel from falling or washing into the concrete base.

If you still have the strength, lift the steelwork — that is, the bearers and the joists, and the angle iron from the base and complete the welds all around to prevent the accumulation of moisture and rusting under them and between the steel pieces. Make sure that the thread on the masonry bolts isn't damaged as the steel is lifted over them.

Your cattle grid will also need sides. These can be constructed from 50 mm by 25 mm by 3.2 mm square hollow tubing welded to the ends of the outer joists at an angle of 15°. The sides should be at fence height (900 mm high). Weld gate infill mesh behind the tubing which forms the frames for the sides.

Prime all the steel thoroughly. The cattle won't appreciate the colour, but it will prevent rusting. The steel will be exposed to all weather conditions for many, many years. Extend its natural life as long as possible with a good quality primer.

48 Pump sled

Move that pump, the floods are coming. Well, perhaps one day it might rain enough for you to have to move your pump above flood level. Here's a plan for a sled I came across recently on a property. The structure has applications for pumps that are on low-lying river banks, or for those located on the wall of a dam that's about to overflow. The sled is easy to construct. It is also double-ended which makes it easy to move so it won't break your back in the process.

The runners

The runners are made from steel 1200 mm long by 150 mm wide and 3 mm thick, cut to shape to facilitate sliding over the ground. Use a rounded template (such as a 4-litre paint tin) to get the shape right, then cut both sides exactly the same. After marking the outlines of the template on the steel, use an oxy torch to cut the steel to shape. Smooth out the resulting ragged edge with a grinder. A rather neater job is obtained when the two sides are clamped together and the grinding is done on both of them together — that way, the curves will be even. Make sure that, when assembled, the two ends that were ground together become either both fronts or both backs.

To increase the surface area of the runners where they are in contact with the ground, and to prevent the narrow edges biting into the wet ground, weld lengths of flat bar 50 mm wide and 3 mm thick to the bottom of them to form a large tee. Pull the flat bar in tight to the sides and curve it around the ends to ensure a good fit — it will curve easily around the formed front and back of the

runners. The flat bar doesn't have to be welded all the way around — 25 mm of weld metal each 100 mm apart will suffice. See also the chapter on making steel stronger.

The cross pieces

The cross pieces or spacers keep the runners firmly in position, parallel to one another, and they add strength to the whole sled. Use angle iron 40 mm by 40 mm by 3 mm at the front and the back, and the same for the mountings for the engine or pump. The runners should be 600 mm apart. Line the two runners up so that they are parallel with one another and on the same plane so that the structure, when welded, is flat. Tack weld the crosspieces to the runners, and check again for flatness. A twist can easily creep into the structure at this stage of construction, throwing out the whole alignment.

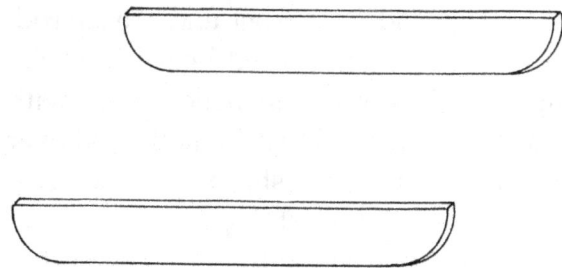

Cut the runners for the sled

Pump mountings

Pump mountings will vary according to the shape of the base of the pump, and the facilities available for attachment of the pump itself. Here's one simple way of

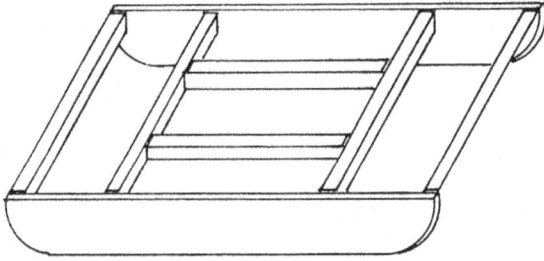

Weld the cross pieces in place to make the structure rigid

attaching the pump, but you will probably need to accommodate your particular piece of machinery.

Weld two more crosspieces of 40 mm by 40 mm by 3 mm angle iron between the two cross pieces. These will be rigid and will be strong enough for all reasonably sized pumps. Measure the width of the pump, and weld the supports accordingly. If the sump of the engine extends beyond a reasonable depth below the mountings, you will need to raise the mountings somehow so the sump doesn't drag on the ground as the sled is being towed.

The pump is secured to the frame according to mountings available for each particular unit.

Towing attachment

The towing attachments are simple. Cut two pieces of 12-mm rod 150 mm long. Mark the centres of the rod, secure one end of each rod, and heat the centres to red heat using oxy equipment. The rod will bend easily with minimal force applied to it. Bend the rod over at the centre to form a sharp vee, and let it cool. Then weld the last 25 mm of each end of both rods, one to the front and the other to the back crosspiece of the sled.

Anchoring points

With the vibration of the engine running over many hours, the sled could well wander away from the creek bed or even off the dam wall and into the water.

At some convenient place along one or both sides — perhaps to the vertical section of one of the angle iron crosspieces — weld a 50 mm piece of a pipe that has an internal diameter of 15 mm. Cut a length of rod long enough to pass through this pipe and then 200 mm into the ground. Cut the rod, heat it and turn over one end 50 mm to form a right angle. This (or these) pin(s) can be pushed into the ground with a hefty boot or with a hammer. It would take many more hours of running for the vibration to dislodge them from even soft ground.

Moving the pump

Moving the pump in times of rising water level is easy. A rope, cable or chain is secured to the attachment hook, and the whole unit (complete with hoses if necessary) is dragged to higher ground. When it needs to be returned to its usual pumping position, it can be slid down a slope to near the water, or dragged back into position. Now you can see the the advantage of making the sled doubled-ended.

Rust prevention

Rust is always a problem with any steel, especially that exposed to the rain and humid conditions. You could use galvanised steel (but take all the usual precautions with welding galvanised steel outlined earlier in this book under the chapter Safety) or you could prime the steel to prevent rusting. However, if the engine of the pump is diesel, that in itself will possibly take care of the rusting problems. There aren't many diesel engines that don't leak oil or spray fuel, just as there aren't many farmers who don't spill sump oil other than into the motor. The light coating of oil should help prevent rusting problems.

But don't think you won't need one of these sleds. Rain is bound to come. Sooner or later.

Index